A VARIETY OF LIVES

Michael Tracey

A Variety of Lives

A BIOGRAPHY OF

SIR HUGH GREENE

THE BODLEY HEAD
LONDON SYDNEY
TORONTO

British Library Cataloguing
in Publication Data
Tracey, Michael
A variety of lives.
1. Greene, *Sir* Hugh
I. Title
384.54'. 0924   HE8699.G7
ISBN 0-370-30026-2

© Michael Tracey 1983
Printed in Great Britain for
The Bodley Head Ltd
9 Bow Street, London WC2E 7AL
by Redwood Burn Ltd
Trowbridge, Wiltshire
Set in 11 on 13pt Linotron Baskerville
by Rowland Phototypesetting Ltd
Bury St Edmunds, Suffolk
First published 1983

For Belka
who made me ask:
Why go to the Louvre
When you have the
Mona Lisa at home.

All of the research and much of the writing for this biography
was done while I was a Research Associate at the Centre for
Mass Communication Research, University of Leicester.
The research would not have been possible without the
support of grants from the German broadcasting organisation, ARD, and also from the Westdeutscher Rundfunk in
Cologne.

The CMCR provided a marvellous place in which to
work, and its secretarial staff displayed consistent and considerable skill in typing the various drafts. My special thanks
must go to the Centre's Director, Professor Jim Halloran.
Jim was always supportive and extremely understanding
when his researcher disappeared in search of the elusive
truth about Hugh Greene. Pam Edwards provided marvellous research assistance during a rather intensive period of
work in the BBC's archives.

There are many individuals, in several different countries,
who spoke with me about Hugh Greene. Rather than trying
to mention them individually which would take an awful lot
of space, I must simply thank them collectively, and say
that their observations and insight were invaluable to whatever understanding of Hugh Greene I was able to attain.

To write a biography of a subject who is still alive is an
unusual activity. In another place I hope to publish an essay
on how I wrote the book, on the trials and tribulations of the
this kind of work, but ultimately on the sheer pleasure of
writing about someone such as Hugh Greene. It became an
essential part of the preparation of this work that I came to
know him extremely well. Nothing so much attests to the
character of Hugh Greene as the fact that he agreed to my
writing the biography in the first place. I first put the idea to
him in 1974 when I had no track-record at all; at that stage I
had not even completed my doctorate. Nevertheless, Hugh
Greene said he would be delighted with the idea of my

writing a book about his life and would offer whatever help he could. And he did just that. He lent me his own personal papers, and then intervened to persuade the BBC that they should give me access to papers relevant to his career, without in any way trying to influence whatever judgments I arrived at having seen those papers. Over a period of several years, I was then in the fascinating position of being able to research his life and to discuss it with him at the same time. It takes a particularly brave and calm personality not just to allow but to encourage someone else to peer into the darker recesses of one's life. But then Hugh Greene is an extraordinary man, whom it was a pleasure and a privilege to come to know.

Finally, my thanks must go to someone who appeared amid my own particular biography about half-way through the work, my wife Belka. She had to put up with my constant distraction with the book. She did it, however, always with understanding that writing about Hugh Greene had entered my life and needed to be worked through to that final full stop. Endless late nights may have made me feel like a researcher, but they sometimes made me also feel like a very bad husband. The addition to our family of young John Henryk, however, proves that not *all* those nights were lonely.

ILLUSTRATIONS

'The Comeback' by Low, by permission of The Standard Newspaper.

The Daily Mail and Illingworth for 'Pirates Galore' by Illingworth.

Syndication International Ltd for the Franklin cartoon.

The British Broadcasting Corporation for:

1

On March 31, 1969 Hugh Greene retired as Director General of the BBC. In the previous nine years he had presided over what was probably the finest period in the history of television. He had not been the 'author' of that moment, but he had been the 'publisher'. The cavalcade of programmes which had marked the passage of those years had been created by other men. Greene's had been the most difficult task of all, producing the mood and the manner in which others—writers, producers, directors—could work and create. The decade is dotted with the names of programmes that have entered legend: *That Was the Week That Was, Not Only But Also, The Wednesday Play, Steptoe and Son, Till Death Us Do Part.*

Greene had somehow managed to capture the times in which he was living, to understand and articulate the deeply-felt need for movement and change, among the young in particular. However, if you add together all the programmes for which the BBC became famous, and controversial, during his director generalship, they amount to only one small part of the total programme output of the Corporation. Picturing it now, those golden moments had the beauty but, alas, the lifespan of a firefly.

Running the BBC was for Hugh Greene but the last of a number of lives. He had been a successful journalist in Berlin, had helped re-create broadcasting in the British zone in war-shattered Germany, been closely involved with the propaganda war against the Soviet bloc and then against the Communist guerillas in Malaya. He had a knack of being in the right place at the right time; for example, drifting into Berlin just as the Nazis had come to power. He also had the knack of attracting the right job at the right time—broadcasting to Eastern Europe, working in Malaya, emerging as Director General at a time which in broad social terms almost exactly matched his own liberal, almost radical, always amusing, highly innocent nature.

He became an immensely controversial figure and stamped his presence on British broadcasting in a manner which has only ever been matched by John Reith. On the day he retired he received many plaudits. One in particular stands out. It was from John Freeman, then British ambassador to Washington, who said that Hugh Greene would be remembered, above all else, as 'the other great DG'. It was a fine epitaph: Reith had created the institution of public service broadcasting in this country; Greene showed what could be achieved with such an idea, given a little courage and not a little mischievousness.

If the public person was that of a great, if controversial figure, the private man was sad and rather lonely. To some of his friends and even to members of his family, he remains an enigma: an aloof character to be admired but not necessarily loved; trusted but only up to a point; frequently inscrutable, unknown and unknowable. Those who have worked with him extend to him the distanced affection and respect often offered to men of charisma.

Once Greene asked one of his governors whether he was happily married. 'Yes,' replied the rather startled Glanmor Williams, and then he added with honesty and simplicity, 'in fact I would go further and say that my marriage is the lynch-pin of my whole life. If it came to an end then I would be totally shattered.' Greene looked at him sadly and said, 'How I envy you that certainty.'

Memories and anecdotes collect around controversial figures: some are golden, others suggest complexity and conflict. This book attempts to separate legend from fact, to disentangle the Director General as a man, from all the issues which constantly swirled around the idea of public service broadcasting during the 1960s. Above all it tries to glimpse Hugh Greene, the individual.

The Greene family fortunes were built around the brewing of beer. Hugh's great-grandfather, Benjamin Greene, was born at Oundle in Northamptonshire in 1780. He began his brewing career with Whitbread's in London and, a very precocious young man, when still only nineteen, in partnership with William Buck he took over the failing brewery belonging to Walter and Mathias Wright in Westgate Street, Bury St Edmunds, in which there is still a Greene family interest. After six years he could proudly advertise:

> Messrs Buck and Greene beg leave respectfully to inform the public that they will be ready by the first week in June, to execute any order they may be favoured with for Table Beer: and will as soon as possible announce when they shall be able to supply such Ale, Porter and old beer, as shall give complete satisfaction to their friends and secure their reputation, particularly in private families.

At the age of twenty five he married as his second wife Catherine Smith, the daughter of a Bedford clergyman, who had inherited a fortune from her maternal grandfather, Zachary Carleton. He was ambitious, energetic and determined and by 1810 his prosperity was such that Benjamin was able to purchase extensive sugar plantations on the island of St Kitts in the West Indies.

Benjamin and Catherine produced thirteen children, of whom eight survived; William, born in 1824, was Hugh's grandfather. William's eldest brother, Benjamin Buck, spent some time in St Kitts and then returned to England to enter the City. Respectable, wealthy and a pillar of Victorian society, he became proprietor of sugar estates in Mauritius, owner of a large fleet of ships and a director of the Bank of England. The next brother, Edward, was also filled with rectitude, entering the family brewing business and becoming

3

a Suffolk country gentleman, Master of Foxhounds and a local Member of Parliament. However, Charles, the brother only three years older than William, was altogether less respectable and a more amusing character, who had fathered thirteen children by the time he died at the age of eighteen.

William and Charles had both attended Bury Grammar School and then at the ages of fifteen and twelve respectively had been sent into the exotic Caribbean world to look after large estates which until a few years before had been worked by slave labour. Young Charles was responsible for the supervision of many hundreds of workers in St Kitts and for all the sugar crop over 2,000 acres. The circumstances surrounding his death remain a mystery. In the family it had always been thought he died of yellow fever. His descendants in St Kitts maintain that he died from the kick of a horse while riding round the estates, and Hugh Greene has written of him:

> One likes to think of Charles, like King Ferdinand of Bulgaria, dismounting and bestowing his casual favours on girls working in the fields. A kick from a horse would, in the circumstances, have been a more appropriate end for Charles than a commonplace dose of yellow fever.

William then returned to England, a rather restless figure compared with his two older, more prosperous brothers, but he eventually settled down, married Charlotte Smith and had four children, the youngest of whom, Charles Henry, was Hugh's father.

The children of Benjamin Greene, the brewer, thus combined brewing, the City and landowning with the more romantic promiscuous life of St Kitts. The next generation combined wealth and respectability with intellect.

Charles Henry, Hugh's father, was born in 1865. Educated at Bedford School and Wadham College, Oxford, he graduated with no obvious distinction, obtaining a Third in Classical Moderations and a Second in History. His initial idea had been to read for the Bar; it was only on a temporary basis that he first went, in 1889, to teach at Berkhamsted public school, then under the influence of the formidable Dr Fry, a fierce Victorian pedagogue.

Within five years he was appointed a housemaster, whereupon he married his cousin, Marion Raymond Greene, a woman of considerable reserve, and they settled down to live at St John's, a 'redbrick monstrosity', where their first five children were born—Molly, Herbert, Raymond, Graham and Hugh. At the age of forty-five, Charles succeeded Fry as headmaster and they all moved into the beautiful mellow sixteenth-century School House, where their last child, Elisabeth, was born.

Charles was a quiet, earnest man of serious mien whereas his wife was described by one of her nieces as:

> Very beautiful, very dignified, but she always knew best. She was a bit cold and we were all a bit frightened of her I think. She never doubted that she was always in the right and I think that made a wall between her and her children. She was also very cool, very aloof, even with her own children, even with the two youngest, Hugh and Elisabeth.

Yet despite the distance she created, this clergyman's daughter could, and did, ultimately generate great devotion in her offspring.

Hugh Carleton Greene was born at five minutes past eight on the evening of November 15th, 1910. He weighed in at 7½ lbs, was brought into the world by Nurse Cross and Dr McBride and was quickly given the pet name, for reasons now unknown, of Cherrybubble. His mother kept a detailed record of his progress in a little book produced by Mellins Foods. His first journey was to Harston to visit his father's brother, William Graham Greene, 'one of the ablest civil servants of his generation'; his first crawl, August 1911; his first walk, April 1912; his first words which, not surprisingly, were 'Mamma, Mamma'. When he saw his first aeroplane on October 10th, 1912, he described it as a 'motorbike in the air'. Mamma even recorded the clothes he wore: his first jersey suit, October 1915—previously he had to wear socks and 'knickers'. His first suit, grey flannel, always a major occasion for any small boy, May 1918. Indeed, his own first memories of childhood were to be of the 'uncomfortable clothes of the period, the itchy woollen combinations, split fore and aft, the thick brown woollen stockings held up by suspenders buttoned to a liberty bodice'.

All the childhood illnesses are recorded: chicken pox, measles, whooping cough, German measles. Under the page headed 'Religious Life—Train up a Child in the Way He Should Go' there is no entry; clearly the pattern in the carpet appeared at an early age and reflected, if nothing else, that he had been born into a household which did not place a massive emphasis on religion and its practice. Neither, however, were there any entries under 'Faults and Virtues'. Perhaps by the time that such qualities might have been expected to exhibit themselves, the excitement of scripting the child's life had died down.

This carefully kept baby's record is a testament not just to a mother's attention to her child's development, but to a regimentation or orderliness in that attention. Marion Greene had detailed each episode with loving care, yet this only served to capture the rigidity in the relationship she had with her children: it was love at a distance. Hugh's emotions shifted between terror and happiness, between a sweat-invoking shyness and a deep affection for his family, between a horror of being seen and a delight in being loved. Looked at with the perspective of the present, when a child's feelings for his parents are less weighed down by inhibition and routine, the mother-child relationship at the beginning of the century is almost beyond comprehension: passions were smothered, the contours of emotion were smoothed out and were there-fore less recognisable both to the observer and the observed.

Part of the explanation for the emotional distance which existed between the parents and the children was that for much of the time they were physically separate. Hugh said later that with both parents the close relationship which could have provided the tenderness needed in childhood only came later in life, 'a very common experience I should imagine with that nurse-ridden generation'. Most of their time as children was spent with nannies, which meant that their happiness or otherwise depended upon the particular women given the task.

There were about six indoor servants in School House, including nurses for the children. Each morning the children would have breakfast in the nursery, where they would remain until about eleven am when they would go down and join their mother. They would stay with her but had to amuse themselves rather than being amused by her. They would then go back to the nursery for lunch. The afternoon would consist of a walk with the nurse and the nursemaid. It was one such walk that provided Hugh Greene with his first memory:

> I am sitting in my four-wheeled pram on the verge of a quiet, dusty country road. I am unscrewing the big brass screws by which the hood is raised or lowered and the whole cumbersome mechanism is held together. I am throwing the screws over a wooden fence into long meadow grass, and I am alone, unobserved and happy. The year must be 1913 and I am 2 or 3 years old.

It is, he says, one of the few vivid memories of his childhood. Tea would follow the walk, again with the nurse in the nursery, and after that a procession was formed to the drawing room where they played or their mother read to them. Then it was time for supper and bed until the following day when the ritual was re-enacted.

Hugh recalls two of the nurses in particular, Olive Dodge and Lillian Hazard. For Olive he had very great affection, but Lillian was a horror who stalked his life for two years:

> She was a mental sadist not a physical sadist. My sister and I absolutely hated her. We never said anything at all

7

to our parents about it, and we invented a secret language which we used to say to each other in the mornings to indicate what sort of mood Lillian Hazard was in. After she left there was one awful day when she came back to visit us and we suspected that she was going to return. Agony.

Holidays were also governed by ritual. Marion would take the children to the seaside, while Charles went off alone on trips to Europe, and in particular to Tuscany. She was unable to accompany him, it was said, because she would get violently seasick and could not bear the thought of the Channel crossing. The visit to the seaside always followed the same pattern: almost all the time would be spent on a beach with only occasional excursions inland; on the first day they were never allowed to go into the sea, on the second paddling was allowed and swimming on the third, but after each swim they had to dry and get dressed rather than just lounge in their swimming costumes. Once they were dressed, there were ginger biscuits.

Even as a child Hugh enjoyed being alone with his own thoughts: he craved privacy. He was nervous and reserved, and isolation brought relief. With the exception of Graham and Elisabeth, the presence of people triggered off his shyness and he preferred to play by himself. He therefore dreaded the thought of school which would destroy all the consolation and joys of his solitary childhood and force him to associate with strangers. It wasn't just a certain blush that he felt, but a suffocating sense of drowning. Sociability, which follows from an open, loving and overtly affectionate relationship with one's parents, simply was not there; he never learned how to mix with other boys or indeed with other adults.

School House itself was divided up into two parts. The private part was where Hugh, his brothers and sisters lived with their parents and where they could find a modicum of contentment despite the rather remote affection of their parents and the occasional sadistic nurse. On the ground floor, past Charles Greene's study, at the end of a narrow, low, dark, stone corridor, beyond a green baize door, lay the school. The green baize door was the frontier between the two worlds. When Hugh was on the private side of the door he felt almost content, but each time he passed through it the mood slipped from him to be replaced by one of distaste and depression.

Originally Charles Greene had thought it would be wrong for his sons to attend the school where their father was a master so he had sent first Herbert and then Raymond to Marlborough, which both hated. Herbert had stayed the course but suffered greatly, Raymond had been removed and made a boarder at Berkhamsted. Graham and Hugh were sent straight through the green baize door when their time came.

Hugh entered as a day boy on September 17th, 1918 into Form One of the preparatory school, and remained a day-boy at Berkhamsted until 1927 when his father retired and he had to become a boarder in School House.

His sons may have dreaded having a headmaster for a father but Charles Greene was successful at his job, given the traditional criteria of success: scholarships won, universities attended, honours gained. He increased the numbers at the school, maintaining a careful balance between boarders and day boys, and also developed the school facilities. He was keen on physical education, on swimming, and one of this major projects was that the school should have new and better playing fields. The money for these was eventually given by an anonymous benefactor calling himself 'Townsman', who was in fact his own brother, Edward Greene.

Edward had made his money from coffee plantations in Brazil. He then returned to England, to The Hall at Berkhamsted, where with his German wife and six children he lived in state with eleven indoor servants and huge gardens. Both Edward's house and that of his civil servant brother, William, at Harston were havens of privacy where nephews and nieces were able to find release from the claustrophobia and embarrassment of their own somewhat arid home.

For Charles was not an easy man to get on with, nor was he

9

an outgoing or cheerfully extrovert father figure. Cecil Parrott, a contemporary of Hugh Greene at Berkhamsted, and
later ambassador in Prague, remembers going to pay the
traditional visit to the headmaster before his confirmation.
He was startled to be told by Charles Greene: 'There is a
whole army of women living on the lusts of men.' Charles
retained a Victorian prudishness and embarrassment at the
mention of any question on religion or sex. At a time when
the central facet of a child's life is his developing sense not
only of his own sexual nature, but also of the existence of a
moral structure around that nature, this prevailing mood of
refined ineptitude created problems and dangers.

If Charles was vulnerable it was largely a vulnerability
born of innocence. The same man who could refer to those
armies of women lurking outside the walls of the school ready
to abuse the virginity of his charges, could also be so appalled
by the picture of the world Graham presented in his first
book that he refused to read any of the others. Raymond
recalled a story which typifies the naïveté of their father:

> I remember an occasion. I was I suppose in my later teens,
> so it must have been when I was an undergraduate. I went
> to the theatre in London and in the interval in the foyer I
> saw the Bishop of St Albans, a gigantic person, about 6′6″
> without his mitre. He was a very human person and he
> said to me, 'Well what do you think of the play?' and I
> said, 'I think it's very good indeed', and he said, 'I think
> it's damned good'. The next day at breakfast I told my
> father that I had run into the Bishop and he said, 'Oh, and
> what did the Bishop think about the play?' and I said,
> 'Well his actual words were that he thought it was damned
> good'. Father said, 'Raymond you must not make up these
> things, Bishops do not use bad language.'

This lack of worldliness was reflected in the atmosphere of
what Graham called 'an appallingly innocent school'. Cecil
Parrott thought that it had to do with the whole atmosphere
of the school:

It was supposed to be an extremely *clean* school—the whole atmosphere was a very gentle one. The tone of the school was extremely good compared with other public schools and in a way I do not think one was encouraged to wake up to the facts of life at the school, at least I was not.

Another old boy said that he could not conceive of either Charles Greene or his wife having 'any capacity to deal with the sexual awakening or sexual problems of the young. Generally within the school this was an absolutely taboo subject with which not even the most daring of the younger masters could possibly deal.'

The school was thus a self-defining, not to say self-denying, inhibited community. There was a girls' school in Berkhamsted but enormous efforts were made to maintain segregation. Nothing was held in common and if a boy had a sister at the girls' school it was probably in his interest not to say anything about her.

Both the boys at his school and his sons therefore found Charles remote and daunting to approach. Graham wrote that as a child, whenever his father talked to him, he wanted 'to crawl under the table'; that the only reason he felt closer to his mother was that, since she was even more distant, she was less likely to embarrass him with questions.

Later on Graham came to view his father as 'an old-fashioned liberal' and to recognise that he possessed a considerable degree of openness and receptivity to new ideas, the obvious example being his surprising decision to allow Graham to undergo psycho-analysis in an effort to remedy the potentially suicidal depressions into which he was sinking, at a time when the science was in its infancy. The anxieties which lay smothered in the boys of Berkhamsted had been heightened in Graham into an escapist folly that teetered on the edge of breakdown. Perhaps even more surprisingly, Charles took the decision on the advice of his son Raymond, who was only a first-year medical student at the time. Raymond commented: 'I had always put him [father] on a pedestal as a godlike figure, and he sent for me in great distress and I found that our roles had been reversed and he was appealing to me for help.'

Charles may have been aloof and moralistic, but he had had the percipience to recognise his son's problem and, as a caring and loving father, he had endeavoured to find a solution.

Hugh managed to cope with his schooldays better than Graham, but all his memories of them are spiced with depression and pain. He was to write later: 'I suppose Berkhamsted was not cruel as compared with most schools at the time but even in one of the outer circles of hell the flames could be hot enough.' The school seemed dark and brooding, the boys threatening, brutal, offensive. It remains a memory he cannot escape which attracts him like a moth to a flame, and still induces a stark reaction: 'As the train gets nearer to Berkhamsted I get deeply depressed, as if I were going back to school.'

He certainly was not the victim of any personal intimidation, though characteristically he recalls with vivid horror incidents of others being bullied. In one ugly redbrick building of the school which housed the junior classrooms, there was a murky cavern of a room where the boys hung their coats. Round its walls were radiators which in winter would burn red hot. On winter evenings when the masters had gone, the older boys seized the younger and weaker ones and held their legs and arms on the radiators: 'I can still hear,' he recalled, 'the screams of the victims and the laughter of the torturers and smell burnt flesh.'

Such a childhood memory is part of the dusty baggage of the mind, but for Hugh Greene, and indeed for many others who went through the English public school system, it was a long, living, lurid horror. In his reaction to school was both the self-pity he felt for his miserable situation in an institution whose only achievements lay in its varieties of physical and emotional discomfort, and also a finer quality:

> To each his suff'rings: all are men,
> Condemned alike to groan;

The tender for another's pain,
Th' unfeeling for their own.

In his final term he began to exert, a little inconsistently, a form of retribution on those who bullied: 'My right to flog I administered sparingly though I must confess to having beaten a rugger playing tough, who had behaved in a particularly disgusting manner in the dormitory, with great satisfaction.'

Academically Hugh progressed surely and steadily through the school. He was a clever boy, regularly winning prizes: Kipling's *Jungle Book*, Spenser's poems, Browning's poems, Chesterton's poems. He remembers few of the boys and only two of the masters with any affection. One helped him to scrape School Certificate marks in Maths, but was later sent to jail for obtaining money under false pretences and ended up as a caddy on the local golf course. 'I can still smell the whisky on his breath as he leant over patiently, kindly and lucidly explaining what was so clear to others but so difficult to me.' It was the beginning of the appeal he felt for amusing rogues. The other master for whom he felt affection was 'Dicker' Dale, the Classics master. He also recalls how in one term he was taught Classics by Claud Cockburn, just down from Oxford, who gave him the most stimulating teaching he ever experienced. At this time Hugh's reading tastes consisted of detective stories, adventure novels, Greek, Latin and Ancient History.

The school was dominated by a set of masters who—with the exception of the affable whisky-swilling embezzler—were usually old boys, bachelors devoted to the school and its prevailing values of sport, empire, Christianity, country, patriotism in the shape of the OTC, clean living and conscientiousness, united in an intense collective sense of bonhomie. Cecil Parrott recalls that often as a boy he would see them coming back from the sports field 'about 6 or 8 of these masters all walking along in a great line, and they looked a really good muscular Christian lot, very friendly and awfully decent, and all that'. They simply continued the mores on which they had been raised, which bordered on what Goronwy Rees described as the 'sexual infantilism' of the time, characterised by intense male-male relationships from which women were excluded.

One person does loom in Hugh's memory, his father's successor as headmaster, Henry Lael Oswald Flecker. Hugh Greene has a capacity to hold an emotion or a feeling towards someone which does not waver or decline with time. Some people, few in number it is true, trigger in him an unforgiving, unforgetting hatred which over decades does not dim, indeed retains the sharpness as if the original cause were only yesterday. From the moment Flecker took over in 1927 Hugh developed a titanic distaste for him which continues nearly sixty years later.

Flecker was only thirty when he took over as headmaster. Before this he had been assistant master at Marlborough under Cyril Norwood. He was intended to be the new broom, the man to shake and stir Berkhamsted which had grown in the Governors' eyes successful but complacent during the thirty-eight years of the Fry-Greene régime. Flecker was to pull up this somewhat low-key minor public school, to give it a new lift, to make it smart, efficient and cost effective. Cricket professionals, for example, became the vogue, something which would never have occurred to Charles Greene's generation. According to one old boy who admires much that Flecker did, he turned the school upside down, and in particular paid much more attention to individual boys than had been the case under Charles Greene.

On Founders' Day 1930 Flecker announced suddenly that he was to take over as headmaster of Christ's Hospital. He had been at Berkhamsted barely three years, a period which was far too short for him to have imposed himself on the school, but long enough to have left an indelible and unfortunate impression on young Greene. Today Hugh refers to him as 'that revolting, oily man', a feeling which he rationalises by mentioning Flecker's extravagant building plans which financially embarrassed the school, as well as by pointing out that, when he first went to Christ's

14

Hospital, he continued to draw his Berkhamsted salary for a while.

Hugh Greene was particularly appalled because Flecker re-introduced flogging by prefects, which Charles Greene had abolished, and failed to support Swedish drill which Charles Greene had initiated. Basically, though, the feeling of animosity was largely personal: 'I just disliked the man. He was so oily, smarmy. I think Flecker was a bad man. It's a very racist remark to make but one could see the Armenian blood in him. There was something physically unattractive about him.'

Either because he was not very perceptive or because young Greene kept his feelings to himself, or because of a certain magnanimity, Flecker did not reciprocate the hostility. There was even one particularly embarrassing moment for the young antagonist when, towards the end of his tenure, Flecker was holding forth in Deans' Hall. To the assembled boys he announced that if there was one person who had helped him to understand the spirit of the school and find his way as head, he was among their number. Necks craned and a ripple of expectation and disgust spread across the sea of youthful faces: 'Hugh Carleton Greene is the boy I am talking about'—a comment which caused Hugh grave embarrassment. Maybe it was no more than Flecker's revenge. He did, however, have a certain insight. When Hugh Greene edited an issue of the school magazine, Flecker read it and commented, 'Greene, you have the mind of a *Daily Mail* journalist.'

Hugh and Graham were not the only members of the family to find their schooldays depressingly sombre. The eldest son Herbert had always been an awkward child but he became worse after his searing experiences at Marlborough. Molly would later tell her younger brothers how much she hated Herbert when they were children, and of how nasty he could be as a little boy in the nursery: they wondered whether he was mentally unstable. To Hugh, Herbert seemed unreliable, anti-intellectual and a total failure. Graham sometimes pondered whether 'there but for the grace of God go I'.

Cousin Barbara said of Herbert:

I can't help now looking back feeling a bit sorry for him. He was not brilliant, not very good at school and all the brothers were so brilliant, and he was just good looking, rather spoilt by my aunt, keen on cricket and was really a very average sort of person in a very brilliant family. He's always been a bit looked down on. They didn't like him. Yet actually he was the most harmless creature except for making debts at times, and I think he was probably spoilt by the girls because he was very, very good looking. At heart he was a very simple ordinary person.

If Herbert was the failure of the family for whom they felt a rather disgusted pity, Graham the troubled genius, Hugh the enigma, then Raymond was the backbone. Despite his initial misery at Marlborough, he was later able to describe his youth as 'happy and free from incident'. Regarded by his contemporaries at Berkhamsted as an over-zealous prefect and 'different from the rest of the Greenes', he later became a distinguished doctor and mountaineer, utterly reliable and straight. Graham considered him to be 'more honest in his morals than Hugh or I. He was certainly more faithful to his wives.'

In his early years, Hugh was not always seen by those around him in an entirely favourable light: a certain reserve was usually expressed, for he was considered clever but distant, perhaps conceited and certainly far from popular. He was also remarkably conformist, and according to one school friend, 'completely docile, completely dedicated to doing the right thing'. He would occasionally be laughed at as 'the little goody-goody boy', although this was largely forgiven because of his difficult position as the headmaster's son. With Uncle Edward's children he was never very popular 'because he was frightfully good', and 'looked' like a good little boy should look, with golden curls and a pink and white complexion. He was acutely aware of a form of victim-isation which was not especially physical or specific, but was contained within the glances of his accusers. Perhaps he merely used this as an excuse to rationalize his lack of close friends at school: maybe his longing for privacy and solitude was a necessary psychological defence against something about which he had no choice.

He remained enigmatic, a stranger in his own land. His judgment is the most revealing statement of all:

> When the time came to leave the world of the nursery and the garden and go to school I left behind a sheltered, if not particularly happy period of my life. I had never had a bicycle or a dog, I had not had much to do with other children and my shyness was overwhelming. I have chosen the word overwhelming with care. It is accurate and precise. Shyness was like a great wave of hot water through which one struggled to the surface, sweating and breathless, in a strange blue light—like the light of the school swimming baths which I hated. The years of school passed slowly by like a long prison sentence: ten years' hard labour with, at the end, one term's remission for good conduct. That is how it seems in retrospect.

The 1920s and 1930s were a transparent, self-conscious age. Libraries are full of books in which the names of Auden, Isherwood, Lehmann, Quennell, Cyril Connolly, and many more rub shoulders in words which try to define and articulate their collective experience. Hugh Greene is not part of that group in any obvious sense, and yet its suppositions and concerns were very much his. He did for example share its common antipathy to the public school system; if anything, he held it in even greater distaste; for him it always remained 'ten years' hard labour'. He had all the basic social characteristics of the Auden generation but none of their ambitions or neuroses. They had defined their position through art and the intellect, and looked to poets such as T. S. Eliot to explain the condition of the human species in between the memory of one war and the fearful possibility of another.

Hugh Greene indulged in none of this and was given more

to the deed than to the word. He had fought his own private war while retaining all the sensibilities of the liberal man—a loathing of those intolerances and rigidities of thought which were so much part and parcel of the public school experiences—the demand for freedom, the impatience with pomp and pomposity. In Edmund Blunden's phrase the iron had entered his soul, but with Hugh Greene the ore from which it had been fashioned was quarried from that place beyond the green baize door and not by the transferred experience of a Flanders field. The self-consciousness of the Auden generation was of the world around them and of how to comprehend and explain it. His was of a private nightmare.

The first war had a crushing impact on a generation which formed its ideas within its shadow. It undermined any sense of traditional values and commitments. Edmund Blunden, who was later to be a close friend of Hugh Greene, wrote: 'I do not claim to discern how deeply the iron has entered into the soul of those who were in the nursery in 1914, but it seems obvious that they have grown up amid unnerving conditions, and such as destroy vision.' This generation of the 1914 nursery grew in a world where ostensibly the orthodoxy was of a games-playing male society—as with Charles Greene's Berkhamsted—but in reality lived, at least in part, with an alternative view of life, 'a life that was free, but emptied of values, requiring action, and specifically sexual action, as the price of maturity'. If one allows for the presence of a value which loathed injustice to the individual, that picture comes close to capturing the personality of Hugh Greene.

John Lehmann referred to the first war as a background 'conditioning the prevalent sensibility, with its preference for tragedy and bitter wit, its rejection of cosy pretences and its refusal to accept any criterion of behaviour except one: does your action cause suffering to another?' That could be taken as a credo which Hugh Greene developed in these years. The difference between him and some of his contemporaries was that he did not express that prevalent sensibility through politics and poetry but in an abandonment of commitment. He understood the rejection of established authority, but his empathy lay in his heart more than his head. There is in some important sense, born in these early years, a vacuum at the heart of Hugh Greene's scheme of things. Rather than preparing him for anything in particular, the first nineteen years of his life prepared him for a period of wandering. He wandered in search of a career, though his sheer intelligence always guaranteed that he would be successful at something. He also wandered in search of that emotional security, stability and commitment which both sides of the green baize door had failed to provide, and which he would never truly find.

2

At the end of December 1928, Hugh Greene won a Classical postmastership to Merton College, Oxford. Freedom was on the horizon, he had only one more term to go at school, his future was assured and his headship of the house provided him with his first experience of the 'heady joys of exercising authority, and also, at times, of behaving with complete irresponsibility'.

For reasons which remain obscure his parents decided that, before going up to Oxford, he should spend some time in Germany, although he had studied French at school. Perhaps Charles and Marion had caught some of the English middle-class obsession at that time for the Weimar Republic, and for Goethe. Hugh himself can only surmise: 'My parents thought it would be a good thing for me to get abroad and learn a language, and I suppose in a sense it was the attraction of Germany at that time even affecting my parents. I don't think before I went that I had any particular urge for Germany.'

Whatever the reason, at the beginning of May 1929 he caught the boat train from Dover to Ostend. His first contact with German soil was a Cologne station crowded with British soldiers of the occupying army which was not to leave the Rhineland for another eight months. From Cologne he travelled on to his destination at Marburg an der Lahn where he lodged with the widowed Frau von Pritzelwitz and her family. Hers was the stiffness and formality of the older Imperial Germany, not the freer, more romantic ways of Weimar. 'After every meal one had to shake one's hostess by the hand with a little bow and say, "Blessed be the meal time".' There was also a strange worship of soup: 'The word "*Suppe*" would be uttered in tones of hushed reverence usually reserved for the Deity and at every meal there would be gigantic tureens full of the stuff which would be ladled out into enormous soup plates while the family sat with heads bent as if in silent prayer.'

His German tutor was the celebrated Fräulein Dietzen who, many years before, had taught Dr Bell, Bishop of Chichester. Her face was long, thin and bearded like that of an ancient dyspeptic goat. She was, however, recognised as an excellent teacher.

While there, Hugh wrote frequently to Graham. Their correspondence then and later was overwhelmingly about books and writing. In reply from 'Hampstead Heath, Broiling gently, May 22', Graham confessed perplexity at his young brother's literary tastes:

> Your lines of liking I do not know any longer. For instance, do you care at all for literary criticism—if so, there is nothing better than *Avowals* by George Moore . . . Or do you like biography—*François Villon* by D. B. Wyndham Lewis is good. On travel in weird places *The Magic Island* is an interesting work telling of black magic and Voodoo worship in Haiti . . . Of novels I have read few that I like better than Joseph Hergesheimer's *Tampico*, scene Mexico. Do you like Aldous Huxley? You ought to try him . . .

Whatever the efforts of Graham to guide Hugh's intellectual and literary development, he remained the shy, gangly youth who found the atmosphere of a dining table awash with soup a little too much for him. That drowning feeling emerged once more, and in order to escape it he would take bread and sausage and wander through the great pine forests that hung over Marburg. With him he took the poems of Catullus: 'As I walked through the woods I translated them into English for a beautiful and wanton (though unfortunately not with me) girl with whom I was very much in love.' The physical effort which, like most young men of his age, he might have preferred to have expended with the wanton girl, he spent instead on the tennis court. The tennis club was a useful introduction to the centre of Marburg social life. Like everything else, however, in this remnant of Imperial society, life in the club was heavily regimented; each time Hugh arrived there he would be expected to walk round shaking hands with everyone who wasn't actually playing.

That summer was exceptionally hot, a vintage year for wine if not for Hugh Greene, who got heat stroke on the tennis court and returned to England sooner than originally intended. It was a crucial period for him: his first time away from home, his first serious dabbles in love and sex, his introduction to German history, politics and culture, but, most important, his first introduction to the German language which would later shape his life. In that summer of 1929, however, that life did not have any particular direction or intent. His ambitions were almost non-existent. All that mattered was to get away from Berkhamsted, and he had already accomplished that by getting into Oxford.

Merton was to be as pleasant a sojourn and as undirectional as Marburg had been. It was to be a time of boisterous uncertainty in which he kept hidden his considerable intellectual gifts, but kept visible his taste for beer and for unconventional women. When Hugh alighted from the train at Oxford station in 1929, his worldliness was limited, his shyness powerful, his eagerness to study present but not in any great doses, his urge to find a certain form of sensual experience considerable, his desire to leave behind those childhood years massive. Goronwy Rees wrote of his own feelings about the young undergraduates of 1929 to whom Oxford 'presented a blissful liberation from the restrictions imposed on them at their public schools'. It was, he says, as if 'they had escaped from some premature form of concentration or labour camp'. The scars though didn't go very deep and 'in no way prevented the victims, while licking their wounds, from enjoying the liberties and pleasures they were now offered; rather they only added a keener and sharper flavour to them'.

The depression which followed the Wall Street crash and the slow but obvious rise to power of the Nazis in Germany began to introduce a new mood among sections of the student population. It was not to be long before 'pleasure gave way to politics, athletes and homosexuals suddenly turned revolutionaries, political agitation took the place of dinner parties and conversation gave way to polemics'. The winds of political change in 1929 and 1930 were no more than a whisper compared to the hurricane that was to come, but they did begin to ruffle leaves, to concern those souls with the disposition to be concerned. Hugh Greene and his friends, John Mann, James Gibson and Christopher Serpell, were not so disposed. Hugh Greene's Oxford was closer to that of Evelyn Waugh than Auden.

Oxford itself was quiet with sparse traffic and even Cowley and its Morris motor works created little disturbance. Hugh especially enjoyed the countryside; walking was always to be a particular pleasure and while at Merton he got to know every village and pub within a radius of about fifteen miles. Little country breweries still existed, and Woodstock, with a population of 900, had eleven pubs owned by nine different breweries, all offering real beer. Bitter was sixpence a pint and mild fourpence a pint. Eggs, sausages and cheese with crusty bread could be obtained in the smallest village pubs, sometimes with home-cured bacon, dark blue in colour and remarkably pungent in taste. Bliss was it—in the gentle evening glow of a dying world—to be alive.

Merton was a small, rich college with just over a hundred undergraduates. It was 'noted for its ancient dons, smelling of dust and cheese, for gaiety, for hard drinking and gentlemanly homosexuality'. Its emphasis was on academic matters rather than sport, and the Merton Eight contained people who would never have dreamed of rowing at a sporting college. For a few weeks the college training crew had Hugh as one of their number, but when a boil appeared on his bottom he abandoned it as a sport fit only for galley slaves.

23

John Mann, who had come up from Bristol Grammar School and was later to become a director of Unilever, arrived at the same time as Hugh Greene:

> The day after I arrived I heard an awful struggle going on on the staircase. I looked out to see what was happening and this was Hugh's own personal bed being brought up the stairs because there was no bed in the College which was long enough for him to sleep in. I had all this explained to me by our scout who was a very bibulous character called Day.

Even the bibulous Day seems to have been taken aback by Hugh Greene's own drinking. It was the custom then for the scout to take into his young gentlemen an early morning cup of tea. On more than one morning Day would inform Mann, 'Mr Greene, sir, up the pole again last night. Had to clear up a terrible mess in the fire place.' Greene developed a reputation for becoming 'rather wild' after drinking bouts and for making far too much noise when trying to clamber unobtrusively back into college after hours. He also took to brandishing his fencing sabre, which, given his inebriated state and his height, did not inspire confidence. Among his personal papers, bills from 'Castle & Co. Ltd., Wine Merchants' are prominent.

To his companions at Merton he was perhaps less extrovert than this description has so far indicated. They detected something of the shyness which he had tried to leave behind in Berkhamsted. He hinted at times that he had an urge to write a book, though those comments were treated with a good deal of scepticism by his drinking partners, since they felt that he did not possess the necessary concentration. His mind was stimulated but directionless, searching to establish points of stability from what went on around him, without itself becoming firmly rooted. In a world in which most people's political ideologies and commitments were becoming increasingly fixed, Hugh's remained adrift.

Was he, however, restless but seeking roots, or rootless

With Doris Day and 'Schnozzle' Durante,
MGM Studios, Hollywood, 1962

The Queen's visit to BBC Television Studios, November 1961, accompanied by Hugh, Sir Arthur fforde and Kenneth Adam (left)

Hugh welcomes Lord Reith, the BBC's first Director General to the Television Services' 25th Anniversary Dinner, 1961

and determined to remain so? Questions of belief, commitment, certainty, began to impinge upon his life but not in any deeply reflective way, more as an ill-defined puzzle. He was not committed to any obvious set of ideas, though he did have a considerable capacity for asking questions.

At Merton he began to display a taste for less orthodox personalities, particularly in his women. John Mann recalls that 'he experimented in some rather unusual friendships', especially in his final year when he was living out of college in rooms in Ship Street. One woman, Ulrica, was described as 'not particularly beautiful but way out intellectually, *avant garde*'. John Mann suggested that:

> . . . there were in Hugh some Germanic elements. There is a certain kind of arrogance amongst Germans. Now Hugh is in no way an arrogant person, quite the reverse. But there were occasions, particularly when he was dealing with women, when he tended to be a little arrogant. And yet mixed up with it, and this you often find in Germans, was a sentimentality which makes for a slightly peculiar mixture. His women always seemed odd to me.

Hugh was what today would be called a male chauvinist; one who wanted to possess a romantic object rather than just to indulge her as a sexual object. That sentimentality, that searching for a different, slightly risqué 'avant garde' object for his emotions as well as his bed was one of the more obvious traits that developed at this stage in Hugh's life.

Shortly before coming up to Oxford he had seen Fritz Lang's silent film, *The Spy*, at a cinema in Tunbridge Wells. 'Three of the main interests in my life immediately coalesced: Germany, the films, espionage.' Once at Oxford he began to review films at the Headington cinema and then later, in conjunction with 'a character called Wurzel, who combined shadiness with naïveté in almost equal proportions', he took over the running of the cinema for several seasons to show old silent films. After a year he obtained permission from the Proctors to start the Oxford University

Film Society, becoming its first President. The front page of the *Oxford Mail* for Monday, February 2nd, 1931 has a photograph of the committee of the OUFS. Dressed like characters straight out of P. G. Wodehouse: 'Mr J. Barber, Mr N. Coghill, Mr A. Wordsworth, Mr James Gibson (hon. sec.) and Mr Hugh Carleton Greene (the president)' are joined by Dr Stobie, Mayor of Oxford and Miss E. Nielsen. Hugh Carleton sits in the centre of the group, legs crossed, mop of hair, very serious, very spruce.

He had much to be pleased with, since in getting the Film Society off the ground he had demonstrated energy, guile, administrative qualities, patience and a talent for handling people. About the Film Society he wrote:

> For one term we had our Sunday evening meetings at the Masonic Hall in the High Street where there was only one projector and there had therefore to be an interval after every reel. We then moved to the Electra Cinema in Queen Street. To belong to the Film Society soon became the fashionable thing to do and the subscriptions enabled me to make frequent visits to London to search for and then book films. Wardour Street was then really a street of adventure and small, and sometimes crooked, renters abounded, particularly for the German, Swedish and Russian silent classics. Even the big men, like Sam Eckman of MGM, were very helpful and it always made a useful impression to visit one of the small fry smoking one of his gigantic cigars. It was then that I started calling myself by my full name, Hugh Carleton Greene. It seemed to fit the Wardour Street of those days.

The bright lights, the tinsel and glamour were beginning to appeal to him, and where other young men of his time went on an existential or political search he was more inclined to follow the trail left by Sam Eckman's cigars. He enjoyed the whole aura of excitement surrounding his London jaunts, which began with a visit to Mr Bowman, the Warden of Merton:

When one knocked on his front door to obtain permission to go to London for the day it would be opened with disconcerting suddenness by a very distinguished butler who bore a marked resemblance to Boris Karloff. One would state one's errand and the butler then mounted a long staircase which stretched upwards from the hall. He would turn a corner, reappear immediately, descend the staircase with slow and easy grace and say, 'The Warden says you may go sir.' I am quite certain that he never spoke to the Warden at all.

The Electra Cinema was run by a small chain to whose senior officials Hugh Greene would give excellent lunches in his room at the expense of the Film Society. He always had an eye to the diplomatic utility of a good lunch. His profligacy resulted from the fact that they charged ten shillings a term membership but had many more members than they anticipated; this became something of a scandal when they threw a huge party to try, unsuccessfully, to soak up the surplus.

The manager of the cinema was a lively character called Roberts, who sported a blond moustache with waxed ends. Hugh proceeded to have an affair with Robert's beautiful, frail, ethereal wife who, unfortunately for her and her young lover, died of consumption. Greene later wrote:

> Our friendship became rather public when the enormous sergeant major who was the commissionaire at the Electra strode one evening into the crowded George bar where I was waiting for her, snapped to attention, saluted and bellowed in his best parade ground voice, 'Mrs Roberts will be twenty minutes late, sir.' I do not think that Roberts minded much, he had other fish to fry.

The Film Society programme itself was eclectic, from Eisenstein's *Battleship Potemkin* and Germaine Dulac's *Seashell and the Clergyman* (which had been banned by the censor, who argued that it was meaningless but that if it had a meaning it was undoubtedly objectionable), to Sennett's *The Fatal Mallet* with Charlie Chaplin.

One might be forgiven for imagining that there was not much going on in the academic area. In fact, Hugh did rather well, if not brilliantly, in his studies. At the end of his fifth term he took Honours Moderations in Classics, which meant that he had had to study all of Homer, Virgil, Demosthenes and Cicero, as well as various other classical authors. His tutor for this was Robert Levens and the two became close friends.

Hugh then had to decide what to read for his finals. The natural thing would have been for him to read Greats, which included Philosophy and Ancient History, but he felt that he did not have the mind of a philosopher and was unlikely to acquire one. An uncomfortably intellectual German girlfriend, Barbara Grautoff, had persuaded him to look at the works of Kant, said to be easier in the English translation than in the original German, but Hugh found that even a page would send him to sleep with not a word understood.

Then he thought he might read German. But after one tutorial with a tutor called Bostock, he felt that he could not spend the next two years in his company without suffering from debilitating boredom. He finally decided to switch to English Literature, which he now regards as one of the better decisions he made in his life.

As there was no English tutor at Merton, he went initially to Nevill Coghill at Exeter but after a term he felt that there was no 'really intimate understanding' between him and Coghill. Relief came in the form of Edmund Blunden who had just been appointed Fellow and Tutor in English Literature at Merton. Greene found him an inspiring teacher and a lasting friend.

Momentarily at the end of his time at Oxford, Hugh toyed with the idea of being a don; he had ambitions to write a thesis on a 17th century poetess called Katharine Phillips, stressing her lesbian characteristics, but Robert Levens never thought that this would have suited Hugh, nor did he think that Hugh would ever have achieved a First, even if he

28

had spent less time enjoying himself. Levens was not one of those who saw Hugh as a shy young man. He thought him ambitious with a 'suppressed self-confidence'. Levens also thought him self-centred, 'the sort of person who tended to have Number One in mind'. Levens said of him: 'Hugh had no nose for error, lacked accuracy, tended to be careless in his work, and anyway could never have settled down to the quiet life of Academe.' He had spotted that Hugh had not the patience, the skill nor the scholar's percipience to sift through detail, to check for truth. Hugh's intelligence has always been keen, but he would never have made a meticulous researcher.

In fact Hugh had already begun to edge towards journalism. On March 31st, 1931 he covered his first story, an eighteen-line account of a fire at Finstock, for the *Oxford Mail*, for which he received, though not until 1959, the minimum payment of two shillings and sixpence with sixpence telephone costs.

He was eager not to waste his time in the backwaters of the provincial press. To achieve his ambitions he enlisted the support of Edmund Blunden who wrote two letters of introduction, one to Phil Tomlinson at *The Times*, the other to R. Ellis Roberts at the *New Statesman*. To Tomlinson he wrote:

Dear Phil, I am encouraging my friend and pupil Mr H. C. Greene to try on *The Times* some articles which he intends to write on his observations in Germany this Christmas. I expect they'll be good; he's in touch with the new world especially. Do oblige me, if you can, by looking out for what he sends in.

However, in case he was not successful in his journalistic enterprises, he asked Sam Eckman of MGM to give him an introduction to Michael Balcon at Gaumont British. Balcon however had nothing to offer and Hugh wrote of his disappointment to his mother. In the same letter he mentioned that he had been in communication with Friedel, his Berkhamsted cousin Barbara's ex-maid, who was now living in

Germany. As Hugh told his mother, 'she's not a hysterical sort of person', yet she had written most aggressively about the pogroms, saying:

> I bought English papers every day and they made me furious with the lies they were writing about the 'poor' German Jews. The government can't be radical enough against the damned Jews, who made millions of marks out of the poor and the state. One scandal after another comes now before the public about the Jews who swindled money into foreign countries to have it safe there if they had to go too. Germany really is poor enough and can't afford such subjects. Heil Hitler more than ever.

Friedel's letter rekindled his interest in Germany and its deviant political developments. However he was still uncertain about his future, so tried yet another tack, publishing. He had an unhappy interview with the managing director of Chatto & Windus which went rather badly, possibly because, he thinks, his shyness was especially acute that day. He was told that there was no job in publishing for him, and so he was once more without anchorage. Blunden tried to help with Harmsworth, but in vain. Blunden wrote: 'I supplied a study of your valued characters and powers, which I think might have helped if anything could have been done.' Blunden also enclosed letters to Kingsley Martin of the *New Statesman*, to Ellis Roberts, now of *Time and Tide*, and J. P. Collins at the *Daily Telegraph*. He stated:

> He begins with a considerable qualification as a Latin and Greek scholar, and an acquaintance with German which he is eagerly extending. In English Literature he is very well informed indeed, and has a special knack of discovering and appreciating the excellent, which, one way or another, has not been sufficiently discussed or lies outside the academic highroad. He writes originally, both in conception and in illustration; he is concise and vigorous and his essays for me almost always gave me something fresh

to think about. Some of his views are perhaps a little difficult to follow, but they are invariably vivid, and they spring from honest individual consideration and not from caprice.

Altogether I believe that he is admirably qualified to teach literature whether he does so as an author or as a lecturer or a tutor. He passes on his own sense of what is vital, both in his ideas and in his brilliant use of words . . . My personal regard for him may be gathered from the above, but apart from it my opinion of his talents would be unaltered.

Blunden added to his protégé, 'meanwhile whatever happens, why not start editing old Byron's narrative'. This was a reference to a publication of 1768 by John Byron, the poet's grandfather. John Byron had been a seventeen-year-old midshipman on board a ship which foundered off the coast of Chile on May 14th, 1741 and had written an account of 'the great distresses' he and his companions had suffered off the coast of Patagonia. Hugh had picked up a leatherbound first edition and found that it greatly stirred his imagination.

Whilst still in the doldrums Kingsley Martin responded to the overtures made to him and agreed that if Greene went to Munich, the *New Statesman* would pay him space rates for anything they printed. Martin also suggested that the *Daily Herald* might be interested. They were, and the Foreign Editor of the *Herald* agreed that they would also pay space rates for anything they used. Hugh wrote to Blunden informing him of developments and asking for his help in contacting people in Germany. Blunden replied: 'Excellent your seizing the *New Statesman*. If only those journals had more sway. Alas, I know nobody in Germany except an ex-pugilist at Emden, and a policeman at Cologne . . .'

However, even with such an encouraging start, journalism was unlikely to earn him enough to meet all his financial needs. His father then agreed to give him £200 on the understanding that if he did not survive and prosper, he would return to England at the end of the year to take the civil service entrance examination.

3

When Hugh left England in December 1933, he demonstrated his instinctive ability, which remained with him all his
life, to be in the right place at the right time doing the right
job. Kingsley Martin had suggested he go to Munich, but
first he went to Berlin, not in search of the grail of excitement,
permissiveness and decadence which had so attracted many
a young Englishman in the previous years. He went there
instead to say goodbye to his frighteningly intellectual girlfriend, Barbara Grautoff, whom he had met at Oxford.

Whilst in Berlin, he went to see the *Daily Herald's* correspondent there, a man called King, a venerable figure with
long grey hair hanging down on both sides of his face and a
waistcoat stained by the droppings of innumerable cigars.
Sardonically, King pointed out that Hugh was unlikely to
survive long in Munich as a correspondent for the *Daily
Herald* and *New Statesman*, papers which the authorities there
would regard as far too left wing. From his wallet King then
produced a visiting card inscribed, 'Correspondent of the
Detroit *Daily News*'.

Thus armed, Hugh arrived in Munich, where he proceeded to register with the local police, the British Consulate
and the Press Department of the National Socialist Party
Munich headquarters, where he duly presented himself as
the correspondent for the Detroit *Daily News* as King had
suggested. He then rushed off to search for stories to send
back to London. There is no question of doubt in his letters,
no worry that he might not succeed, though it wasn't long
before the difficulties of life as a stringer became apparent.

His immediate need was for contacts, and he hoped Graham might help. He wrote to ask for introductions to Jesuits in Southern Germany, thinking that perhaps he might be able to send back reports on the role of the Church in Germany. Graham replied:

> I don't know any of the Jesuits, but I saw Bede Jarrett who has just come to an end of his term as Provincial of the Dominicans. He's going to ring me up with introductions to Jesuits and to some of the leading lay Catholics in Munich. They'll be first-class introductions. I don't have to give him any reason. Tell me if you become a Catholic.

Graham sent off the introductions and added, 'No need to feign with these people an interest in Catholicism; though, of course, if you are interested . . .' These introductions may not have affected Hugh theologically, but they did give him an insight into the Catholic opposition to the Nazis which became one of the focal points of his work as a correspondent.

Slowly in his mind he began to build up a picture of Nazi Germany. He saw the true dimensions of the horror of the régime, but also that its grip upon the German people was far from total, that there was an active opposition which deserved and needed to be written about. It was at this time that he became increasingly bitter about the appeasement policy of the British government which in its ignorant cowardice guaranteed the holocaust.

He soon 'caught the true reporter's fever, the conviction that just round the corner something horrible or important was bound to be going on. And in Nazi Germany there really was always something horrible going on just round the corner. Terror had become part of ordinary respectable bourgeois daily life.' His rooms were with one such respectable bourgeois family from whom he quickly learned the lines:

Lieber Gott, mach mich stumm
Das ich nicht nach Dachau komm.

Dear God, make me dumb
So that I don't to Dachau come.

He spent his first Christmas, he wrote to his mother, at the home of Donald St Clair Gainer, the British Consul, where he met 'one very charming person, a Mrs Vavasour Barber, who is acquainted with the Bells (I mean Oxford Bells). She has a lovely house here where I've been several times since, and I'm going again tonight.'

Lodging with Mrs Barber was Helga Guinness, the precocious seventeen-year-old daughter of a Norwegian mother and of Samuel Guinness, the very successful Irish director of the merchant bank Guinness Mahon. Helga did not get on very well with her parents and had been sent to Munich because of the trouble she was having with her eyes. Apparently her mother did not like girls wearing glasses, but without them Helga could not see very well, so her mother took her away from peering at her school books and sent her abroad to learn German instead. Hugh immediately liked her very much. For her part, she found him very tall, very young and very clever, 'but not clever-clever', very serious but with a nice sense of humour. They began to see a great deal of each other.

In January 1934 Hugh managed to earn 200 marks, the equivalent of about £10. This, combined with the money from his father and that earned from giving English lessons, meant that at least he was not in penury. He would send back items of local news, small feature pieces including an article on the working of marriage bureaux and features on German and Swiss life:

My most interesting thing since I last wrote is that I have had half an hour's conversation with Grock [the clown], who is now appearing in Munich. A worried tired and melancholy man off the stage but wonderful on it. I was given a box free for myself and companion. I have also seen Hitler for the first time. I have taken to going to a café where he often is, in the hope of seeing him, and last week I went in one evening and there he was in the corner. Later Goebbels came in as well. Goebbels is a tiny little man with a limp, but most attractive looking with a charming smile. Things are becoming considerably more interesting here with the New Year.

His inclination, however, was not to the easy features but to the more exciting life of opposition to the Nazis. On one occasion this had potentially disastrous results. Towards the end of December 1933 he went to the SS headquarters, still pretending to represent the Detroit *Daily News*, requesting permission to visit Dachau. While there they asked for his passport which he handed over. To his horror he suddenly realised that the passport contained an unsealed envelope with an underground Communist pamphlet in it which one of his contacts in the Communist resistance had given him. He was finally called into another office where an SS officer returned his passport and told him that arrangements would be made for him to visit Dachau in a week or so. The envelope remained untouched. It was a salutary lesson in two ways: if his career was to prosper he must be a little more careful in his contacts with Nazi officials; at the same time he would never again overestimate the thoroughness of their security.

He wrote his mother:

I went over to Dachau concentration camp the other day. Though of course I saw no trace of cruelty, the general impression was pretty ghastly. But to be fair I might have felt the same in any prison anywhere. There are 400 SS guards, all with steel helmets and rifles to look after 2,300 prisoners. The guards were quite the most brutal and criminal looking collection of men I've ever seen, quite different from the prisoners. One is no longer allowed to speak to the prisoners, because in the past, the commandant told me, the foreign journalists who came used to tell lies about what the prisoners had told them! The eyes of the prisoners were horrible. I shan't forget that. I must stop this letter and take it to the person who is going to England. Please make no comment on its contents except to let me know you've received it, as all my correspondence is tampered with.

The camp was, he later wrote, 'evil, in broad daylight, not in the shadows of nightmare'.

The British Consul, Donald Gainer, not only introduced Hugh to Mrs Barber and so to Helga, but to Eustace Wareing, the *Daily Telegraph* correspondent in Germany. Wareing was a fussy, irascible, ruddy-faced man with a short body and stumbling flat-footed walk, who was also extremely randy. His Munich assistant had just been expelled so he was looking for a replacement; he liked Hugh but feared that lack of experience might count against him at the London office.

The Munich job didn't go to Hugh Greene, instead it was given to the one-legged Rhea Clyman. Nevertheless Hugh had impressed Wareing sufficiently for him to say that there might be an opening for him as his assistant in the Berlin office, but Hugh would first have to do a month's trial without pay. As a mere stringer in Munich Hugh had not been able to afford to use the telephone and knew that much of his copy going in the mail was being intercepted and destroyed by the Nazi authorities. Before accepting Wareing's offer therefore he decided to ask the editor of the *Herald* if he could become their regular correspondent in Munich. If they refused, he would go to Berlin.

Christopher Isherwood and his friends had gone to Berlin in the 1920s because it spelt freedom and because, as he later wrote:

> . . . an elderly relative had warned me against it, saying that it was the vilest place since Sodom . . . But Berlin offered more than sexual freedom: to be intimate with Germans was to cast off the emotions and rhetoric of the First World War, and so to reject childhood and become free and adult.

More prosaically he later admitted that 'Berlin meant boys'. They had been tourists in search of sin, whereas Greene and his colleagues, such as Norman Ebbutt and Karl Robson, were there because that was where the news was. Berlin was a theatre in which were playing the forces of good and evil: Hugh Greene was about to be given a front-row seat.

He arrived at the beginning of February 1934 and immediately began to work in the Berlin *Daily Telegraph* office on a month's trial, but his mind was not totally on the job and kept wandering back to Mrs Barber's. He was in love with Helga and missed her greatly. On arrival he had written to her to say he badly wanted to return to Munich to see her. Two days later he wrote again:

> Dear Helga, many thanks for your letter and the so charming photograph. I was so moved by the various emotions running in different directions across its pages that I nearly broke down in Cooks Mail Dept . . . But seriously I was much more homesick for Munich than I have ever been for England . . . I am now one of the world's real workers . . . I started doing a bit of work at the *Telegraph* office on Sunday morning. I read about 20 newspapers a day (which isn't quite as bad as it sounds) making marks with my nice new red pencil, and I've also been doing all the filing of documents which they've left over for the past two months . . .

Despite being lovelorn, Wareing's apparent confidence that Hugh would make a journalist was quickly shown to be correct. Before the end of February a story by him was given the best display, three headlines and head of the column, on the foreign pages of the *Telegraph*. Though he received no payment even when his stories appeared, he wrote to his mother, 'these weeks have at least been excellent experience'. These weeks were also for Hugh poor times and on one occasion his hunger and poverty were such that all he had to eat was a whole tin of hay-fever lozenges.

The first Sunday in March 1934 the news came over the

phone that the *Telegraph* had decided to give him the temporary post of assistant to Wareing on a salary of 500 marks a month, representing the NUJ minimum of nine guineas a week. His job entailed scanning the various German papers, looking especially for 'reaction' stories in which Germany was responding to English news, developing his contacts with members of the government, party, the banking world, as well as the opposition to the regime. He also read *Mein Kampf*, rapidly concluding that it contained the gist of Hitler's plans, which were malevolent, and thereafter could never understand the obtuseness which seemed to prevent leaders in the West from picking up the book.

Full of confidence, he finally expressed his love to Helga. Much later she was to argue that obtaining a wife was merely part and parcel of a much broader schema he had in mind in which marriage was the right thing to do. On the evidence of his letters that seems a too cynical view of the affair. She observed recently: 'The next girl he was actually interested in, once he'd got the job, would probably be the one he'd marry. He got the job and so he married.' His letters to her tell a rather different story. He felt himself to be genuinely in love with Helga, and longed for the certainty, commitment and sharing which he believed marriage could offer. On March 14th he wrote:

> I am no good at writing how much I love you. I prefer to kiss you very hard and tell you that way. Though I laugh when I think I am describing myself as a man of deeds and not of words! It's easier to write about the limitations of armaments than about my love for you which hasn't got any end or any beginning. I should certainly have hated it if you had cried when you left! I felt too near to that myself. Just to say I love you is better than any further protestations. But that you love me as you do is something I never dreamed of before you came.

He became lyrical in his writings: 'Now we need never be uncertain any more. I is we, and we is I. I love we, we love we, we love I, I love I. I'm sorry to be ungrammatical, perhaps I had better just say I love you.' They decided that they wanted to get married, even though Helga was still not eighteen, and they had only known each other spasmodically for three months. 'Tell your mother that we want to get married as soon as possible, but that when that will be cannot yet be said. I agree with you that by August I ought to know my fate.' Wareing was due to go on holiday in June, so his young protégé would be left in charge of the office alone for a month. If he could survive that without, as he put it, 'dropping any bricks', then his future as a correspondent would almost certainly be assured.

Raymond Greene was just about to be married when Hugh wrote to his mother, who was not even aware that Helga existed: 'You may be interested to know that I am following my brothers down the primrose path—in other words that I am engaged . . . The name is Helga Guinness.' He took the family by surprise. Graham wrote to him:

> Many congratulations on your engagement. The church was noisy with the news. Everyone seems to have seen the photograph [of Helga] but me. You seem to have timed your letter to perfection. Excitement however and maternal pride fought on Mamma's face throughout the service; there seemed to be a general impression that you had done something rather clever if perhaps, like my novels, a little risqué.

It wasn't however until a later letter that Hugh mentioned Helga's age, which he described as 'a continental seventeen'.

The Guinnesses apparently were 'indiscriminately delighted' with the news, making immediate plans to travel to Berlin to meet their prospective son-in-law; they arrived at the beginning of April. This first meeting 'went off pretty well I think. I worked pretty hard on the mother and apparently had my reward by winning her heart completely. I also got on well enough with the father. They are fairly pleasant people . . .' By May 1st he had changed his mind:

39

The mother for someone exceptionally silly, has a curious amount of intelligence. I like her faintly. The father whom I have not seen since they were first here I do not think I should ever like. There was something about him which vaguely repelled me from the first moment I heard his voice, even before I saw him. But that is not to deny that he has been of the greatest use to me in the way of introductions in these days when most of the news is financial.

It is difficult to know just why Hugh's feelings about the Guinnesses changed so rapidly. His genuine love for Helga contained a desire to possess her in order to know, and be certain, that his love was reciprocated; so long as the Guinnesses were there fluttering around their daughter, they could possibly have represented a challenge to that total possession and total immersion in a relationship which he wanted so very much, and which for a time he thought he had found:

> I can't tell you how incredibly happy your letters make me. That you should love me so much, as much as I love you, still seems to me almost a dream. And in a way such an incredible happiness almost frightens me. I shan't commit the terrible cliché, however true it is, of writing that I'm not worthy of you. But to have so much love committed to one is a responsibility. But never I hope will you want or have to say 'I love you' to anybody else in the world—for ever. There is a sort of calmness, quietness and completeness (though the calmness and quietness disappear when we are alone together somewhat!) about my love for you, a feeling of everlastingness, which is a new thing for me.

The correspondents of the Western press used as their drinking hole, club and, often, office, an establishment called Taverne, where they had a table permanently reserved. There they would meet each evening, get drunk on wine, swap stories and make ribald comments about the men from

40

the Gestapo, who sat at the next table trying to listen in to their conversations. Greene was a frequent visitor and while his relations with other journalists were friendly, they were also remote. Karl Robson, who was in Berlin at this time working for the *Morning Post*, observed that Hugh was 'not what the English call clubable, he wasn't a bird for staying up late drinking or anything like that when I first met him.' Neither did he show any particular passion for politics or social questions; he just did his job with all his feelings, impressions, conclusions submerged beneath the surface of his apparent aloofness. A correspondent for the Austrian News Agency, Ernst Albert, found Hugh to be 'a pretty cold fish, but I don't think deliberately so. When you worked with him you had the feeling that there was a barrier . . . it was nothing positive to put you off, but a lack of warmth.'

Despite these comments Hugh seemed to be leading a busy social life, playing tennis, swimming, sailing, having lunch with other correspondents, or with a contact, going out to dinner and attending balls. Much of this was, however, in the line of work; he socialised to hide his loneliness, for this bustling, gossipy, restless existence was not the life he sought. He wanted, or thought he wanted, the peace and security of a home. In an undated letter, probably written sometime during the spring of 1934, he mentioned he had met an old friend of Helga's and added with confidence and bravado:

It always amazes me to think that all these people I meet who have known you for years longer than I have and yet how little all of them including your parents know about my Helly. It gives me a nice comfortable feeling inside to think that I know you better than anybody else, even though I have enough to learn to keep me amused for years.'

Journalistically there would be periods of quiet when he became bored and his mind turned to other possible occupations, including the persistent murmur at the back of his mind that maybe he should still try to pursue a career in films. For a correspondent the quiet days were not just boring, but unnerving: '. . . even less news today than yesterday, but that's not really restful. When there's very little I am always worried by the feeling that I may have missed something right in front of my nose.' When things *did* happen in Hitler's Germany, however, they happened on a mind-numbing scale.

On the morning of June 30th, 1934, Hugh went to play tennis with *The Times* correspondent, Norman Ebbutt. They were both nervous, feeling that something momentous was about to occur, something which they knew would be important but the nature of which they had no idea, because thirteen days earlier von Papen had attacked, in a speech at Marburg, Nazi propaganda, Nazi Byzantinism and all the talk of a 'Second Revolution'. When someone like von Papen indulged in such polemic, it was obvious that something was either going to happen or was happening already. They finished playing at about noon, walked out from the tennis club in the Tiergartenstrasse, turning right past the head-quarters of the Berlin-Brandenburg SA stormtroopers, which they now saw was surrounded by men in greyish-green uniforms, armed with carbines and light machine-guns. Men in brown uniforms were coming out of the building with their arms in the air. For a moment they had the wild hope that the army had turned on the Nazi régime. But the men in the greyish-green uniforms did not belong to the Reichswehr: they belonged to the special State Police detachment of Hermann Goering, Prime Minister of Prussia, for General Goering was in charge of everything that was happening that day in Berlin.

Norman Ebbutt and Hugh Greene hurried to their offices, on opposite sides of Unter den Linden. 'I remember that I had a sinking feeling in my stomach. I had only been engaged by the *Daily Telegraph* four months before, my boss was away and, with all my inexperience, I had to cover as best I could one of the biggest stories of the decade.'

The news at the office was that all telephone connections

to foreign countries had been cut off and that General Goering had summoned a meeting of the foreign press for three pm at the Propaganda Ministry, where Goebbels, whom he hated and despised, normally presided. Goering, in the uniform of a General of the Luftwaffe, strode in, looking properly grim. He always had a sense of the dramatic. 'You boys like a story,' he said using the English word. 'I've got one for you today all right.' He explained that for some time he and Himmler, the chief of the SS, had been keeping their eyes open for possible insurrection by Ernst Roehm, Chief of Staff of the SA and other ambitious stormtroop leaders against Hitler. He, Goering, had been entrusted by Hitler with special powers to strike at those who thought they could overthrow the state. Hitler had arrested Roehm and other stormtroop leaders near Munich, some had been killed, some had committed suicide.

Hugh Greene was hearing at first hand about what is now known as the Night of the Long Knives, when Hitler decided to settle old scores and dominate through the SS.

More than any other event June 30th revealed to Hugh Greene the real nature of the Nazi state. He wasn't surprised, it was just that the slaughter sharpened his senses to the horror around him. All he could do was to try to communicate something of that horror in his journalism. Hitler had come to power as the man who would bring order to the crumbling chaos of the Weimar Republic. His appearance merely heightened the disorder, and June 30th, 1934 was the worst example of the chaos and conflict which would follow in his wake. It was the day when the revolution turned upon itself. Hugh saw that Hitler's was:

. . . a gangster's régime. It didn't come in to restore order. This was the street taking over a modern state in a way which hasn't happened, I think, at any other time in our history. It was rather as if this country had been taken over by the Black and Tans. And of course they were not ashamed of killing off another lot of gangsters. One was living in a gangster world.

To get away from the gangster state, Hugh often went to a suburb in the woods outside Berlin with the curious name of Onkel Tom's Hütte. There he could get a very good meal whilst a band played sentimental music. At other times, in other moods, he would go to the cinema: 'There's nothing I enjoy more than a good custard pie comedy.' There was also the cabaret which managed to survive for two or three years after Hitler's accession to power. Such places as the Tingel Tangel and the Katakombe were a breath of fresh air in the oxygen-starved world of Nazi culture. They were, he says, 'remarkably frank at times in their satirisation of the régime'. Another journalist thought the cabaret was 'brave but tame', perhaps more daring in Munich than in Berlin. The mood though in Germany, in the months after January 1933, was becoming so oppressive that even the slightest criticism of the régime gave tremendous relief. On the stage of the Katakombe he saw for the first time Tatjana Sais who, though he had no inkling of it then, was to be the great love of his later life and his third wife.

Although Helga's family were still dubious about their relationship because of her age, Hugh felt happy during these months: he had covered the startling events of June 30th with considerable skill for someone of such limited experience, he had developed a wide range of friends, and he was in love. For the first time in his life he felt professionally and emotionally secure.

Most days were still spent reading as many German newspapers as possible, keeping an eye all the time, rather like an intelligence officer, on the small pieces at the bottom of the page which might contain a hint about some strange activity or event. Each day there were two booked calls to London, one in the late afternoon, one in the late evening. His letters to Helga and his mother are dotted by references to the need to break off to talk to London. Each day there were also several deliveries from DNB, the official German news agency. Other colleagues were also invaluable sources, particularly when they were as well informed as Norman Ebbutt. Talent lay not in soaking up the gossip which drenched the city, but in interpreting its meaning and then slipping that interpretation into copy without its being so apparent that it would lead to expulsion.

To be successful, a journalist has to develop a range of personal contacts so that he is not solely reliant on official sources. In a Germany dancing on the edge of chaos, such souls were legion and Hugh had additional help from Sam Guinness, who arranged some useful banking contacts, notably Paul Wallich and Emil Puhl of the Reichsbank. It was dangerous to write or telephone a really good informant, so either secret meetings had to be arranged or else Hugh, who was hardly an inconspicuous figure, would ask Helga to deliver a message.

It was a standard practice to develop a contact with a government or military official. Greene's main contact here was Hitler's adjutant, Captain Wiedemann, whom he got to know through a shady character called Bernard Lescrinier. Lescrinier was known to one and all as 'Fatty' and worked principally for the *Daily Telegraph* and United Press. His importance was that he had direct access to Goering, and many contacts in the Reichskanzlei. He remained a puzzling character because no one was ever quite certain precisely what his relations and intentions actually were. His main role seems to have been to keep Goering in touch with opinions among the foreign press, in return for which he was allowed to supply them with occasional scoops. He was, Greene thought, despite his mystery 'a likeable man. Honest. No Nazi and extremely useful.' Lescrinier was one of the very few who was open about his contact with the foreign press, he did not mind being seen entering their offices where he obviously felt quite at home: indeed there is a photograph of Hugh sitting at his desk reading Goebbel's *Angriff*, with Lescrinier nearby tucking into the latest edition of the *Daily Telegraph*.

Other sources kept themselves submerged, including a local Frankfurt correspondent who continually rang the office with news of the latest outrage at a synagogue or a Jewish cemetery, and an Evangelical Protestant pastor who

45

regularly supplied information about clergy and parishioners who had been arrested and sent to concentration camps. The pastor also gave Hugh a whole sequence of stories about Pastor Niemöller of the Bekenntnis Kirche, a former U-boat commander who had become a leading opponent of the Nazi government. Hugh's main contact with the Communist underground was with Stefan Grzeszkowiak, known as Peter the Pole.

Though Hugh didn't have the same access to the very highest levels of the Nazi party, he did occasionally meet some of the bizarre luminaries who had come to the fore. To Helga he wrote:

Last Saturday we didn't play vingt-et-un because going to Taverne after the party we joined up with Diels, the head of the secret police who was there with some people and later went on with him to a boring hole where those who dance danced. But it was most interesting to meet Diels. He is I believe only 26.

His journalistic career was progressing well, he was now employed on a monthly basis, so he and Helga could think about the details of their wedding. They decided to have a church ceremony, although neither of them had 'any particular belief'. Indeed he wrote to Helga, saying:

I feel that the Christian view of children as a 'primary purpose' is very degrading. I marry you because I believe that I can only get the greatest happiness possible for me living with you. It is 'primary' that I want you enormously. But there's no procreation instinct in that.

Sex, he believed, was solely and simply important for what he described to Helga as:

. . . the pleasure and exaltation of the moment, and not in the least for results, which we shall anyhow be trying to prevent. The only reason why I should wish to have

46

children at all—after some years—is because I know it
would make you happier and therefore by derivation
probably myself.

His indifference to children, rather than something to be
resolved, was like a bomb ticking away beneath the surface of
their life together, waiting to explode when their efforts at
'prevention' failed.

However, outwardly the summer of 1934 seemed particularly serene for Hugh, for he had much to be content about.
His marriage plans were coming to fruition and he had found
a job he enjoyed enormously, at which he was a success: 'I
hear from Wareing that my name 'breathes forth a sweet
odour' in the London office'. He continued in this letter to his
mother:

> I'm feeling pretty sure now that this has got into my blood
> too much for me to be happy at any other job. In fact I've
> got much more of the journalist's instinct than Wareing.
> He's glad to be away while exciting things are happening
> and there's a lot to do, whereas I should be mad if I was out
> of the country during any really big story. I've fallen under
> the drug all right.

Emotionally, too, he had found fulfilment in companionship.
He wrote to Helga, 'I am happy even though you have gone
away, because I know that you are really here too, and
knowing that the worst sort of loneliness is impossible any
more.' The wedding ceremony was at Chelsea Old Church
on October 24th. Neither of them was particularly impressed by the fact that their relationship was being solemnised
and legitimised by the Church. He wrote to Helga:

> I entirely agree with you about the wedding. I shouldn't
> feel in the slightest degree different if you came out to live
> with me without our being married. All that hocus pocus
> means nothing to me whatever, only the fact that I love
> you and hope I shall always love you . . . Wareing said

today that he admired the way I preserved my sangfroid with the wedding service ordeal pressing so close upon me—I don't know what he expects me to do. I hope I manage to preserve it through the ceremony. Let's try to make ourselves heard with the responses we have to make and show them that they can't get us down.

Nor did actuality alter his attitude, indeed he asked his mother to 'tell Da that neither of us enjoyed the wedding! My disapproval of the ceremony is considerably increased by experience.'

His relationship with the Guinnesses continued to deteriorate. Why he should have developed such a sharp antipathy to them is difficult to say. An intriguing facet of his character was a tendency to develop sudden harsh judgments about people. He was also undoubtedly reflecting Helga's confused and unfavourable feelings towards her parents. She was actually allergic to their visits and would break out in a rash whenever they were about to arrive. Hugh later wrote to his mother:

Apart from anything else there has been the visit of those terrible Guinnesses. Really I know no people whom I dislike more . . . I had a considerable set to with Sam from which fortunately I emerged victorious. He did not think we were displaying enough wealth and said we ought to have two servants (in a three-roomed flat). Said he did not like Helga ever opening the door and reams more sickening nonsense. But in the end I managed to silence him because he's not quite armoured against sarcasm. One of his best remarks to Helga (not to me) was that he wished we could get another telephone beside the one which is connected with the office because he did not like people to think of her in any way in connection with the *Daily Telegraph*! If one met such an impossible *nouveau riche* character in a book, one would say 'how far fetched'.

Later still he described the effect of their visits on Helga as 'equivalent to a bad attack of influenza . . .' Helga now says that she felt that Hugh wanted to cut her off from her family altogether:

> He didn't see why we should be involved with the Guinness family and in one sense I sympathised with him because I got on better with his family than I did with my own, because I thought they were much more my sort of people. But I just didn't feel the same way about it. I thought it was a sign of childishness on his part, I thought it illogical that he should want to be grown up and married and that he shouldn't be able to do a bit of give and take.'

Unfortunately Sam Guinness was a snob and an interfering father: he also had an over-developed sense of propriety, which Hugh felt was irrational, and with which he had no patience.

Nineteen thirty-four had been an interesting year, a passionate year, a crucial year. At the end of it Hugh emerged a reasonably successful foreign correspondent of a major British newspaper. He emerged too with a young wife with whom he believed himself to be deeply in love. He had begun the year in penury and ended it with an annual salary of £500 and an income to Helga from her father of £100 a year.

Hugh retained an affectionate relationship with his mother. Indeed they probably found in their letters much of the communication which had been missing in Berkhamsted. They are warm letters full of talk about books and films, which they both loved. He recommended her to see '*The Bengal Lancer* film if you get a chance. It's complete bunk but immensely exciting and very well done. And it has your dear Gary Cooper at his very best.'

Hugh was also involved at this time in the problems of his brother Herbert. Uncle Edward had stepped in at one point and given Herbert a job in Brazil, only to find he had to sack him because of his corrupting influence on the workers. Charles Green was now worried about his eldest son, who seemed to be frittering his life away while his younger brothers went from success to success. Marion Greene wrote to Hugh to see if he thought it would be possible for Sam Guinness to find Herbert a job in banking. In the meantime Herbert had to be supported financially, and Helga suggested to Hugh that they contribute a pound a week to his father Charles' bank account as a way of channelling money to Herbert without him knowing it. Herbert was to become a permanent problem which was neither understood, nor solved.

Nineteen thirty-five turned out to be dull, and the first months of 1936 proved the same. The excitement of being a journalist was beginning to pall. Hugh wrote to his mother in March that things 'are pretty quiet here just now. In fact I'm bored. When I'm in England this summer I mean to study seriously the possibility of getting a job at home.' He next wrote to Graham to ask if he would make enquiries about the chance of work at the National Film Institute. Graham was amazed: 'I thought you were permanently wedded to journalism.' Graham then wrote:

> The Camerons were to dinner here last night. The post of General Manager of the Film Institute (£750 a year, rising I think as things are to £1,000) is to be advertised in the papers next Wednesday. Cameron is chairman of the selection board. He hopes you will put in.

Graham was, however, as he explained in a letter three days later, 'frankly surprised that you are interested. I would have thought the *Daily Telegraph* was safer and better. And do you want to live in London? Certainly I should have thought it was dangerous to let the editor know of your intentions.'

However, the mood of restless boredom and the desire to change jobs quickly passed as events began to move again in the spring. By April Hugh was informing his mother that in the previous six weeks he had only had two free days and about half a dozen free nights. By September he had begun to sense the imminence of war. By December he had come to recognise the appalling nature of National Socialism; to see it for the evil it contained and the threat it posed. The whole experience of Nazi Germany served to amplify his hatred for bullies which he had begun to develop at school years before. The brutality, torment and pain, the bigotry, prejudice and intolerance of Germany were certainly on a grander scale, but they nevertheless retained echoes of those dark caverns at Berkhamsted where flesh scorched on red hot radiators and little boys screamed. Hugh had few illusions about what was to come; he was no appeaser. He thought:

> . . . the editor of *The Times* an absolute tragic disaster at that time in our history. The *Telegraph*, I think, took a while to catch up, and I can remember an occasion after the German march into the Rhineland, when Eustace Wareing and I put together an article about what would happen next, when we said it was quite obvious that after the Rhineland would come Austria, and after Austria would come Czechoslovakia, and after Czechoslovakia would come Danzig and Poland, and that didn't require much foresight. We did it. But Ribbentrop, who was at that time in London as a special emissary of Hitler, managed to persuade Lord Camrose that their correspondents in Berlin were talking a lot of nonsense, and the article was never printed, but that was a very rare aberration on the part of the *Daily Telegraph* in those years.

On his return to Berlin, Ribbentrop invited Greene to lunch in the vain hope of continuing the process of persuasion.

Apart from this, Hugh's copy was never tampered with, unlike that of *The Times* correspondents. Hugh's own most vivid memory of the attitude of *The Times* was in Austria at the time of the plebiscite which followed the Anschluss in 1938. He was covering the story with Darsie Gillie of *The Times*. Together they went round to watch the voting. They both wrote very similar dispatches, pointing out that armed stormtroopers watched the way people filled in their voting forms. Greene's account appeared on the main page of the *Telegraph*, whereas Darsie Gillie's only appeared on the foreign news page. Every single word Gillie had written which indicated that this was not a perfectly normal democratic election had been removed.

A key reason why Hugh Greene had so little difficulty with his copy was that his views on the Nazis were in step with those of his London office. Norman Ebbutt was basically out of step with the editorial policy of his paper. Both Dawson, the Editor of *The Times* and Robert Barrington-Ward, the Deputy Editor, believed that the 1919 Treaty of Versailles had been a mistake; they acquiesced in Chamberlain's policy of appeasement, to the horror of the internal opposition to Hitler, and accepted the expansion of German military power.

It appalled Hugh that this nascent opposition to Hitler was confronted with a pussyfooting, ill-conceived, basically cowardly British foreign policy. The German opposition was desperate because it was clear to them, as it was to every journalist in Berlin, what Hitler was up to. Greene dearly wished that members of the British government, instead of reading their ambassador Sir Nevile Henderson's mealy-mouthed appeasement despatches, would take the trouble to read *Mein Kampf*.

The German opposition had read the book and did not need English journalists to tell them which way the wind was blowing. Dachau was full of those Germans who had defied, disobeyed, criticised. They were not Jews; they were mainly Communists and they suffered. Theirs were the frightened faces which had made such an impact on Hugh's mind on that first visit to Dachau; men whose opposition to Hitler's dictatorship had been persistent and courageous. There were other men too, who had been picked off one by one through a careless word or gesture, abominably tortured, confined for years, or sometimes returned contemptuously to their families as broken, twitching scarecrows. It saddened Hugh that theirs could be no more than the courage of despair as they watched their countrymen fall at the feet of their new political maestro and saviour, to whom indeed foreign politicians came to pay homage.

Much later on, with hindsight, Hugh came to believe that if the opposition to Hitler had received more support, it might have acted. If, Greene was later to suggest, at the time of the Jewish pogroms in November 1938, the general commanding the army in the Berlin district had called out the troops to clear the streets and restore order, '. . . he would have lit a flame throughout Germany that nothing could have put out. One saw then in a blinding instant that given the time and the man, even something as firmly founded as the Nazi regime seemed to be might disappear in a puff of smoke.'

However, it must be said that whatever Hugh Greene's later feelings of the necessity to convince the British government and public to support and encourage the German opposition to Hitler, his actual dispatches to the *Daily Telegraph* at the time tended to be straight factual accounts. When reporting the arrest of Pastor Niemöller on July 1st, 1937, for instance, he treated it as a news story rather than as an event which had any broader context. One comes away from reading this account today with the feeling that Niemöller was a brave but isolated intellectual who happened to have annoyed the Nazis. Had Hugh's reports been written more persuasively, with more detailed contexts, maybe the notion that this opposition should be encouraged by British government foreign policy would have been taken up. As it is, the main impression one has from the *Telegraph* coverage is that the opposition was splintered, without organisation, therefore ineffective against the monolith of the Nazi state and not a serious part of the equation of how to deal with Hitler. The kinds of stories Hugh filed always followed a basic format, with only the occasional exception; a number of different points would be made, each given as a straightforward statement of news but which cumulatively could be taken as a picture of the gradual strengthening of Nazi Germany. The message was there for anyone to see who wished to see, but the message was not explicit.

The whole world was falling apart around him as he sent out words from the eye of the storm to ears which were

53

partially deaf. His marriage too seemed to be in an equally rocky state. Hugh spent the Christmas of 1936 alone. Helga had gone to New York and the newly born Graham had been left with a nurse in Berlin: 'I don't think I told you that I actually went to see how the baby was last Monday. He seemed very well and the woman he is with very nice. I didn't give him a present, I'm afraid!' His colleagues had sensed that things were not at all well between him and Helga. There were no rows, they just appeared to be drifting apart. His job meant many late nights in the office; Helga was still only eighteen. They had not planned to have Graham and, to Helga, Hugh's feelings towards the child seemed ambivalent suggesting that he was not over-enamoured with fatherhood. Whether this was actually the case or not was less important than the fact that his young wife felt it to be so.

His letters to his mother were a harbinger of the new mood: in the early years they bristled with his enthusiasm for Helga, but through 1935, 1936 and 1937 the references became less, there was much more on other people, work, pastimes, books and films. Children just weren't very important to him. When James was born in January 1938, he wrote to his mother: 'It looks exactly like Graham did, not red which is something, though all babies seem to me rather disgusting.' He also expressed some liking for the nurse they had hired to deal with the baby 'partly because she didn't take it as a personal insult that babies do not interest me in the slightest'.

In March 1938 Hitler invaded Austria. The *Daily Telegraph* man in Vienna was Gedye, who reported the vicious anti-semitism which swept the Austrian capital. Gedye's reporting was so effective and powerful that he was expelled from Austria on March 28th. Hugh Greene was sent down to Vienna temporarily to replace him and to cover Central Europe and the Balkans. He therefore appeared in the paper under a number of guises, 'Our own correspondent in Budapest', or 'Bucharest', though his real ambition was to be 'Our own correspondent in Tirana', for the coverage of King Zog of Albania's wedding.

Then in May 1938 Wareing was transferred to Paris and Hugh Greene was made chief correspondent in Berlin. His cousin Barbara had arrived from England and was with him when the news of his appointment came through. She remembers him 'dancing round the room because his salary was put up to £1,000 per annum, saying, 'I'm a four figure man, I'm a four figure man'''. Once more the timing for him was perfect. At the age of twenty-seven he had been made chief correspondent of a major newspaper at the heart of world politics.

That May he displayed a capacity for seeing and describing the comic side of the Nazis. Hitler and Goebbels were to depart from the Potsdamer Bahnhof to visit Mussolini. Security measures were stringent and strict instructions had been issued that the foreign press was not to be allowed anywhere near the ceremonies. Hugh Greene decided that he would wander down to the station to see if there was some way in. He arrived at the same time as Goebbels:

> There was a long staircase lined by members of the Hitler Youth, and Goebbels, with his staff around him, started limping up it. So I fell in immediately behind him. Goebbels was about 18 inches shorter than me, and as we climbed that interminable staircase the lines of Hitler Youth on both sides started roaring with laughter. This was not the sort of reception to which Goebbels was accustomed, and he kept turning his head in a puzzled sort of way. I kept right behind him and I do not think that he saw me.

On the platform he ran into his friend, Captain Wiedemann, Hitler's adjutant. Wiedemann was astonished to see the tall Englishman but made no effort to have him removed. Greene strolled along the platform and took up a position next to Hitler, who was talking to the Italian Consul-General excitedly, and beating his left palm with his fist. 'Only,' Hitler was overhead to say, 'only in this way can we win.' The journalist's pulse began to race as visions of the world scoop on the declaration of war scurried through his mind. Disappointingly, Hitler was discussing motor-cycle racing.

Hitler and Goebbels were to travel in two trains and as Hitler left, Greene wandered over to the other platform where Goebbels was talking to a group of people seeing him off. Suddenly the train began to move with Goebbels still on the platform, 'as it went by a large SS man leant out of a carriage window, caught Goebbels under the arms and hauled him into the train with his short little legs kicking in the air'. This reminded Greene of some lines current in the General Strike of 1926:

> Early in the morning
> Down upon the station
> See the little puff puffs
> All in a row.
> Man upon the engine
> Pulls a little lever . . .

It was a lovely story which Hugh Greene made the most of, much, he now assumes, to Goebbel's chagrin. But what puzzled him then, and puzzles him still, 'is what happened to the man upon the engine who pulled the little lever'.

Thoughts of home began to beckon. It was clear now that the moment of departure could not be too far away. The whole of Germany was becoming a stage on which was being enacted a terrible tragedy, and Hugh could less and less stomach the role of theatre critic. Painful signs were everywhere: Paul Wallich, who had befriended Hugh Greene, and had been godfather to his first son, Graham, threw himself in the Rhine at Cologne and extinguished a life which could no longer face up to the nightmare of Germany. By November the *Telegraph* was making plans to withdraw the office members by March 1939. Hugh wrote home:

We hope it may be postponed until the end of September, and what may have happened by then, Lord knows. There doesn't seem anything much one can write in a letter these

With Sir Arthur fforde, 1960

With Lord Normanbrook, 1965

Hugh with his two predecessors, Sir Ian Jacob and
Sir William Haley (centre)

THE COMEBACK

PIRATES GALORE!

WELL, THEY'RE DIFFERENT, AIN'T THEY?

days. But I've been hitting out in my messages without any diplomatic beating about the bush.

In the early hours of March 15th, 1939 German troops marched into Prague. Gedye, who had been acting as the *Telegraph*'s correspondent since his expulsion from Vienna, was definitely *persona non grata* with the Nazis and immediately took refuge in the British legation. Hugh Greene was sent to replace him. Hugh's article on Goebbels had not done his reputation much good with the German authorities, and he was refused a pass to go into Bohemia, so he bought a railway ticket to Vienna, which would take him via Prague. When he arrived at the frontier, the SS came and looked at everybody's passes. He recalls:

> They came to me and said, 'Where is your pass?' And I said, 'I haven't got one.' And they said, 'Why not?' I said, 'Well, look, I've got a ticket to Vienna.' 'But you need a pass.' And then I put on my best Prussian officer's manner and said, 'Can't you read your own announcements? All that it says is that you need a pass for travelling into Bohemia–Moravia and not through it.' They scratched their heads for a bit and said, 'Oh, all right, but don't do it again.' And I got off the train in Prague, went up to the office of the German Commander-in-Chief in the castle, asked for a permit to travel in and out of the Protectorate. They just assumed because I was there I had every right to be there—German literal-mindedness—and I got my pass to travel in and out.

Despite the feeling of despair, the fearful foreboding at the way events were moving, he was pleased and amused to see that the sometimes exhausting efforts of the past six years had reaped some kind of reward when through the post came a form from *Who's Who*. Wareing had never been in this register of the great and good, nor for that matter had any of the other correspondents in Berlin. It was a remarkable achievement for the whole Greene family: 'Assuming that the next edition ever appears I should think Da will be able to claim a record with himself and three sons in it!'

On May 4th, 1939 the *Daily Telegraph* carried the announcement that Hugh Greene, along with five others, had been ordered to leave Germany by May 24th. The Germans made it clear that this had nothing to do with his reporting. It was a straight reprisal for the expulsion from London of Dr Rösel, who was ostensibly the correspondent of the *National Zeitung*, but in practice the leading *Partei* man and chief pro-Nazi propagandist in Britain.

Helga, the children and their nurse had already gone, so Hugh now set about storing the furniture and making arrangements to leave, although where he was going was not decided until the 17th, when he was told that he was to replace the *Telegraph* correspondent in Warsaw, an American who wished to return to the States.

On the evening of May 23rd he left aboard the Nord Express from the Friedrichstrasse railway station, seen off by a large group of foreign correspondents, his old contact Lescrinier, and a small group of Gestapo to make sure he did go. As the train pulled away he leaned out of the carriage window, fencing sabre in hand, waving at the Gestapo men, shouting '*Ich komme als Gauleiter zurück*' (I will return as a District leader).

Hugh Greene was leaving a city which had transformed him in five years from a rather gangly, diffident youth with no real sense of direction into a foreign correspondent of international repute. Life in the city had also forged, in a fire fuelled by fascism, his deep disgust with the politics of intolerance. Berlin may have meant and done things to many people, but it *made* Hugh Greene.

The only chink in the façade was the souring of his relationship with Helga. He had written to her in the romantic days of 1934 that the worst kind of loneliness was no longer possible. He had presumed, mistakenly, that he had *known* the worst. It is difficult now to disentangle what went wrong. Circumstances had created an ambivalence in his feelings between the desire to be secure in his marriage and his commitment to being a successful correspondent at an extraordinary moment in history. It was this dichotomy which slowly split the stability of their marriage. The rift, however, was not to occur for six years.

4

Greene arrived in Warsaw in June 1939 and was amazed to find Poland wallowing in foolish complacency. There were obvious signs of considerable poverty but, despite being controlled by what was in effect a military dictatorship, the city felt free and lively after the oppressive brutality of Berlin.

Rather in the way he established strong and immediate feelings for or against people, so did he for whole nations and Poland, oppressed, threatened, romantic, slightly naïve and about to be brutalised, was a good candidate for his affection. There were also elements to Polish life which appealed to him. He recalls the amazing number of times that he wore white tie and tails while in Warsaw, more than at any other time in his early life. There were nightclubs and cabarets with a good deal of satire at the expense of the military government. The aristocracy was still prominent, there were long dinner parties and all manner of diplomatic parties. The mood in Poland was one of totally unrealistic confidence. He spent one day with the Polish cavalry, was served splendid food and drink, watched their marvellous horsemanship and knew all the while that they were gallant, blind heroes on their way to slaughter.

Hugh planned to stay on as a correspondent in Poland if war broke out, thereby displaying a surprising and exaggerated faith in that army's ability to survive. On August 5th he was expressing his feeling that:

War is probable this year, although no longer so certain. What an awful show Chamberlain put up in the House of

Commons on Wednesday. Everybody in Poland from the top to the bottom seems to regard him as the biggest danger to peace—even more so than Hitler.

By August 21st even his limited optimism had disappeared and he told his mother:

> I'm afraid it rather looks as if we may be heading straight for it now . . . If things start up, don't worry if you hear nothing from me. It may not be possible to write letters. I shall stay in this country as long as there is any possibility of getting news out.

By the 24th he was expecting the attack:

> . . . any hour now. This waiting is rather unpleasant. My only hope is that Hitler has always preferred surprise and on this occasion we are ready for him. But that's rather a slender hope and he may yet try another twist. One must take off one's hat to him about this Russian pact. It really was a magnificent stroke.

On the brink of disaster his mind turned to the likely possibility that his life, along with many others, would not have much further to go. There was the question of his will, which he spelled out to his mother: 'My last will and testament is that you should keep the children out of the hands of the Guinnesses whatever happens!' The Poles though—'these extraordinary people'—continued to impress him with their calm indifference to the possibility of war. He signed off, 'Well, see you after it's all over—one way or another. Love to Da.'

He was by now the longest serving English correspondent in Warsaw and as such he settled down to filing copy which heralded doomsday. Claire Hollingworth, another young *Daily Telegraph* journalist, had travelled down to Katowice in the latter part of August and was present when the German attack came at five thirty am on Friday, September 1st. She immediately telephoned Hugh Greene in Warsaw to say that Katowice was being bombed. Hugh in turn at once phoned Mr Kulikowski, the Head of the Press Department at the Polish Foreign Office. Kulikowski refused to believe the news until halfway through their telephone conversation the Warsaw sirens began to sound to usher in the awful truth of total war.

Greene's anxiety was that Britain and France might *not* declare war on Germany. He felt more than a little nervous about his physical safety if the two governments did not do so: 'We were terrified that this Chamberlain government would let us all down and it was a moment of great relief when at eleven o'clock on Sunday morning Chamberlain broadcast that Britain had declared war.' There followed fantastic scenes in Warsaw as the Polish crowds greeted the news, carried Greene and any other Englishman shoulder high past the British embassy.

The city started to dig in. The problem of reporting the war became almost insurmountable because of the lack of reliable information and the restrictions of Polish censorship, and he never really knew how much of what he was writing was actually getting through. *The Times* correspondent, Patrick Maitland, had come to like Greene as a friendly, kind, thoughtful man with a rather sardonic sense of humour. He was also, in Maitland's eyes, a very modest person, professional, competent, with an able analytical brain. Maitland now moved into Hugh Greene's flat on the Aleja Szucha. Living together provided plenty of opportunity for conversation and Maitland formed the impression of Hugh Greene as someone who, despite his abilities, was never emotionally engaged because he was fundamentally agnostic, bringing very few preconceptions to anything he thought and did.

The accounts emerging from the Polish government told nothing of the crushing defeats that their army were undergoing, so Hugh's dispatches told of orderly retreat, even though the mood in Warsaw was that the Germans were not very far away and a flood of people began to move across to the possible security of the east bank of the Vistula.

Greene and Maitland decided to leave Warsaw when they learned that the Polish government and the British, French and American Embassies would be leaving on September 5th for the little spa of Nalenzow, near Lublin. Travelling at the same time was Sefton Delmer, who recalls in his memoirs the journey as:

> . . . a nightmare retreat of ours out of Warsaw, across bridges crammed with small, skinny horses, pulling low-wheeled carts piled to the top with bedding, bits of furniture and refugees . . . Past them slid shiny American and German limousines. They carried staff officers and their ladies, or civil servants with their families. Official Warsaw was moving out . . . I followed behind the other car with British journalists. It contained Carlton [sic] Greene of the *Telegraph*, Willie Forrest of the *News Chronicle* and Patrick Maitland of *The Times*.

He added that he could easily have passed them in his car and got to the frontier with the news before them:

> . . . but in time of war Fleet Street holds together. The car which my colleagues were in was a slow and decrepit affair which they had managed to buy in Warsaw. It looked as though it might break down at any moment. I wanted to be around to pick them up if it did.

It was a sentiment which was far from credible and one of his colleagues said, 'if you believe that you will believe anything'.

The young Englishmen must have been a curious sight amid the fleeing nation. Maitland in particular created more than passing interest. He was, recalls Greene, a strange, romantic figure on the journey, dressed in a fur hat, a heavy black leather coat, baggy riding breeches, top boots and on one arm he had a band with the Union Jack, on the other a pale blue band on which was embroidered in white the words 'The Times, London'. The weather was sweltering but he was prepared for a winter fighting in the Pripet Marshes in the far east of Poland.

Nalenzow was quiet, offering a moment of calm amid the surrounding chaos. The calm dulled the senses and it is not a place that Hugh Greene can remember much about, with incidents that are no more than bright flashes in a surrounding fog. The excitement of events had bred a self-confidence and mutual interest that Maitland and Greene forged in a symbolic agreement to cooperate and collaborate in reporting events, 'because we were the two greatest newspapers in England. Thank goodness we took ourselves seriously then.'

The relief offered by the calm of Nalenzow was brief. On the evening of September 6th they were in the post office which was acting as the British Embassy, drinking champagne, only to be suddenly told that the Germans were ten miles away. That was the end of the champagne as they made all possible speed to Rumania. After a journey of increasing difficulty, amid masses of refugees with their livestock and household goods and frequent air attacks, they arrived in Czernowitz on the Rumanian side of the border on September 9th. In a cable to his mother on that day he described his condition as 'safe Rumania, future movements uncertain'.

He then moved on to Bucharest, obtained rooms at the Athenee Palace Hotel and wrote to his mother, describing the adventure—for that is what it was becoming:

I had an amusing trip out of Poland. Between leaving Warsaw on Tuesday and crossing into Rumania on Friday night I didn't take off my clothes or sleep in a bed and I was singularly filthy. . . . I walked into this country through a delightful ornamental gate inscribed 'Rumania' carrying a bottle of beer and a gas mask. Except for what I'd got on I'd abandoned everything I own . . . We all left Warsaw because of the danger of getting captured. I got quite used to air raids which aren't nearly as bad as one might imagine. The first day of war I was pretty scared but after a day or two raids ceased to be anything but rather a nuisance. I suppose I've been in about 40 and it wastes an awful lot of time . . . Covering the war from here is pretty hopeless so I don't know how long I shall be here. What are all the family doing?

English public school understatement at its most quintessential: the most startling and successful attack in the history of warfare was 'rather a nuisance', and difficult mainly because it wasted time. For someone raised on the love of adventure stories, of daring exploits and devil-may-care comradeship it was as if one had become part of an adventure novel, but this time the bullets and bombs were real. Amid the pain, the horror and the long shadow of the coming genocide drifted these Englishmen of whom Hugh Greene was the archetype —young, courageous, sipping champagne, reporting from the eye of the storm, self-consciously filling a role which they had learned in a thousand adventure stories. His colleague in these events, Patrick Maitland, summed it all up: 'The foreign correspondents were romantic figures in those pre-war days. It may seem strange now, the two of us saying that, but we regarded ourselves as romantic figures and were regarded by the public as romantic figures in a way that doesn't exist now.'

Hugh and Claire Hollingworth went back to the Polish-Rumanian border, and watched the arrival of the fleeing Polish government with the excitement of journalists who suddenly find themselves in the eye of an historical storm. One day, on the Polish side of the border, they suddenly came across a tank which at first they did not recognise. Slowly the full horror of it became apparent: it was Russian. Hugh turned to Claire Hollingworth and said, 'I think it's time to go', and they headed straight back to Bucharest.

The London office told him to stay in Rumania for a while to see how events broke. There was then one of those examples of his uncanny ability to be in the right place at the right time. He was there when Calinescu the Prime Minister

65

was murdered by a fascist group on September 21st. The telephone and other links between Rumania and the rest of the world were cut. Most correspondents had therefore hurried to the border with Bulgaria to try to get their stories out. Hugh Greene had been suffering from colitis since he left Warsaw and stayed on in the capital. In the evening telephone connections were restored. He got through to the *Daily Telegraph* man in Budapest, who took down his account of the murder. The Budapest correspondent couldn't get through to London direct, and so cabled the story to the *Telegraph* office in New York, from where it was cabled to London. The other eager correspondents were stranded on the Bulgarian border and did not get their stories through at all.

In November 1939 the London office asked Hugh to cover Germany from Holland and in December he moved to Amsterdam. His stories, with their suggestion that Holland was on the point of being invaded, infuriated financial interests in the Amsterdam Bourse and the Dutch Foreign Office. He was summoned to the Hague to see the head of the Dutch Foreign Office, who threatened him with expulsion for infringing the principles of Dutch neutrality. They were worried that his stories had only referred to German plans to invade Holland. Greene simply said that he would have gladly reported British invasion plans if he had been aware of any.

The *Daily Telegraph* had planned in April 1940 to send him to Norway with the British Expeditionary Force. The army then decided that it would only take one 'pool' reporter from Reuters on what proved to be this ill-fated venture. It had been a lucky escape for Greene—similar in fact to the luck in his not being sent to Abyssinia and then Spain as had been planned by the London *Telegraph* office earlier on. He had another uncanny ability: not to be in the wrong place at the wrong time.

At the beginning of May 1940 he was moved to Brussels to await the German attack. On the early morning of May 10th, he was woken up by a phone call from a military contact to say that the German invasion had begun. He quickly went to the telegraph office and realising that there was no time to write a story, just sent one brief telegram: 'Balloon up gone.' It did not arrive in time.

The day after he left Brussels the Germans entered. He had left with Geoffrey Cox of the *Daily Express* and Eddie Ward of the BBC. On the first night they got to Tournai where during an air raid the blast from one explosion flung him, somehow appropriately, into a wine cellar. The three of them were then picked up by the British army field security police as spies. Taken before the commanding officer, the tension was broken with the exclamation, 'Hello Eddie, haven't seen you since Eton.' The officer commandeered a taxi, which already had a complement of fat Belgian ladies dressed in black. In this they cruised into Amiens from where they went by train to Paris, where the *Telegraph*'s office was being run by Eustace Wareing.

On June 10th they left in Wareing's car for the coast. They reached Bordeaux and boarded the *Madura*, on its way from East Africa, carrying 240 passengers, but now packed with 1,500 frightened, demoralised expatriates. Hugh Greene was no exception, he felt like a 'beaten dog'. This mood of despair was partly lifted on the first evening when a bell went and out from their cabins stepped men in dinner jackets, women in formal evening dresses. It was, he says, the moment he decided that any nation which produced such eccentrics could not possibly lose the war. The voyage itself was uneventful, if lucky, since a ship behind them was torpedoed. Hugh spent most of it lying on an upper deck reading John Hayward's anthology of nineteenth-century poets.

On June 24th, 1940 the *Madura* docked at Falmouth after a two-day journey from Bordeaux. The passengers received a rapturous reception from the people of Falmouth, who did not regard them as fleeing from the Nazis, but merely returning home safely.

Hugh Greene's reports had come from all over Europe, but now he had no idea of what his fate would be. He soon saw that there was not much for him to do in the London office and to his alarm learnt that his age group was due to be called up in the autumn. He decided to strike first in an effort to make his future service life as comfortable as possible, and set about getting a commission as a volunteer. His first introduction was to Ian Fleming, who quickly dashed any hopes he might have had of working for Naval Intelligence. Hugh's mind then turned to the army, until the day he lunched at White's with Victor Gordon Lennox, the *Telegraph*'s Diplomatic Correspondent, and Air Commodore Coope, the Air Correspondent, who were both horrified to hear that Greene was thinking of joining the army. 'Good God, old boy, we can't have that. You're the type we need in the RAF.' A few days later he sat before an RAF appointments officer in Ryder Street. He was asked whether he spoke French and German. His reply of 'oui' and 'jawohl' convinced the officer that he was a great linguist. He then appeared before an appointments board—the first and last time in his life that he was on the wrong side of the table. He describes the scene when a white-haired Air Vice-Marshal who was presiding asked him if he spoke Bulgarian:

That was a question I was not in the least prepared for and since I did not even know the Bulgarian for 'Yes', I lost my nerve and said 'No'. I learnt afterwards that the members of the Board did not speak Bulgarian either and that if I had been bold enough to say 'Yes' I should immediately have been appointed Assistant Air Attaché in Sofia.

Then I got an even greater shock. The Air Vice-Marshal turned over some papers and asked me why I had never taken Certificate A in the school OTC and had never risen above the rank of Lance Corporal.

This called for some quick thinking and I replied that at the relevant time the Locarno pact had just been signed, it appeared that we were in for a long period of peace and the OTC seemed rather a waste of time.

I could not have given a better answer. The Air Vice-Marshal launched into a long tirade against pacifist schoolmasters who misled the young—while I sat there thinking of the earnest attempts made by those masters to

68

make me conform. This put him in such a good humour that he dismissed me with every sign of friendliness and soon I heard that I was being commissioned as a pilot officer in the Royal Air Force Volunteer Reserve and posted to AI 1 K, the branch of Air Intelligence which dealt with the interrogation of German Luftwaffe prisoners.

The only training I was given before reporting to AI 1 K Headquarters at Cockfosters was in giving and receiving salutes. I was fascinated to hear that an officer should always salute a Chelsea Pensioner and I spent several evenings in Chelsea searching for a Pensioner to salute —in vain.

His commission as pilot officer formally began on July 29th, 1940. He was then posted to Cockfosters under Wing Commander Felkin. The commander was a likeable if eccentric character, but his deputy was loathed by one and all, and described by Hugh Greene as 'a slimy little man whom we decided could only have been a French letter merchant in private life'.

Greene's job in RAF Intelligence was to be on the spot as quickly as possible whenever a German aircraft was shot down, to log its type, where it had come from and any other information which might be of tactical importance. He was then to interrogate any surviving German flyers. It was taken as a matter of course that the use of physical methods was unprofessional and likely to produce unreliable results. Mental pressure and deception were, naturally, another matter. Members of AI 1 K were each assigned two counties to cover, where they were known as 'branch managers'. But Hugh's first brief job was at Plymouth for two weeks where things were not exactly pressing, since he managed to read *War and Peace* for the second time. Next he was sent to Dorset where he had his first confrontation with corpses, washed up on Chesil Beach near Bridport, and became eternally grateful to the village policeman who searched the bodies for him, handing over their identity discs and sodden papers which smelled appalling.

He was then posted to the fighter station at Tangmere near Chichester, where he lodged comfortably at the Dolphin Hotel and shared an office with Superintendent Savage of the West Sussex Constabulary. With the Battle of Britain at its height he was moved to RAF Kenley in Kent, from where he had to deal with every aircraft shot down in West Kent and East Sussex. When prisoners fell into the hands of the police they would be put into a cell to await the 'branch manager's' arrival:

> This was just what I wanted . . . a sympathetic figure wearing more or less the same uniform and speaking their language could work wonders. If they fell into the hands of the army they would be given cups of tea and biscuits and generally cheered up and then often they were not in the mood to talk when I reached them.

The vital day in the Battle of Britain was September 15th. It was therefore also his busiest day:

> One of my first clients—a German fighter pilot—was lying stretched out as though asleep in a field. His parachute had failed to open and I imagine that every bone in his body was broken. He was very handsome—one could even say beautiful, with long flowing golden hair. We searched his pockets and in addition to his papers found a powder puff and lipstick. I opened his tunic to get his identity disc and he was wearing a woman's pink silk underclothes. We went on to find more of the living and dead, scattered across the countryside on this extraordinary day. By a strange coincidence the last wrecked aircraft I examined just as dusk was falling was in the outskirts of Crowborough. My WRAF driver and I had supper with my parents. It was almost the last time I saw my father alive.

Even while he was examining transvestite German fighter pilots, plans were being made for Hugh Greene to join the BBC's European Services.

5

In the summer of 1940, while still under training at the RAF station at Cockfosters, Hugh Greene had been asked to go to the BBC to see Arthur Barker, who had asked him if he would be interested in taking charge of the news to Germany should they be able to obtain his release. Hugh had said that he would of course consider such a proposal, and then had returned to the fascinating and sometimes amusing work of RAF Intelligence, which was much closer to his own sense of solitary adventure. Precisely why he had been approached remains unclear. He had left the *Telegraph* to join the RAF with a reference from Arthur Watson, the Managing Editor, which observed that in his six years with the paper he had 'been able to acquire an intimate knowledge of Germany, Poland and South-Eastern Europe which few men of his age can possess'. He certainly spoke very good German, had obviously been a success as the correspondent in Berlin for the *Daily Telegraph*, had covered the retreat from Warsaw and the Low Countries with skill and a certain gung-ho bravado, but he was not yet thirty and had no managerial experience.

The proposal that he should join the BBC had then slipped his mind, and he had volunteered to go and work in RAF Intelligence in North Africa, when suddenly the BBC post was formally offered to him. It was difficult to refuse, if only because it was clearly an important job to which his skills acquired in Berlin were well suited. A measure of the seriousness with which his release was taken by the BBC was that they had approached both Duff Cooper, the Minister of

Information, and Sir Archibald Sinclair, the Secretary for Air, to ensure that they got their man. Leaving the RAF was not easy for Greene. He had come to enjoy his position out in the field as 'branch manager', with sometimes truculent, sometimes frightened, sometimes dead German flyers as his clients.

Before he could take up his new appointment, one slight hiccup occurred. It was routine procedure for all new recruits to the BBC's overseas and European services to be 'cleared' by MI5. Someone had suggested that Hugh had been a Communist. No one seemed to know for certain, but doubts had been sown. Quickly an old friend of Greene's, Foley, who had been the Passport Control Officer in the Berlin Embassy and therefore the MI5 representative there, disabused the authorities of any feeling that this man Greene had been anything more extreme than somewhere in the centre of the Labour party.

On October 15th, 1940 Greene arrived at Broadcasting House as German Editor. He was only twenty-nine, had no radio experience to speak of and had never had control over more than one or two other souls. If there was ever a moment of doubt, a feeling of trepidation, a trickle of anxiety about this new job, he kept it very, very well hidden.

Those who worked in the German Service during the war remember it as a time of total commitment, exhausting work, youthful bravado and much laughter. An army of dispossessed writers and poets, actors and singers, intellectuals, university professors and journalists, they were a kaleidoscope of talent united by language and exile who had been brought together to wage a war in which their only weapons were wit, intelligence and a passionate conviction that they were going to win. As a generation they were to dominate the BBC for the next thirty years.

During the First World War, both sides' propaganda efforts had been aimed at establishing the guilt of the other through the documentation of atrocity stories. In 1940 it was very different, for Britain stood alone and it was clear to everyone that the Nazis were the aggressive party and were aiming at European domination: Austria, Czechoslovakia and Poland had already been overrun and the persecution of the Jews was known to all. This meant that British propaganda began with a number of distinct advantages, at the heart of which was the ability to stick to the facts. Truth was a much more potent weapon, a sentiment totally shared by Greene and his colleagues.

Since Germany was the enemy, the German Service occupied a special role in this war of truth. Hands reached out from the rest of the BBC and from government departments to caress and cajole this special service doing battle with the enemy through a war of words. Inevitably this led to a multiplicity of pressures and interferences. No comprehension of Greene's work in the service can be gained without understanding these various complex links which had both the capacity to support and to bind. Indeed, no grasp of Hugh Greene's later career is possible without seeing the way in which he handled this, for him, new and difficult situation. The abilities he learnt now were later to stand him in good stead.

The BBC European Services were responsible to a secret government organisation during the war called the Political Warfare Executive (PWE) which was headed jointly by the Foreign Secretary, the Ministry of Information and the Ministry of Economic Warfare. Below them initially was an executive committee of representatives from the BBC, the Ministry of Information and Special Operations, who were jointly responsible for the coordination of propaganda policy. This executive was organised into two parts: on the one hand the regional directorates, for the separate territories controlled from Political Warfare Executive's country headquarters at Woburn: on the other, the Central Organisation which functioned with the liaison sections of the MOI, SOE and BBC. Overt cover for the PWE was provided by the Political Intelligence Department of the Foreign Office.

In February 1941 Ivone Kirkpatrick was appointed foreign adviser to the BBC, paid by the Ministry of Information but based at Broadcasting House; he had no executive function but was the sole channel of official information and guidance to the BBC. He explained the government's war policy, kept in touch with BBC departments, advised on the general treatment of news with an overseas interest, advised on individual scripts 'and in particular kept an eye on the performance and development of the broadcasts to Europe'.

After the Germans attacked Russia on June 21st, 1941, it became clear that the European Services should be expanded and organised into a service separate from the rest of the overseas operation. The reorganisation happened in September 1941 and Ivone Kirkpatrick was made Controller, European Services, receiving political guidance from PWE, obliged to accept policy guidance, though the manner in which the policy was executed was entirely his affair. In administrative, financial and technical matters he was responsible to the Director General and Board of Governors of the BBC. During the war, then, the BBC's independence existed within a tightly defined framework.

Hugh Greene had originally arrived at Broadcasting House to run the German news output of the European Services, but by the autumn and early winter of 1940 the thoughts of the Director of the European Services, Noel Newsome, were turning to the idea of 'the formation of a German programme unit', and this was created during the next year.

The European Service itself was organised around a series of meetings: the weekly European board meeting which coordinated the general policy, development and maintenance of the European Service; the policy meeting, held four times a week, which discussed the daily programme and the coordination of the European output; and individual service meetings. The German meeting was a daily affair, with Hugh Greene in the chair, along with one or more of the sub-editors, the German translators, German language supervisors, German features unit, Greene's deputy, Lindley Fraser and Richard Crossman, who represented the Political Warfare Executive.

Initially, when Hugh Greene was only responsible for the

74

news service to Germany, he was directly responsible to the European News Editor. The basic idea was that every language broadcast should be saying exactly the same thing. The news was therefore written at the central news desk and then translated into the various languages. The initiative to break this arrangement came first of all from the French Service under Darsie Gillie, with whom Hugh had covered the Anschluss in 1938 when Darsie had been working for *The Times*. This development fitted with Hugh Greene's own notion that if news was to be the most important part of the output and clearly it was, then that news had to be written to suit the particular needs and conditions of the country to which it was being addressed.

The emergence of a relatively autonomous German news service was well suited to Hugh Greene's own personal attitudes. It was also a reflection of the general sense of independence which dominated the whole of the European Services, which tended to be populated by individuals freshly recruited for the war effort, who had less of the traditional, deferential, slightly bureaucratic disposition of the rest of the BBC. The emerging race of 'Bushmen' felt themselves to be a 'a very different sort of creature' from those in Broadcasting House. The BBC itself, Greene said:

. . . seemed to be awfully stuffy and odd. I was only aware of the BBC from the angle of Bush House. The Director General at that time, Robert Foot, one never saw at all . . . There were in the early days one or two old administrators from Broadcasting House who were around. But for old journalists like myself, and Darsie Gillie, the BBC itself was a strange and alien affair. The people we'd met who were old BBC people, from the Home Service, from Reith's days, seemed to us to be curious, stuffy individuals whose minds we just could not fathom at all. And I think that anybody who worked in Bush House in those years would probably agree that we went our own way without paying really any attention to what was going on in Broadcasting House; we hardly knew it existed.

The very pace of the news process also made it difficult for anyone from outside to control the language services in an immediate sense, so Hugh Greene and Darsie Gillie became increasingly independent and did their best to ignore their boss, Noel Newsome. In his official history of the BBC, Asa Briggs is fulsome in his praise for Newsome, whom he describes as getting his own way by using 'the weapon of responsible journalism and through the instruments of the clever advertiser'. To Hugh Greene, Newsome was a fool whose idiocies had to be neutralised if the services were to do any meaningful broadcasting at all.

Robert Lucas, who worked in the German Service, felt that Newsome was 'blissfully ignorant of Europe', an opinion with which Greene concurred, adding, 'Yes, but also completely ignorant of the basic tenets of propaganda'. When Newsome held meetings about the news for the day and the lines to be taken, Hugh would often send Maurice Latey, a senior member of the German Service, instead of attending himself, but if he did come, he would sit there cold and silent, with a look of contempt on his face.

Hugh Greene's job was to see that the news beamed at Germany was as near to the truth as he could get it, given the limitations and needs of the war effort. His self-appointed task was to resist as many outside pressures as was possible, and to establish as much autonomy for his service as was feasible: he walked the tightrope between constitutional propriety and his desire for an independent service. Marius Goring observed that 'he had just as many pressures from the BBC to follow certain lines, which he did not want to follow, as he had from the government through PWE'.

Weekly directives were long and detailed, acting as pointers to what the forthcoming news might be and the overall line to be taken on, for example, oil or rationing, but they did not always fit in easily with daily problems. Often something came up for which a line had not been devised and, as Hugh pointed out, clashes were inevitable:

One example of a divergence between government and the German Service, was an incident not of any very great importance but it comes back into my mind. Churchill was visited one day by Sir George Frankenstein, the Austrian Ambassador in London, who although Austria had ceased to exist, still had some honorary existence as Ambassador. After lunch one day, it was in February 1942, he went along to present Churchill with, of all things, a tea-caddy. Churchill came out from what had obviously been a very good lunch in No 10, and accepted the tea-caddy and made a most incoherent speech, in which he said things, as I remember it, like, millions of men had marched millions of miles through the desert and thousands of men had flown millions of miles through the skies, in order that Austria may be free. Well I was sitting on the German newsdesk, and I'd seen the tape and it was an interesting story, when I got a call from somebody who was acting as our liaison officer in the Foreign Office who was in a great state. He said to me, you've seen the speech by the Prime Minister? I said yes. He said you can't possibly put it out. He said the Allied powers are still discussing the future of Austria, they haven't yet decided Austria will be free. So I said I'm sorry old boy, the story is on the tape just about to go out in a few minutes in our next German bulletin, so Austria will have to be free, won't it? And with a groan, he went off the telephone.

Kirkpatrick and his assistant Grisewood had to mediate between the strong-willed men at Woburn and the individualists at Bush House. Kirkpatrick rarely interfered in day-to-day affairs but tried to protect Greene and Gillie from outside pressures in order to maintain the BBC's objectivity, and to enable the Services to get on with their work in peace.

Hugh Greene did not personally like Kirkpatrick, 'because he was too much Munich minded', but he does accept that 'Kirk', as he was always known, was of considerable importance:

. . . to me, because I couldn't stand Noel Newsome, and Noel Newsome couldn't stand me. Newsome used to issue a daily directive and they were really quite fantastically silly. He was very energetic, but extremely ignorant, and as far as Darsie Gillie and I were concerned, we regarded it as one of our contributions to the war effort to see that no traces of Newsome's directives were ever seen.

Newsome's efforts to control the European Service's news output floundered occasionally on the stubborn-minded refusal of Hugh Greene to be anything other than his own man. It was not surprising then that when, many years later, Hugh Greene was able to see his own personal report—the definitive document which the BBC keeps on all its personnel—he found bitter memos written by Newsome to Kirkpatrick about this stubborn maverick within the Service. Briggs places a great deal of emphasis on the fact that it was Newsome who originated all the directives about news and talks in the Services. The comments by Greene and Goring, and Newsome's own notes of complaint, seem to indicate that these were perhaps a little less significant than he may have wished.

Even when Britain was suffering serious defeats, Greene stuck firmly and uncompromisingly to his belief that news and information in war should be as near to the truth as possible and that disaster should not be hidden, but lead the bulletins. There was a cold rationale to this position. 'If we lost the war, if there was a German invasion, we'd all be shot anyway, so why not tell the truth. Whereas if we held out and the tide turned, the fact that we told the truth would mean that the German people would believe us, as indeed they did.'

Julius Gellner, who worked with Greene and Richard Crossman at this time, gives a lively description of a morning meeting when the line to be taken by the German Service is under discussion and Hugh is in the chair:

Crossman gave the most fascinating talk, full of ideas, but he was so full of love for his own voice and his own brain and ideas that he couldn't stop and kept on seeing the other side of the question—he always played the '*advocatus diaboli*'. I don't think Hugh Greene would say more than a few sentences in an hour's meeting. Crossman, who was extremely powerful then would never contradict because Greene would have said in one sentence, clearly, what the line should be. Hugh was a real leader, not Crossman, not Gordon Walker and not Lindley Fraser. And yet how could one be a leader without any trimmings of power —the power was there, but none was displayed. He had a certain amount of humour and his was the most analytical mind; he could reduce complex arguments to a few words, and I never met anybody who impressed me so much.

Not everyone was so impressed by Hugh's single-mindedness. Many found him a cold fish, unflappable and fair maybe, but somewhat bleak. Martin Esslin, a German Service member in his early twenties at the time, believes that Greene was able to sustain his authority by maintaining that aloofness which came to him so easily. He was the amateur from the public school, capable and authoritative, 'never showing his back to the natives', never taking things too seriously, but always doing them well. Greene's height and his general bearing, his personality, his whole appearance, his ability to look dominating, all served to create around him an air of distinction. A former member of the German Service commented:

Once seen, never forgotten, he impressed himself on one's mind straight away. But also you must imagine him then being surrounded by a lot of Germans who had been professional people in Germany, who had come over as refugees and who somehow or other, because they had a literary career, or were from a publishing firm, had got into broadcasting and were totally at a loss as to what to make of this strange man. I do remember conversations about his walking along the corridor with his head in the air and not looking at anyone in particular, just looking and gazing and having this very vague look about him, which other people took literally and thought he was totally vague and not very bright—vague that is in a dim-witted sense, that somehow he was not quite there.

The emigrés were kept at some distance, not only from editorial decisions, since this was to be a manifestly British station, but also as far as possible from the microphone. Whenever a German was on the air, an English member of staff stood by a control switch in case anything untoward should be said, like 'Heil Hitler'.

The division within the service was further reflected in the social habits of the different groups. The emigrés spent their breaks in the canteen at Bush House where they would talk of the past: 'Do you remember Reinhardt's version of *Midsummer Night's Dream* in Berlin . . .' Greene and his colleagues Lindley Fraser, Leonard Miall, Patrick Gordon Walker and Maurice Latey spent their breaks in Finch's pub. One German member of staff who did occasionally go to Finch's with them recalled how appalled he was by 'their schoolboy humour. I was flabbergasted, there were only lavatory jokes, they satisfied themselves with beer and sex jokes of the lowest standard'. The pub was undoubtedly the principal source of rest and recreation. They were all, it should be pointed out, working extremely long hours, always under considerable stress, often very tired.

One of Hugh Greene's most persistent problems was how his service should view the German people and how these people should be encouraged to see their future. Unconditional surrender meant no negotiation with any part of German society, yet should not a distinction be made between ordinary German people and Nazis? How far were the people to be held responsible for what the Nazis were doing in their name? Finally Greene decided that there could be subtlety in his programmes; some might be aimed at particular audiences, women, seamen, the Luftwaffe and so on, but within that variation there would always be one consistent theme, the breaking down of the will of the Germans to fight by convincing them that while defeat at the hands of the Allies was certain, that defeat need not necessarily have intolerable consequences for the ordinary citizen. As one internal document put it: 'In short we have sought to provide a judicious blend of "despair" and "hope" propaganda.'

A distinction was always made between the German war machine and the German people, along the lines that the former was to be destroyed, come what may, whereas the latter could surrender and be saved. As the war developed during 1942 and 1943, the general tendency was towards a greater toughness with the German people, a constant argument that they themselves must get rid of the Nazis or share their fate. By August 1943 they were no longer being called upon to revolt openly but rather to dissociate themselves from the régime through, for example, acts of kindness to foreign workers and support for leaders of the Churches. By the autumn of that year, the main focus of the broadcasts was retribution for war crimes. A report at the time noted that while

> . . . attitudes varied between the Services, the German Service had made it clear that though it was Hitler's objective to implicate the German people in his criminal actions, we ourselves would still be prepared to accept evidence that those crimes had been rejected by the German conscience.

The consistent theme offered in addition, however, was that the longer the war lasted the worse the consequences would be for the German people themselves.

The German Service's attitude was that the German 'war machine' consisted of three elements: the Nazi party and the SS; the generals; and the industrialists. Towards the first the attitude was one of implacable hostility. Towards the third there was no particularly special attention, even if one internal paper noted that 'it cannot be said that we have shown any tenderness'. The generals however posed a difficulty. When Hitler took over command of the army there was a crisis in the relationship between him and the military. Hugh Greene and Crossman both immediately felt that this was an opportunity to drive a wedge between the Nazi party and the army. Greene wrote a piece when Field Marshal von Brauchitsch was removed from his command, encouraging the army to turn against the party. This caused a sharp reaction among those of his staff who thought this was too cynically pragmatic. Greene commented that:

A large number of people under me in the German service, including Christina Gibson, Tangye Lean, who I think was really the ringleader, James Monahan and Patrick Gordon Walker, regarded this as immoral because, to them, all Germans were bad Germans, the army was no better than the party and we were, by attempting this wedge-driving, inevitably taking the side, to some extent, of the army. I remember we had a meeting in the conference room at Bush House at which they challenged this new line. Dick Crossman came to the meeting, I was in the chair and I made it clear that this was going to be the line whether people liked it or not. I rather think that I said that anybody who doesn't like it can seek a job elsewhere.

Feeling about this decision, and about Hugh Greene in particular, reached such a pitch that several members conspired to have him removed. The two main conspirators were Stephen Haggard and Tangye Lean, with whom Hugh had been at Oxford, and who had been a vociferous critic of Hugh even in those days. The fact that they 'conspired' has only recently emerged in conversation with Marius Goring, whom they had tried to recruit. Goring says that the dissension was not only over Greene's attitude towards the German generals, but also over the whole style of programming, with Lean, Haggard and others demanding a more intellectual, artistic service instead of Greene's insistence that the emphasis be on news. Their idea was to persuade the Political Intelligence Department of the Foreign Office, which was the front organisation for PWE, that Greene should be removed. To this end a letter was composed, with Haggard as the principal author, outlining their opposition to Greene. The plot was always doomed to failure because Greene clearly had the support of Crossman, and inevitably the BBC would have fought bitterly to prevent the removal of any of its personnel by PWE, even if that agency could claim the reserve powers to do so.

Lean and Haggard were both artistic, sensitive, rather volatile characters united not only in their temperament but also in their loathing for Greene. Marius Goring thinks that Haggard's attitude towards Greene, which was not at all unfavourable in the early stages of the war, changed because his 'poetic nature' and his ambition for the service as a creative enterprise, were badly bruised by Hugh Greene's antipathy towards such ideas. Haggard was also, in Goring's eyes, 'hot headed' and intemperate in his criticism of Greene, whereas Lean was 'after blood'.

James Monahan, a close friend of Lean and himself opposed to aspects of Greene's policy, though not part of the conspiracy, observed that despite the hate which flowed from Lean to Greene, Greene himself showed 'remarkably little hostility to his adversary'. All the acrimony, he said, 'came from Tangye, Hugh remained extremely serene and unaggressive about it. Hugh wasn't quarrelling with Tangye, but Tangye very much quarrelling with him. It was basically temperamental.' The difference was really between the professional, calm, balanced, tough—'much tougher than Tangye'—Greene, and the tremendously artistic, intellectual, emotional character, deep into psychoanalysis, which was Lean: 'To Tangye's eyes Hugh seemed like a tough power man and that he didn't like. To Hugh's eyes I suspect Tangye seemed a rather more likeable, brilliant and awkward character.'

As head of the German Service Greene had begun to develop, with his sense of power, an aloofness which teetered on the edge of being autocratic and imperial. He remained almost totally unconcerned about the heaving and seething hostility beneath him. Of Lean he said, 'I thought he was rather a silly little man, then and later. Very emotional and highly strung, not much logic in his make-up.'

The peak of the effort in wedge-driving between the generals and the Nazis came after the failure of the attempt to overthrow Hitler on July 20th, 1944. In the early hours of July 21st, Hugh Greene was at home in bed when the phone went, asking him to return to Bush House. As he walked to the office through a particularly heavy display of VIs, he thought up the opening line of a news story: 'Civil war has broken out in Germany'. It was, he says, the only occasion when he knowingly exaggerated because, he thought to himself, there may be people holding out in different places who would be encouraged by the opening phrase 'civil war has broken out in Germany'. The Foreign Office next morning was utterly furious because the government line was still one of unconditional surrender and they thought any idea of Germans fighting Germans would arouse Russian suspicions. Greene merely says of their anger: 'One had to make up one's mind on the spur of the moment.'

Another major difficulty facing Hugh Greene was the dreary, heavy style in which the old-fashioned German staff wrote the news bulletins. The German mind expresses itself in ways which are ponderous and complex, and the presence of so many German emigrés tended to make the programmes boring and unimaginative. The emigrés believed that as Germans they understood how to broadcast to the German people. Not so, said the English staff. Hugh Greene overcame this problem in a way which was to characterise the rest of his broadcasting life: he gave authority to new people who could realise what he wished done. One of them was Carl Brinitzer, a well-known and rather extrovert German man of letters who was asked by Greene radically to transform the style of broadcasts. Brinitzer concentrated his efforts of persuasion on those people who were not too encrusted with age and tradition. There was even a recognisable 'Brinitzer group' among the translators who

. . . were all really very excited by the scope we had in writing stories, translating them into the kind of German which would really register on the listener. Don't forget that all our listeners were in mortal danger, they were people who were listening in extremely difficult circumstances and so it was very important that the sentences should not only be short but written in such a way that the vital thing should register very quickly and should penetrate through the interference.

In August and September of 1942 Hugh Greene visited Stockholm to experience for himself the problems faced by those who were trying to listen to a service which was being jammed. He found that the transmissions remained audible so long as the speaker spoke clearly, did not go too fast, and when presentation was simple and straightforward, but that listening to programmes which were being jammed was tiring. When he returned he therefore made plans to eliminate the more elaborate type of feature programme; he decided that news and talks would concentrate on clear speaking with fewer words per minute, that they should recruit people who had the deep and resonant voices which best penetrated the jamming, and he introduced two announcers to read the bulletins in order to maintain listeners' attention by sharpening the detail through contrast. He had already tried to improve the quality of the transmissions by bringing together, in November 1941, the news editors, talks assistants, translators, features section and language supervisors on to the fourth floor of Bush House. He now merged the functions of the language supervisors and the sub-editors so that the final German version sounded much less like a translation. He also arranged for Julius Gellner, Fritz Wendhausen and Hans Buxbaum to teach the English members of staff, including himself, to perform well in German, to read their scripts naturally, as if they were talking. Ernst Albert, himself an emigré working in the Service, commented: 'They invented a special broadcasting style which was one of the reasons why I finally couldn't stand it any more and left . . . the kind of pidgin-German which they produced, and which I think Greene liked very much, was self-defeating.'

To some minds, Hugh Greene's passion for clarity demonstrated his exclusive concern with the tactics of the propaganda effort. Even Julius Gellner, a great admirer of Greene, thought that there was 'a certain lack of imagination' in his make-up. Marius Goring, who had been brought in to transform talks material into entertaining features, immediately ran up against what seemed to be Greene's lack of interest in this kind of item: 'To be quite honest, there was something philistine about Hugh's approach.'

If the question of his artistic insensitivity remained ill-defined, no such doubts existed about Hugh's ability to make hard, even brutal decisions, to dismiss men from the service without a flicker of emotion. The most obvious example of this concerned his appointing Goring to take over from Walter Rilla, who, Greene felt, was partly responsible for the ponderous nature of features' output. Goring was in his office on his first morning in the new post, only to be confronted by his predecessor, Walter Rilla, who had not been informed of his removal. Greene sacked a man called Hamilton, 'on the spot', according to Martin Esslin, for an anti-semitic remark. Robert Lucas recalled an occasion when Greene had dismissed someone whom Lucas respected and thought a great asset to the German Service. He went to ask Greene whether he would reconsider the decision. As he was putting his arguments to Greene in his office, Hugh leaned back in his chair, his face growing redder and redder and said, in a very cold voice, 'It is not open to discussion.' It was, Lucas added, 'a frightening experience'. Gellner argued that one of Greene's principal attributes was that 'he was quite prepared to tell you you are wrong; quite prepared to be even cold about it. I don't think he would ever be swayed in his opinion by sympathy or antipathy, or by being a friend or not a friend.'

In his history of broadcasting, Asa Briggs quotes an anonymous source describing Hugh Greene during those years as 'a beast, but a just beast'. The words were in fact taken from an unsigned review in *The Times Literary Supplement* which had actually been written by Hugh Greene himself when he had felt the need to sum up his own career. To describe himself as a beast attests both to Hugh Greene's self-awareness and his occasional sense of self-mocking humour.

The German Service carried programmes for workers, the armed forces, intellectuals, talks on economic subjects and feature programmes. For example, Lindley Fraser gave regular weekly analyses of the latest Hitler or Goebbels speech and created a masterly series on War Guilt. Eminent Germans living in exile in the West, such as Thomas Mann and Professor Richard Barth, gave talks with the aim of 'the upholding of the great cultural values of the past which the Nazis are fast trying to destroy'. Especially important and successful were the programmes aimed at women anxious to receive news about their men on the Eastern front, about casualties and prisoners of war. One of the most famous programmes was a scripted *Any Questions*, with a panel of Richard Crossman, Lindley Fraser and Hugh Greene answering questions put to them by Marius Goring, alias 'Charles Richardson'. At first the programme made up its own questions, but soon it began to receive questions from listeners all over Europe.

Hugh Greene performed well during those long, long days of war. The German Service, he was later to learn, had genuinely made an impact on Germany, creating not only reputations for its broadcasters but for the BBC as a whole, which probably did much to make the job of Occupation that little bit easier. The work had absorbed him as perhaps no other work would ever absorb him again. With energy, creativity, passion and, where necessary, ruthlessness, he had provided the core of Britain's anti-Nazi propaganda war. He had gained a sense of the BBC, of its traditions —some of which appalled him—and its values; he came to understand the underlying concept of public service broadcasting and its need for independence. He had displayed an ability to work with people and to create an atmosphere of liberal autocracy in a self-defined framework which he understood how to control with subtlety.

As the war drew to a close he took time off to visit the newly liberated areas of France and Germany. On Saturday, April 28th, 1945, he walked into Dachau concentration camp. He had travelled there from Paris with an American colleague and friend, Bill Hale. Once in Germany they were following the tracks of a retreating German army. The roads had been cleared but the verges were covered with the flotsam and jetsam of war.

The first thing he remembers seeing on his arrival at Dachau were American soldiers outside the gates lying on the ground in a state of collapse and vomiting. He wondered how he would react to what lay behind the entrance. It was early in the morning, just after the first American troops had arrived to liberate the camp.

Death was everywhere. In a large hall he saw an incinerator. Piled all around were the emaciated corpses waiting to be cremated. On one wall hung a notice saying, *'Reinlichkeit ist hier Pflicht: bitte Hände waschen'* (cleanliness is a duty here: please wash your hands). The dead were lucky compared to the living. He and Hale walked through barrack buildings where the prisoners had lived and slept with several men having to share the same narrow plank. The smell was indescribable. Emaciated scarecrows in striped pyjamas crowded round to kiss their hands. Smiles were impossible to summon to a face that was pale with the horror that lay before their eyes. Their instinct was to hurry away from the grasping hands and the demanding, pleading eyes. Suddenly one of the scarecrows spoke and identified himself. He was a French journalist whom Hugh Greene had known in Berlin, but who was now beyond recognition.

In a railway siding just outside the camp stood a train, made up mostly of cattle trucks. It was loaded with thousands of corpses, dead from starvation and typhus. The removal of the corpses for incineration in Dachau had been interrupted by the arrival of the Americans. The image which stayed in his mind, however, was that of young

Richard Crossman, Hugh Greene, Marius Goring and Lindley Fraser
with Leonard Miall in cubicle broadcasting to Germany in
the programme *Was wollen Sie wissen?*

Morning conference in the BBC German Service

Broadcasting to Germany during the War

Farewell dinner given by members of BBC German Service,
September 1946

mothers taking their children for a walk along the road which ran beside the siding. Not one cast a glance at the train. It was that Sunday afternoon that a group of the leading citizens of Dachau were forced to see the horror which had been perpetrated within their locality but not, they would disingenuously claim, with their knowledge.

When he returned to London he could be confident that his work in the German Service had been one small part of the battle to end such horrors as he had just seen on this Dachau Sunday. He returned, however, to an ever deepening marital crisis.

Helga had been the seventeen-year-old bride of a very youthful foreign correspondent. Whether she married Hugh in order to get away from her parents is impossible to know, though she herself feels now that whatever the difficulties that arose between her and Hugh, she did at least make an effort. Hugh's problem, she felt, and still feels, was that his main concerns were professional, not personal. While he was a very mature young man in many ways, in his attitude to politics, to literature and to his work, she feels that he did not have the ability to create a warm home atmosphere. He was not, to her mind, domesticated enough. During the war, for example, it rankled with her that he could not carry out the black-out procedures, which she therefore had to do. She felt that the reason he wasn't very domesticated was that he married too soon and she did not make sufficient demands on him to force him to become more involved in their home life.

When asked to comment on the observation by those who knew him, that basically Hugh did not care for other people, Helga replied bluntly:

He neither considered other people, nor did he need other people much, I think. Professionally he did, but emotionally I don't think he did. He liked his drinking companions and he liked his critics. But otherwise he liked to read or relax or go to the theatre or a film . . . He didn't make a lot of close friends.'

89

Indeed it is true that Hugh Greene up to then seems to have had no one in his life to whom he was particularly close, with the notable exception of Graham.

The war work in the German Service of the BBC was an important job but a necessarily busy one which left Hugh little time for home life. A friend put it this way: 'He is the kind of man who cannot serve two masters. He was married to the defeat of Hitler, though the fact that Helga somehow, without wishing to, carried with her the Guinness banking ethos did not help.' The gap which had appeared in Berlin between Hugh and Helga less than a year into their marriage became wider as the stresses and strains of two different personalities with different needs, different moods, different intentions built up like pressure along a geological fault.

By 1945 the gap was unbreachable, and Helga basically blames Hugh. By the end of the war too, there was, according to her, practically no contact with her parents, which was awkward for her. 'They were perfectly willing to be nice, but he wasn't prepared to meet them half way.' She says that she would never have broken up with Hugh if only because of the children. The children had not been planned for and he left her with the impression that he did not want to have a family:

> To a certain extent I lost my respect for him as an adult when I realised that he wasn't really living up to what I thought he should in being grown up. Now I realise that this was unfair, he was too young, he put all his energy into his work, which is OK, but then he shouldn't be married. You can't have things both ways. I don't mean that he didn't have every reason to look elsewhere because to some extent we were in different camps and I made a lot of mistakes, because he didn't want children. I kept them, not away from him, but I saw that he wasn't bothered by them. He opted out of fatherhood, I thought, but I made the mistake of not forcing him back in. I realise now that he should have been more grown up, but I should have been more adult too.

90

She says that it was not until after the war that he began to enjoy being with the children—by which time it was too late: 'He said that he always felt about them as if they were rather nice nephews. He was very direct. He never wrapped anything up, he never pretended.'

The fact that he poured most of his energy into his job rather than his family is something he now acknowledges. At the time it could be rationalised because the war seemed all-demanding and important. Of the possibility that marriage might have domesticated him, he says, 'Well it didn't . . . one couldn't live the life of a married man; that didn't go along with being a journalist.' Hugh Greene was seen by his wife, and to an extent by himself, as a man whose professional life took precedence over his marriage and his children. To this personal problem were added further complications created by the war itself: 'Many families were broken up because of the bombing. The children stayed in Crowborough . . . and one had to be at work every day late into the evening. It meant that Helga was alone during the raids. Certainly that involved tension.'

There clearly was a private man who did try to seek the emotional security and nourishment which a family can sometimes provide but his professional involvements froze the family out. Once he had made a success of journalism and broadcasting, he felt he could then afford to concentrate on Helga, Graham and James, but it was too late. When the war ended the silence which had emerged at the heart of the marriage suddenly became very loud. It hurt him. He sought to reconstruct, to try to tell her that he loved her still, that the passion of those first few months when he was in Berlin and she in Munich still remained. He wanted her very much. His letters tell it all.

In July 1945 Robert Skelton of the *News of the World* offered him a job as the paper's European Correspondent, based in Paris, with discretion to travel where and when he liked, a guarantee that nothing he wrote would be altered to fit in with editorial policy and a salary of about £2,500, apart from expenses. He wrote to Helga, who was in Wales, about the offer but she did not reply and he became anxious:

> I've heard nothing from you since you left which makes me wonder a bit if everything is all right with you . . . Since I wrote to you in a somewhat dizzy condition about the possible new job the scales have evened up more in my mind . . . Is there any way of phoning you if I wanted to talk with you about it?

He wrote again and again but answers from Helga failed to appear with any regularity: 'Sorry to have bothered you with the telegram. But you usually write so promptly and you know how when one is lonely reason has a hard fight against the black spectres.' Even in July 1945 he was not anticipating, at least in his letters, the possible end of the marriage.

The BBC had promised him that some time after the spring of 1946 he would be given the opportunity to go abroad for at least three months. He therefore decided to turn down the offer from the *News of the World*. He wrote to Helga:

> I have had plenty of time to think over this by myself and I feel pretty sure that I have made the right decision. As I wrote before, you matter to me infinitely more than any particular job. But what I must aim at is you plus a job in which I can feel that I am doing something which is of a certain importance to the world in general. And in the end I was not satisfied that I could feel the second part of that with the *News of the World*, despite my first excitement with the offer. But the whole thing has been well worthwhile. It has given me an opportunity to remind the BBC of my market value outside, it has made me think about the sort of things which I really want to do and it has made it possible for me, without sacrificing anything, to secure the period abroad which I hope will be helpful so far as our personal future is concerned. So I really must be grateful to Skelton! . . . This is my 18th letter in 16 days. I don't

suppose I shall keep up quite such a high average in the remaining ten days. Goodnight, my darling, and all my love.'

Those are not the words of a man who has fallen out of love, they are the words of a man desperate to hold on to all that glorious promise and joy of 1934, while at the same time balancing that with the achievement of that self-respect which would flow from maintaining, and then enhancing, a successful professional life. Time and again he expresses his love for her and the boys, of how he is pained at their separation. But she rarely answered; in one more letter he yet again reminded her that 'I look forward to hearing how things have gone since I left. To you still there it probably seems a very short time. To me, here, it seems an age.'

A sense of permanence in life is never worked out through any grandiose statements as to the future. Once one has to start planning for the future or talking about the shape of things to come, one is already the victim. A knowledge of permanence is reflected in the precious unstated assumptions one can make about the continuing relationship. Here was a man who knew this and who tried to cling to the assumption he wished to make that his wife, his family, would be there. He knew they wouldn't be, but he had to try, which he did, by discussing the minutiae of their life together. They had been working together on a play to be called *Bellamy*, and his letters discuss the details of particular scenes. He is always trying to suggest that life will soon return to normal again and Helga and the boys will soon be back in London. But a faintly shrill, somewhat frantic underlying note persists in coming through. He was off to Berlin for a brief visit: 'It would be nice if you could write so that I found a letter with the latest news waiting for me (and the date of your return) when I get back.'

He was back on September 18th, but there was no letter waiting. He implored her: 'Please write and tell me about how you are and your doings. If not at this length, still something! There was nothing waiting for me. Goodbye, sweetheart and I hope I shall hear your voice later this morning or this evening.' He ended with a PS: 'I hope you will soon be back.'

The visit to Germany had filled him with apprehension: 'Dachau was in some ways remote in its extreme horror. I think that to see the people and places one has known really well will, in its way, be much worse. Goodbye, darling. I wish I could tell you how much I love you.'

In Berlin he tried to find old friends, only to discover that the Russians had been there before him. He heard atrocious tales of murder and rape. Some people had just disappeared. He wrote to Helga of their former home: 'Our house is completely destroyed; just a few outside walls standing and all the inside completely collapsed. The sight of the ruin really depressed me. It seemed that a whole bit of our life had been wiped out.'

'Our house is completely destroyed'; whether he was conscious of the poignancy is difficult to know, but that burnt-out shell was their marriage.

There is a letter from Vienna, written on March 8th, 1946. It seems to be the last one, but his love and hope had not diminished, even though he was effectively only weeks away from the final break with Helga. He toured the city, met people, but his thoughts were not there, nor were they on his work. His thoughts lay amid the memories of ten or more years past, amid what was no more than a charred shell, with a small young girl, with glasses and self-confidence, with whom he would talk lovers' talk in the dead of night on the phone from the *Telegraph* office. She it was who had borne him two boys whom he could never quite love as fathers should love, not because he didn't want to but because he didn't really know how to; had made him for a moment very happy, had let him escape from the well of loneliness in to which his childhood had placed him. His thoughts were there, and Vienna was merely the lens through which he gazed to see them: 'There's quite a touch of spring in the air now and there's nothing I'd like so much as another Vienna honeymoon with you. I miss you and love you always.'

6

After the initial conquest of Germany in 1945, the Allied mood switched from subjugation to a positive desire to construct a liberal democratic community. The members of the Allied Control Commission were well aware that in order to create such a new society, they had to re-educate the people, to bring about a lasting change of heart in a population which they regarded as hard-working, efficient but ruthless and war-loving. They had to make post-Nazi Germany understand democratic ideas, to create an empathy in the population for the central principles which provide the political morality upon which Western liberal democracy is based. It was not enough, they knew, to establish institutional artefacts, and to re-vamp the economy: they had to create a new consciousness, a new set of intellectual commitments and imperatives. However they were realistic enough to realise that to set up a new culture in the midst of a spiritual wasteland would be a Herculean task.

To read accounts of those early post-war years in Germany is to read chronicles in which hope and despair, perception and perplexity are inextricably linked. In the journal of his travels through the British Zone at this time, Stephen Spender was much taken with the enigmas of German culture and society, and his diary contains the details of many conversations and thoughts in which he poured over, considered, tried to digest this intractable problem.

Spender describes 'a special kind of German suggestibility —a willingness to obey orders, thinking in generalisations, the search for panaceas, faith in power which made many

Germans capable of falling to deeper depths than many people of other nations'. George Grosz was more satirical:

> They are fine people, but they are quick to catch the disease of anti-humanity which is very close to many people, but my poor Germans are unusually susceptible. I think it is, on the whole, because of their poor elimination. Yes, I am sorry to say, I think Germany is the head-quarters of constipation.

Whatever the explanation, and there seem to be as many as there are people to offer them, it was taken for granted in 1945 that something had gone drastically wrong with German society under Hitler, and the men of the Allied Control Commission spent endless hours in conversation with their German subjects, trying to work out just what it was: the Allies knew that they were fighting 1,200 years of German history and they worried over the apparent absence of humanity, tolerance and compassion in the German character.

Broadcasting was seen to be a very important re-building tool and the newly-created Information Services were expected:

> . . . to bring home to the German people the progress and reality of disarmament, and also to help in their re-education and in the re-orientation of their minds, and to stimulate in them a mental attitude which it is hoped will be helpful to themselves, to us and to the world.

The man chosen to re-create the mental life of a shattered society, to develop information services, newspapers, radio and film throughout the British Zone of occupied Germany in December 1945 was Major General Alex Bishop. He began by initiating a broadcasting service run on the lines of the BBC's Home Service, based on Hamburg with studios in Cologne, entitled the Nordwestdeutscher Rundfunk or NWDR. This was not to be a British mouthpiece but 'an

instrument which, though serving our purposes and con-
forming to our general ideas, could be regarded by the
Germans as essentially their own'. Bishop transferred a
considerable measure of responsibility to the German staff,
'while retaining a small English staff at all the key controlling
points'. It was the illusion of democratic control with not
much of the substance, until such time as the occupying
powers allowed an independent Germany to emerge.

However, Bishop soon found that the first organiser,
W. A. Palmer, was insufficiently forceful as a personality, he
could neither enthuse nor inspire the German staff with new
ideas, nor did he seem likely to have the vision necessary to
create from scratch the structure for an independent public
broadcasting service which could eventually be handed over
to the Germans. Bishop therefore wrote in July 1940 to
William Haley, the Director General of the BBC, to ask him
if he could recommend someone who would be 'adequate for
the onerous task' of creating what would be a BBC for
Germany.

Haley consulted with his colleagues and recommended
Hugh Greene who was particularly receptive to the idea, if
only because it would enable him to get away from his
domestic problems.

The move to Hamburg was the right offer at the right time.
Hugh felt moreover that he was ready for the challenge
involved in transplanting the concept of the BBC to a new
and very different society. He had a very 'soft spot' for
Germany, although he was well aware of the crudities of
some aspects of its political culture. He felt, too, that he had
much to offer the job and that he possessed many of the
attributes necessary to do it well: he had learned how to
impose discipline without excessive interference, how to
guide with dextrous subtlety, he knew how to govern
through example and he felt he would be able to handle the
Control Commission and all its sub-committees and sub-
sections. Above all, he thought that he would be able to set
up a new broadcasting framework, train the people and then
relinquish control gracefully.

But it was one thing to run a branch of a renowned organisation; quite another to try to inculcate the seeds of liberal democracy into a war-shattered populace. Could he, could indeed anyone, successfully plant and nurture those seeds in a soil which was barren through long neglect and from which Nazism had sucked out much of the goodness that it once contained? Was it possible to create, along with the new roads and buildings, a new consciousness, a new sense of commitment, to tolerance and compassion, a genuine belief in freedom of thought and expression?

His immediate task was to continue to enhance the relatively liberal atmosphere at NWDR; to obtain legal status for it; and to ensure that the nature of the latter guaranteed the future of the former after his departure. His view was that the station should be an institution in public law, independent of the government, centralised, financed by licence fee.

Shortly after he arrived in Hamburg in October 1946, he collected together the employees of NWDR in the station's large concert hall to tell them of his intentions and hopes for the future. The station, he said, would not be the voice of the conqueror, but the voice of the conquered, of the new Germany. On one point he was clear, '. . . that one of the tasks of the coming months and years will be to secure the independence of the broadcasting service . . . from the individual political parties and from any essential future government agency.'

He summarised the policy of the station as he saw it as being committed to 'objectivity and being factual in all areas'. That did not mean, he argued, that they had to be boring. The model for the station would be the BBC, but though that would be the ideal against which their success or failure would be measured, it would be a German broadcasting service which meant that he was 'here to make myself superfluous'. He summarised his function as being 'to make available the experience I have been able to gain for the further setting up and securing of a new German broadcasting system which accords with German needs'.

But who was to define German needs? It would not be long

before the emergent ruling élites would insist on delineating them their way. Greene's belief was that it was for the broadcasters themselves to define them since the presiding assumption within the basic model, the BBC, was that it had, in an almost metaphysical sense, a *relationship* with 'The Public' not as a group of partial interests, but as a collective entity which was composed of different interests and different needs. That core to the public service ideal was extremely difficult to grasp; it was certainly not readily apprehended by the key figures in the new Germany.

In his first letter to his mother, he commented on his new position and the excitement of the very real power which had become his:

> After being so long in a job I knew backwards it has seemed strange starting on something new among new people (probably very good for me!). But I think I'm beginning to find my feet. It's a funny sort of job where one has to be switching all the time from thinking 'English' to thinking 'German'—both literally so far as the language is concerned, and in one's attitude.
>
> . . . It's curious too being complete lord and master in internal administration matters and being able to affect, very seriously, the lives of over 1,000 people by signing or not signing something. Life in general is a curious mixture of luxury and discomfort. I have an office which would have made Goering green with envy; a car about the size of a railway engine which used to belong to an SS general and a very big pleasant room in the mess, looking out over the Alster, with my own bathroom. But there is only hot water once a week, so far no heating and only expectations of sort of semi-heating throughout the winter. Still, I suppose it's a good thing to share, even to a minor extent, some of the discomforts of the people among whom one lives.

It was clear to him from the very beginning that his main problems would lie with the attitudes of the political parties.

Inevitably broadcasters and politicians were antagonists, but Greene expected them to be effectively co-equal within a framework of law and political principle which enclosed them both. For Greene this was and is grist to the mill of the liberal democratic tradition; to politicians it could be borne with all the grace of severe arthritis:

> It started with the introduction of political discussion programmes in which representatives of the parties took part. The larger political parties demanded the right to speak for longer than the smaller parties, as if one can ration argument and as if he who speaks longest always speaks most effectively. One of the main parties even withdrew for a time in protest, but soon returned when we carried on without them.

Greene's knowledge of the history of broadcasting in Germany before 1933 also gave him cause to worry. He knew that it had been over-centralised, state controlled and a-political in a bad sense: the independence and freedom of speech which might have made it an effective weapon in the defence of the Weimar Republic had been unknown. The regional broadcasting organisations had been grouped together into one company in which the Post Office had held the majority of shares. All the broadcasting units had been closely controlled by political committees on which representatives of the government and of the political parties sat side by side. This supervision had developed, in the Germany of the Weimar Republic, into regular pre-censorship by the political parties of talks and any programmes dealing even remotely with a political subject. The grand old man of German broadcasting, Dr Bredow, himself described how the dead hand of party political control led to colourless reporting and an unnatural neutrality towards the events of the day.

Bredow encouraged Greene to make sure that the transmitters for NWDR should be owned and run by the broadcasting organisation and not by the Post Office. Greene was searching for those vital mechanisms and conventions which would distance NWDR from the political establishment but which would not, in so doing, isolate it. Of course he knew the problems that were likely to arise from the parties no matter what his intentions, and he was trying to buy time for the development of those traditions of independence, open-mindedness, and tolerance which were the real bedrocks of the reputation which was the BBC's. The BBC's work in practice depended on its being suspended in a life-giving atmosphere of acquiescence to its role, status, and position within British culture. Without that atmosphere, all the institutional devices in the world could not safeguard an independent organisation. It was unfortunately never possible for Greene, as the chief architect of NWDR, to reproduce those conditions in Germany.

Historically, Greene's claim to fame in Germany is as architect of the first constitution of NWDR and as a major influence on the institutional development of the whole of post-war Western German broadcasting. There is another aspect to his work, which lives on, not in the institutional histories but in the hearts and minds of those who worked under him in NWDR. As Controller of the station Greene was his own one-man illustration of the kind of broadcasting organisation he wished to develop. He was obviously a joy to work for.

When he arrived in 1946, Greene inherited a considerable body of talent, not just men who had a professional competence, but 'characters' with drive and imagination who had an intuitive empathy for what Greene was trying to do. In conversation now he picks out as central to this body of talent Peter von Zahn, Axel Eggebrecht and Ernst Schnabel. It is interesting to note that two of these three principals did not last long in the station after Greene's departure.

Perhaps the main reason why Greene had such a good reputation among the German staff was that he did not intrude. Von Zahn noted that 'he never interfered with programmes. The only thing that I remember worked the other way around, when he went on the air defending things that we had done against party pressure.' As Controller in Hamburg Greene had more power over the lives and work of his employees than at any other time in his career, before or since. That he did not choose to use this power reflected an important feature of his personality which was rapidly developing into the central aspect of his executive style: the ability to stand back and trust others to get on with the task of making programmes. It is an ability which should not be under-estimated.

In his writings Greene refers to 'the gaiety and irreverence of those days', and on the available evidence they do seem to have been just that. Certainly those Germans who worked with him confirm this impression. The stance he developed —the benign remoteness, the sense of fun and particularly his gentle mockery—were core elements of his whole broadcasting style. At no point did he articulate precisely what it was he wanted done; his ambitions, desires and intentions were expressed telepathically rather than didactically, yet they were understood and acted upon.

February 1947 was bitterly cold, Hamburg froze over and twenty-two degrees of frost were recorded. Coal was scarce and Hamburg was only receiving half her daily needs. Coal pilfering became serious and 1,500 police were called out to deal with the problem, but their efforts were thwarted by NWDR which proceeded to announce the times of the arrival of coal trains and points in their journeys when they would be going slowest. The youth of Hamburg immediately leapt aboard the trains at these places to divest them of their cargo. When irate German bureaucrats complained to Greene, he dismissed them with the observation that this was a German problem and therefore nothing to do with him.

The frightful cold created a mood of discontent and ambivalence among the local people. They had shaken off much of the angst of defeat, and their joy at having been spared the Russians, but now they began to grumble about their new masters. As Greene described it to his mother:

First there was the feeling that the British were living in comfort while they were freezing, 'those wicked British . . .' and then when it got round that the British were freezing too the attitude changed, 'Oh, those inefficient people, they can't even heat themselves.'

It was in this demoralising context that Peter von Zahn wrote a mocking little satire called *How to Get on with the Conquerors*, which gently poked fun at the British and urged the Germans to put up with their strange ways. This programme epitomised what Greene was trying to encourage NWDR to do, to tease, to reassure, to create German self-confidence and independence of thought. As von Zahn himself said, the NWDR was trying to be 'an instrument of political and cultural education in liberal democracy, tolerance and compromise'.

Eberhard Schütz also suggested that they were trying to ask pertinent questions so that people would think about the past and not cloud over the issues.

What were the Germans not allowed to know during the Nazi period? What was eliminated, starting with school books, and what kind of literature was burned? What happened in the world during those years and was only known in a distorted fashion? We systematically tried to get this kind of material into the programme.

Greene's years in the station were an opportunity to begin the slow process of re-colonising German society for civilisation. Eggebrecht summed up their mood and their sentiments: 'There was special freedom with Greene in the station. There were special possibilities.' But would this spirit survive Greene's departure? Would key figures such as Eggebrecht, Schnabel and von Zahn be able to retain their integrity and to insulate themselves from overt pressures once Greene had gone?

What became rapidly clear was that the rest of German society was developing in ways which would make it very difficult to sustain the ideal. Almost as soon as the political parties gained legal status, they were at odds with the broadcasters. The politicians sought, perhaps understandably, party advantage on the air, to make people vote for them, an attitude of mind which was poles apart from the view that public service broadcasting should avoid commitment but should endeavour to make Germans *think*; think about the issues facing the nation as a whole, think about attitudes, values and ideals.

Nor were all members of Greene's staff enamoured with NWDR's espousal of liberal democratic values. Karl Eduard von Schnitzler, the son of a banker and industrialist, had spent much of the war as a prisoner in England, where he had refined his open commitment to Communism. In early 1946 he took over the '*Politisches Wort*' department of the Cologne station which he shared with Max Burghardt, a man of similar sentiments, who had been made Intendant of Cologne in May 1946. Inevitably the presence of these two men provoked attacks from the right wing of the Christian Democratic Union, led by Konrad Adenauer. In the summer of 1946, Burghardt was reproached by the CDU for his 'Marxist programme structuring'. This prompted a letter from Schnitzler to Adenauer arguing that it was not the party political or ideological ties of the staff of NWDR which had led to the reproach, but the fact that the CDU were not prepared to cooperate in the development of an independent NWDR. The station was also accused of being red and there were further occasional attacks from the American Zone, but none which Greene regarded initially as especially serious. Eventually however he decided that he had to remove both Schnitzler and Burghardt:

'It was very much a personal decision. It started with Burghardt . . . I got rid of him, and he went to East Germany. Schnitzler was removed from Cologne to Hamburg for a trial period where he continued to do political commentaries, because he was a good broadcaster and a clever man, and I wasn't anxious to get rid of him, but he continued to slip Communist propaganda into his commentaries and in the end I decided he had to go.

The Control Commission's attitude to Communism and the German Communist party, the KPD, was summed up by Brownjohn, Deputy Military Governor, in a note to Bishop:

We cannot preach objectivity one moment and severe bias the next, without risking creating the very type of radio organisation which we have been seeking to destroy. NWDR does not give equal prominence to the activities of the Communists, but only equitable treatment. Unless and until the KPD is banned, it is not possible to go further than this. NWDR is carefully monitored and any tendency to give the KPD more than equitable treatment will at once be checked. I am assured that the action taken against Communist infiltration into the staff of NWDR was fully effective.

On the same day Brownjohn issued a note asking that the news coverage of the KPD be kept at the same level as its numerical support, which was about eight per cent.

At the other end of the political spectrum there was a similar, but more emphasised, problem. Directive Number 24 of the Control Council, issued in January 1946, called for the removal 'from office and from positions of responsibility of Nazis and of persons hostile to Allied purposes'. Such persons were to be replaced 'by persons who, by their political and moral qualities, are deemed capable of assisting in developing genuine democratic institutions in Germany'. If there was evidence that the person had been no more than a nominal Nazi, was not a militarist or hostile to the Allied cause, then he could be retained despite the mandatory clauses.

Greene had to sack a number of his employees who turned out to have been a little too involved with the Nazis. In June 1947 he was attacked by the *Hamburger Echo* for refusing to give the names of the dismissed men, and for describing them as 'valuable colleagues'. He later commented on this: 'I do not regret the description. Perhaps I might add at this point that my dismissal of some Communist members of the staff, most of whom were working in Cologne, took place in somewhat less painful circumstances.' Over the de-Nazification process, Schütz describes Greene as being 'very, very decent. We protested in most cases and some came before tribunals and in all cases where some doubt was left Greene refused to dismiss them.'

Nineteen forty-seven had not been an easy year. The problems with personnel were difficult, but essentially beyond his control in so far as de-Nazification was concerned. More important is that it was the year in which Greene drafted, argued about and redrafted the constitution of the NWDR. He set out to transform an ideal which had been underpinned by benign dictatorship, into a living organisation which could stand by itself once benevolence had been removed. He almost did it.

He covered endless miles of the Zone in his Maybach, driven everywhere by his ever-faithful German driver, Stricker. He talked to politicians, trade unionists, religious leaders, anyone who had something to say or, more crucially, anyone who would listen to the message which he was spreading, the message of public service broadcasting—independent, financed by licence fees, committed to the collective entity of 'the public', free from the pressures of any partial interest. In a formal sense, whether they liked the message or not was immaterial since the station was to be a creation of the Control Commission. The day of the conqueror's departure however was drawing ever closer and it was therefore only common sense to try to persuade the future leaders of Germany that in NWDR they had a model of broadcasting at its best, and that their only chance of keeping it that way was for the station to be independent of all organised political groups.

Greene's immediate concern therefore was to establish a broadcasting organisation so structured that it could guarantee this independence. The executive would need to be responsible to a board of governors or Verwaltung-srat, but who would appoint this board in the absence of a monarch? How could they be seen to be above party politics?

He decided on the creation of a body known as the Hauptausschuss, the members of which would be there by virtue of holding certain offices; the Minister Presidents of the three Länder in the British zone, the Mayor of Hamburg, the Rector of Göttingen University, the President of the Zonal Trades Union Council, and the presidents of the most important women's, youth and cultural organisations in the zone. These people would appoint the board of governors, who in their turn would appoint the Director General. However, unlike a monarch, many of the ex-officio trustees had been appointed to their initial offices because they represented a specific political party. It could therefore happen in theory that members of the trustee group all belonged to one political party. Even if this did not occur, it was inevitable that many members of the trustee group were heavily involved in party politics, and retained strong vested interests.

On December 30th, 1947, the NWDR Charter was officially handed over and on January 1st, 1948, what had been previously only an institutional extension of the political will of the military government gained legal status. For the time being, however, the military government retained the power of censorship and the power to approve any appointments made to NWDR.

On that first day of the New Year, Greene could look back on his work with considerable satisfaction. The German staff *were* closely involved in making programmes which were widely praised. One journalist wrote at the time: 'The radio play is treated with loving care and above all those plays which deal with the problems of our time earn acclaim.' The station was gaining a considerable reputation in music broadcasting under the direction of the orchestra leader, Dr Hans Schmidt-Isserstedt. It was known for its topical output; programmes for schools were also well developed, and the training centre under Alex Maass was gaining a considerable reputation. A Swiss correspondent at the time wrote that the developments were '. . . particularly astonishing since they are achieved under very unfavourable circumstances . . . In the misery of contemporary Germany, the work achieved by NWDR is one of the few rays of light.'

In March 1948 Greene wrote to his mother:

> On Friday the first NWDR board of governors was elected . . . I shall now be in the curious position of taking instructions from the governors in my German capacity and being able to overrule them any time I like in my English capacity. Now it remains to find a DG and then my job will be drawing to a close.

Adolf Grimme, the Minister of Culture in Niedersachsen, was elected Chairman of the Board of Governors. On this subject Greene wrote to William Haley at the BBC: 'It is a somewhat unusual position to have the Minister of a Land government in such a position but Herr Grimme is an unusual man and, in my opinion, one could have no better chairman.' Haley replied: 'The Chairman is rather a surprise, but as you say it is personality that counts.' This was only true so long as that personality was allied to a real sense of authority, and so long as it was willing to pursue the interests of the public service broadcasting system rather than particular vested interests. Grimme was a questionable choice, although Greene still thinks that in the circumstances of the time, the right one.

Greene's remaining task was to find the first German Director General. It was eventually decided to ask Grimme to switch from his position as Chairman to that of the chief executive. Again, it was not a good choice, though in the circumstances it may well have been the only one possible. Grimme had earned his credentials during a period of imprisonment under the Nazis, he had a good reputation as an administrator, and clearly Greene was delighted with his emergence in NWDR. Greene commented on his choice:

It was because he'd had a very good political record. I liked him and he had great prestige in Germany. He was involved in the SPD but he was very much on the right wing of the SPD so he was politically acceptable, even for the CDU and was one of the most respected people in Germany at the time. I thought it would be very good for the future of broadcasting to have as the first DG a man really of great prestige, rather than going for a professional broadcaster.'

In reality it was not actually as simple as this. Initially Grimme seemed to have all the right ideas, he saw broadcasting as a cultural instrument although he understood its political implications. Broadcasting, he said, was more than just news, more than just entertainment, more even than edification—it was the centre of family life, instructive, an instrument for making people conscious of the new Europe and Germany's role within it. German broadcasting was to be 'an ambassador of the German spirit and also the spirit of the good European'. These views sound so straightforward, but in no time at all Adolf Grimme had become a controversial figure: 'Grimme didn't know people, couldn't judge people. He took the wrong persons for the wrong job.' 'Greene was right to take Grimme, but he couldn't have known that Grimme was not a person for a leading position.' 'He was the wrong man—a good man, but the wrong man for the job,' were some of the differing assessments made by colleagues.

But this was not all: Grimme had come to NWDR under what some observers regarded as rather suspicious circumstances. In 1954 the German magazine *ABZ* carried an article which implied that Grimme had been moved from his post as Minister of Culture to Director General of NWDR because 'he had taken too much interest in the wife of a minister in Niedersachsen called Kopf'. Greene had total control over the appointment of the Director General and knew all about Grimme's involvement with Kopf's wife, but denies that it had anything to do with the appointment of

Grimme, if only because Kopf cared little about his wife's extra-marital activities.

Greene says that he, and he alone, made the decision to offer Grimme the appointment and in so doing, he says, he was not influenced by party political considerations. But there is an internal BBC memorandum written by Greene which shows very clearly that he was influenced. It states:

> Before the appointment of Grimme as Director General, I made an agreement with Herr Arnold, Prime Minister of Nordrhein Westfalen, that if he would agree to Grimme's appointment it should be regarded as reasonable that the Chairman of the administrative board should be a member of the CDU and a Catholic. Grimme of course is a member of the SPD and a protestant. This agreement has since been regarded as binding.

Hugh Greene therefore must bear some responsibility for the deep-seated problem which emerged almost as soon as his aeroplane had left the ground, when the political parties began to assert themselves on the station and in effect to undermine Greene's central principle that NWDR should be, and should be seen to be, independent of party politics. The compromise which Greene was forced into accepting can be seen historically to be the moment when the leading role of the political parties in German broadcasting was born. There was fierce disharmony between Grimme, the Protestant SPD Director General, and Raskop the Catholic CDU member who had been appointed Chairman of the governing body. Neither man had much time for what one internal memo described as 'the old guard of NWDR, some of whom are intellectuals of a very left wing tendency, are strongly individualist, often temperamental, and unwilling to submit to any kind of discipline from above'. Instantly a wedge was driven between the Greene years and the new régime. For months the station teetered on the edge of chaos.

Greene had left Hamburg with a considerable reputation. He had done an excellent job both in creating the formal structure of NWDR and in creating a feeling of freedom and creativity which his German employees found exhilarating. In some ways, however, he had done too good a job because he created expectations among members of the staff which any successor would find difficult to meet. Moreover, the combination of his strong personality, the very real power which he possessed as a member of the Control Commission, and his considerable tolerance in dealing with his German employees could not easily be reproduced. Inevitably his successor, Grimme, ran into immediate difficulties in his relations with his staff. He was accused of favouring right-wing, even ex-Nazi figures over those characters, such as Eggebrecht, in whom Greene had placed so much faith as the foundation for the new public broadcasting system in Germany. The Control Commission became increasingly anxious about developments after Greene's departure. One memo at the time argued, 'it remains an open question whether he [Grimme] will succeed in pacifying the house and, at the same time, safeguard its development as a free and independent institution'.

The Control Commission now had to decide whether these were teething problems or whether they reflected a much more fundamental flaw, for when Grimme became Director General, pre-censorship of all material had ended but should the Germans misbehave, censorship could still be restored immediately.

In the British camp there was more than a hint of dis-appointment at the way things had gone. In May 1950, the CCG was referring to the 'dangerous trends' developing within NWDR. They noted that when he was appointed, Grimme:

> . . . took over an organisation in which the team spirit, healthy outlook and goodwill towards the British was of a high order. Dr Grimme entered upon his duties backed up by the maximum of good-will and cooperation on our side. Had he been of the calibre required, he would have met few difficulties which would not have been easily overcome.

Grimme has, in fact, proved to have certain marked failings, the chief of which is his complete lack of judgment . . . He is weak and likes to surround himself with favourites. He lacks a broad conception of his functions as DG . . . [and has] a genius for selecting bad advisers.

To be fair, it was not only Grimme who lacked these so-called 'broader conceptions'. There did not seem to be either the understanding or the willingness within the new German Republic to come to grips with the idea of public broadcasting. Fundamentally, any public service broadcasting organisation exists because it is allowed to exist. The other side of that coin is that any public broadcasting organisation exists under a perpetual threat of annihilation. Britain had successfully developed a political culture in which free comment and critique were tolerated; a tradition that had been a long time growing and even then rested uneasily on its base at any time of crisis. NWDR was created in a society in which the state, let alone benign liberal traditions, did not at that time even exist. The battle was on, not only for the soul of NWDR, but for the soul of the new Germany. NWDR was no more than one front in that campaign.

Perhaps it was inevitable that the new political class in Germany—appearing out of camps and exile, pained and frustrated—would be eager to control and guide emerging institutions within the new society. It was and is the basic instinct of the politician to take for himself the means of creating the future, to scratch the itch and mute the sharpness of the bite. It is a universal phenomenon and only the most self-confident of societies, the most assured of political establishments are willing to grant freedom for a separate definition and exploration of its own nature. In only a handful of instances have these conditions prevailed. Amid the physical, emotional and intellectual rubble of defeat in Germany, it was almost inevitable that the architects of the new state would not have the self-confidence. The bickering between Raskop and Grimme became more than just pettiness, representing the birth pangs of the emerging struggle between the SPD and the CDU. The various other hostilities, the accusations of right-wing bias and left-wing bias, of conspiracy and corruption, were battles linked to the emergent struggle to define the ways in which the new state would fashion itself. To whose rhythms would its feet tap?

On November 15th, 1948, at the end of his stay in Hamburg, Greene addressed the personnel of NWDR, and many of the leading British and German personalities in the British Zone, for the last time. He later described the event:

In my speech in the big concert hall, where I had first spoken to the staff of NWDR more than two years before, I referred, not for the first or the last time, to the need for public service broadcasting to be as independent as possible of state and party political influences . . . I came down from the platform. Herr Brauer, the Bürgermeister of Hamburg, growled softly, but with an unmistakable tone of hostility, in my ear, 'You will not succeed, Mr Greene. You will not succeed.'

With the passage of a quarter of a century, it has become clear year by year that Herr Brauer was right. I did not succeed. NWDR, which might have become the pillar of a less decentralised German broadcasting system, was divided up. New constitutional instruments came into force which placed the political parties in a dominant position. More and more the election of *Intendanten* and other senior staff took place along party lines and the *Proporz* system came to rule in the broadcasting houses.'

In a personal sense Greene's time in Hamburg was far from a failure; he had become a great figure in European broadcasting, much admired and respected by his colleagues; he had built up an enterprising, successful station from small beginnings to the third largest in Europe, with three and a half million licence holders, and he had imbued his staff with the spirit of independence. His reputation had grown and in many ways he had done a first-class job in establishing NWDR. It was, as the formal letter of thanks from the

Foreign Office stated, 'an example of the constructive work carried out by the Control Commission and one of which all concerned, and in particular you yourself, can well be proud'. Bishop also congratulated Greene, and told him that 'you have the satisfaction of knowing that the result of your work will continue; you have built up a structure that has very firm foundations'.

But time would show these tributes to be faulty. Greene had made errors of judgment; from its birth NWDR had been deformed and for that Greene was partially responsible; he had also made unfortunate appointments in Grimme and Raskop, whom he had thought when they emerged, 'two of the best and nicest people I know, so I shall be able to leave here with a quiet mind'. When Greene, therefore, offered his own response to Herr Brauer more than a quarter of a century later, he was right to be despondent about the way things had gone. He had to acknowledge that the political parties had gained a level of involvement in post-war German broadcasting which was totally incompatible with the notion of public service broadcasting conceived with the BBC as its model.

Germany had changed him; between 1946 and 1948 the contours of Hugh's character became sharper. As he moved away from the war years, through the break-up of his marriage, to wield the greater power given him in Germany, he grew in stature. The many disparate parts of his personality were now more closely woven together: a certain aloofness, a hatred of pomposity and intolerance, an impish humour, power and authority, all combined to give him a calm inner strength which enabled him to allow those under him to use their creative talents to the full without fear of interference or jealousy. His passionate opposition to illiberal thought and action led him to welcome those who would prick or attack authority and the established orders: his mind was neither narrow, petty nor restricted. He possessed, too, the crucial quality of not being worried when people outside the organisation, receiving the programmes, were occasionally shocked by what they heard or saw.

By 1948 Germany had become the prime influence in his life, as formative an experience as his school days. It was not just Nazi Germany and its aftermath that had affected him; it was something in Germany itself, another side of German life which persisted briefly until about 1936 and re-emerged after 1945, that particularly appealed to him. It was the sensuality and dissidence which bordered German culture like rich satin embroidered round the edge of a calico skirt.

He was amused by the wit and sharp truths of its political cabaret and was open-minded, tolerant and courageous enough to believe that it might appeal to others. The country also offered him long, languid trips down the Rhine, trying out innumerable wines, or somewhat raucous evenings in nightclubs. One of his former colleagues said: 'I suppose his first German love had been Berlin. He also loved the Rhineland, definitely he loved wine, definitely he didn't hate girls. He loved to feel being accepted and loved.' Peter von Zahn said how Greene loved 'the biting fun of German cabaret', though perhaps one of his colleagues, Franz Reinholz, came nearer the truth when slowly, deliberately and with a wry smile he said, 'He didn't like the cabaret, he liked Tatjana', referring to Hugh Greene's third wife, the German actress, Tatjana Sais. One of the more perceptive English officers working at the station said:

> Hugh was very close about his private affairs. One really knew nothing about it. I think he was very lonely and later on he and I, who also had a broken marriage, used to go out to dinner and would get talking and the curtain began to draw back. And what appeared from behind the curtain? A very lovable man. I will say that straight away. A man who was trying to sort out his life . . . He was a lonely, unhappy man who wasn't really quite sure whether he could achieve happiness.

Helga had left him. Perhaps she and Hugh were victims of his total absorption in his work. Perhaps they were victims of their own personalities. Theirs had been a passionate and youthful relationship. He wanted her back, but she would not go back. He arrived in Hamburg disillusioned and sad, but, as is sometimes the case, the solution was not far off. He met Tatjana, a German actress, cabaret performer and wife of a well-known German writer for radio, screen and stage, Günter Neumann. The affair developed.

Anthony Mann, who had been his assistant in Berlin before his expulsion, recalls a curious incident. He had been interned in Denmark for five years, and then returned to Germany, again as a correspondent. On an icy night in the winter of 1947 he was making the 120-mile journey through the Russian Zone in a non-weather-proofed jeep:

> It was bitterly cold, and my army driver and I reached the British border at Helmstedt half frozen. We made for the wooden hutment in which NAAFI provided meals and hot drinks for interzonal travellers. We went up to the bar, and I ordered tea, soup, and other restoratives. The place was completely empty except for one table near the window, where a tall man and a woman were in earnest conversation. The man glanced over at us, and to my surprise I recognised HG. I was about to walk across when I noticed that his face wore a completely blank and distant look, as if he had never seen me in his life.
>
> The hint was unmistakable, and I engaged my driver hastily in conversation about the quality of the soup. The lady's face seemed vaguely familiar, then she looked briefly in our direction and I remembered her name. She was the German actress Tatjana Sais. We finished our soup and left.

The family were largely unaware of this development and wrote to him expressing their sorrow at the breakdown of his marriage, implicitly siding with him against Helga. In May 1948 he wrote to his mother: 'I think it's time sombody expressed sympathy with Helga instead of me! I don't need it. I can quite truthfully say that I've never been so happy in my life.'

7

In September 1948 Hugh Greene wrote to the Director General of the BBC, William Haley, to enquire about his future. He approached the end of his contract at the Control Commission with little or no idea about his fate. There followed what the Director of the Overseas Service, Sir Ian Jacob, described as 'rather prolonged contortions' before they found a new post for the exile in Hamburg. They wanted him to accept the post of head of the East European Services broadcasts to Russia, Rumania, Bulgaria, Yugoslavia, Albania and Greece. Jacob hoped this job would become vacant because he particularly wanted it to be done by Hugh Greene. To this end he forced out Gordon Fraser, the former head of the service, who then took up a post with UNESCO. Jacob had felt that Fraser was not strong enough to run such an important and difficult service as the East European operation: Fraser was, he felt, a bit 'soft' at a time when toughness was the order of the day. In Greene he saw just the right kinds of qualities—his journalistic background, his administrative experience in Hamburg, his powerful personality. He was, Jacob felt, 'head and shoulders' above any other possible candidate. The key to the operation was inevitably the service to Russia, and Greene was specifically asked by Jacob to beef up that service's output.

Hugh Greene's response to the offer was polite but uncertain. He knew little about the countries which the service covered, even if he was confident enough to feel that this would not be a major problem. More seriously, he had been advised by a heart specialist to have a long rest, to take things very quietly for at least six or seven weeks, and not to commit himself to another job before January 1st. His contract with the Control Commission ran until the end of December and therefore he would have no chance for any holiday if he accepted Jacob's offer and, as he told Jacob, since 'the end of 1933 I have, as you may know, been engaged in one fairly exacting job after another'. He therefore left his answer hanging in the balance, allowing himself more time to assess the state of his health.

It did not take him long to decide that the post offered to him in London was too attractive to turn down. At the beginning of December he wrote saying that he would accept the post, at the same time trying to convince them that he was worth more than they were offering. He did get more. He was offered £1,800 a year for a post which normally would have received £1,570. From December 22nd, 1948, he was once more a member of the BBC's staff, but was not to take up his post until January 15th, 1949.

Hugh Greene had returned to Bush House, to the war of words, and while the methods remained essentially the same as those used during the war, the target was very different. The shape of the battle, the strategy and tactics, were not to be Hugh Greene's to decide. These had already been determined by a small quiet man with a powerful intelligence and personality, and a certain vision about how he wished to develop the European Services, the Overseas Services and ultimately the BBC itself. Jacob is, perhaps because of his rather shy character and inconspicuous appearance, one of the least well-known of the BBC's major post-war figures. However he is particularly important in the life of Hugh Greene, since he became Hugh Greene's mentor and carefully groomed him for the higher echelons of the BBC. Jacob's ideas, attitudes and opinions enormously influenced the whole of the BBC in the later 1940s and throughout the whole of the 1950s. He, more than any other individual, was to be responsible for the rise to power of Hugh Greene. One must therefore look a little more closely at this interesting but largely unknown character.

Lieutenant General Sir Ian Jacob, KBE, CB, joined the BBC in the middle of May 1946 from the Cabinet Office. Born on the Indian Frontier at Quetta on September 27th, 1899, son of the late Field Marshal Sir Claud Jacob and his wife, Aileen, he had been educated at Wellington College, Royal Military Academy, where he passed out top in his year, and King's College, Cambridge. He rapidly established himself as a brilliant young soldier with a keen analytical mind and a superb capacity for organisation. He joined the Committee of Imperial Defence in 1938, and in 1939 became Assistant Military Secretary to the War Cabinet, a post he held until he joined the BBC. The *Sunday Times* described his rise to prominence:

'He won the special confidence of Mr Churchill, attended many important conferences, and established himself as one of the best brains in the Chief of Staff organisation. Promotion followed rapidly, and it seemed that the highest position in the new defence organisation was already within his reach.'

The end of the war, however, saw the return to promotion by seniority rather than ability. It was not a system geared to furthering the career of an officer who, though he had made an enormous contribution to the war effort, was notably lacking in battlefield experience. The point was not lost on Jacob, and he decided that there was not much future for him in the army and therefore he had 'better get into something else while he was young enough to do so'. Various jobs were offered, but none of them matched his desire to retain involvement in the public affairs of the country about which his war work had made him enthusiastic. The BBC, at the suggestion of Ivone Kirkpatrick, approached him with the idea that he might like to run their European Services. He smiled at the possibility:

'I knew the Foreign Office very well; I knew the government machine, policy and all the rest of it, I'd been at the centre the whole time; and this was where the Cold War was being waged. That seemed to be a more suitable line of country than going into industry or something of that sort.

It was therefore a way of remaining at the heart of things while not suffering the indignity of being overlooked for promotion.

There were undoubtedly doubts and queries in some minds that Jacob's path to the door of Bush House would lead him to excessive acceptance of the government line of the day, or at best to a reluctance to upset or deny his former masters. Jacob, however, immediately made it clear that his propaganda vision encompassed vistas far greater than those of daily foreign affairs. Under him the BBC's European Service began seriously to view itself as not just a national agent and voice for British intellectual and institutional forms, but rather as a supra-national agent transmitting those forms not as one version of how the world should be ordered, but rather as something akin to an absolute truth untainted by petty nationalism. This was to be an important part of the continuing political education of Hugh Greene. On reflection now Jacob recalls that his policy was a rather mild effort to 'make friends with the people of a country while exposing any of the things which their government is doing which is inimical to our interests . . . the BBC has got to be regarded as the one truthful station in the world.'

Jacob described his first, and all-important directive, as a 'Statement of Policy for the European Service'. It contains, however, a paradox: the BBC would provide a comprehensive, well-balanced and objective service of news and at the same time project 'Britain, British activities and aims and the British way of life and thinking'.

Jacob possessed to the full the unbelievable self-confidence, arrogance and righteousness, attitudes which so characterised the BBC after the war. His wish that peacetime news bulletins and other programmes should be objec-

Hamburg, 1946

Hamburg, 1947

Christmas, 1950 in Malacca,
photographed by Graham

With Alex Josey at the Lake Club
Kuala Lumpur, 1951

Greene's Propaganda Army at Emergency Information Services
Headquarters, Bluff Road, Kuala Lumpur

tive and yet demonstrate Britain's greatness was to create problems. Hugh Greene was soon to discover that for the BBC to claim independence and objectivity, and then also to define its own concepts of Britishness and morality, was only possible if those officials and leaders who made up the government and the nation agreed with the BBC about just what the elements of that consensus actually were.

Such problems, however, lay in the future; for the moment Jacob's polemic was useful. When Hugh arrived on January 15th, 1949 to run the East European Service, its mission had been defined, the subtlety of its relationship to official policy had been worked out and attitudes to key issues of international politics established; all Hugh had to do was to give his programmes a journalistic edge and hardness which Jacob felt had been lacking under Gordon Fraser. Almost immediately Hugh was helped in this resolve by being able to put on the Russian Service a series of talks by Colonel Tokaiev, who was, the Governors were informed, 'what is known as a "defector"'. Soon the USSR responded by commencing a major jamming campaign to block BBC Russian broadcasts. A battle was on which was to run for nearly two decades and was eventually to be temporarily resolved by Hugh Greene when, as Director General, he invited his Soviet opposite number, Mr Kharlomov, to London. The jamming created a profound sense of déjà vu. It meant that broadcasts had to be at a slower tempo than other language services, that elaborate forms of presentation were avoided, that stress had to be on a maximum clarity of style. In other words, all those skills which he had learnt and employed in the German Service once more surfaced in the context of this new, Cold War.

The East European Service was but one part of an extensive body of foreign broadcasts in the BBC's Overseas Services. When Greene arrived the services were offering something like 700 hours a week in forty-seven languages at a cost of £4 million annually, of which one and a half million were spent on the European Services. 'The cost,' someone observed at the time, 'of a battleship—and the value of a fleet.' The East European and Central European Services covered ten countries, of which a number—Czechoslovakia, Hungary, Poland, Albania, Bulgaria and Rumania—were seen as the Soviet Union's satellite countries. The major difference in terms of policy was that the audiences of the satellite countries were regarded as friendly to the BBC's broadcasts, whereas no such friendliness was presumed in the Russian audience. The trick which Greene's service had to perform in broadcasting to the 'satellites' was to exploit the audiences' latent anti-Communism, without recourse to what one internal paper called 'a dangerous provision of unfounded promises'. The declared purpose of the Eastern Zone programmes of the German Service was:

> . . . to pillory the Communist régime and display it as being ridiculous as well as cynical and evil, to restate and expound the principles of Western civilisation with special reference to democracy, freedom of thought, respect for human dignity and the basic message of Christianity.

Hugh Greene's own view could be equally pugnacious. He had been brought in to make the East European Service tougher and more aggressive, and tougher and more aggressive it became. In September 1949 he looked at events in Albania and decided that the situation was ripe for initiative. He proposed to his old rival Tangye Lean, now senior to him and Controller of the European Service, 'that a situation now seems to be arising in Albania which offers a great opportunity for our broadcasts. All the available information goes to show that the present régime is facing a crisis.' He asked for, and got, an extra fifteen minutes for news and comment to be broadcast to Albania. The Foreign Office's attitude was that though 'plain news may be regarded as a form of softening up—the punch comes in the comment, and in their present mood the Albanians are probably worth punching'. Hugh Greene saw his role as one of taking the initiative in recommending that broadcasts be stepped up in the hope of further de-stabilising the Albanian government.

Unfortunately it was almost impossible to have any precise knowledge of just what the impact of any particular service was, especially when jamming of broadcasts became significant. A joke, current in Bush House at the end of 1949 about a particularly well-known broadcast to Czechoslovakia each Friday evening, captures something of the confident assumptions which the services had about their impact. At a Communist party factory meeting on a Friday evening, the hall was only quarter full. As the meeting progressed people began to drift away in twos and threes. Finally, looking round the empty hall, the chairman looked at his watch, shuffled his feet and said, 'Well, we'd better be getting along home or we'll miss it too.' There was, however, as Ian Jacob recognised, always great difficulty in actually proving that anyone was listening, a fact which undermined the credibility of any request for further funds, which in turn indicated that maybe the foreign language services of the BBC were not held in quite the esteem by the Foreign Office that the BBC sometimes liked to imagine. At the time Hugh Greene was quoted as saying, 'We're working tremendously in the dark. But despite the jamming, we believe that the man who is really hungry for information can still get us. How many are they? Well, enough to make it worthwhile.'

At the daily meetings with Jacob, which formed the administrative heart of all the services, Hugh Greene once more played his rather quiet, distanced role, while all the time being perfectly well aware of what was expected of his own department. Indeed, he began to show a certain level of initiative and independence which was none too welcome to his old antagonist, Tangye Lean.

One consequence of Hugh Greene's absence in Hamburg was that some former subordinates, such as Lean, had risen higher in the BBC hierarchy than Greene had. Lean had become Controller of the whole European Service whilst Greene was only head of the East European section. One particular incident captured something of the hostility between the two men, demonstrating how Greene's independence of mind made the sensitive Controller seethe.

At the beginning of June 1950, while Lean was absent abroad, Hugh Greene conducted the Chairman of the BBC, Lord Simon, and a number of Conservative MPs around the European Services. At the request of Simon, Greene drafted an account of the essence of their talks, a copy of which was waiting on Lean's desk on his return. He read it and exploded because, as he put it in a memo of complaint to Jacob, ominously headed 'Personality of H.E. European Service', of Greene's:

> . . . omission of any reference to the Controller of the European Services as being in any way responsible or organisationally involved in the important matters under discussion. Indeed, he is quite clearly ruled out of existence by the statement that criticism by MPs 'should be directed against me, or above me, against General Jacob'. I take it that they can only have concluded that Greene works direct to General Jacob and is independent of other control. This is in line with Greene's eccentric attitude last month in writing to the Allied authorities in charge of Radio Trieste with whom I was in negotiation. His indifference to my views at that point damaged those negotiations seriously enough to have nuisance value. I have already rebuked him for it, but I wish to record in advance of a more formal report that Greene's shortcomings in the sense of exaggerated independence have not grown less since my last annual report.

Lean was not a happy man. How could he be when his arch enemy, who was manifestly more able than him, if also temporarily more junior, was displaying that indifference and contempt which had so antagonised him in the past. Greene, however, did not see it quite that way and set out to defend himself, suggesting that while he may not have referred to Lean personally in the discussions he had given a relatively brief but adequate formal description of the services which, at least implicitly, referred to Lean's position. It obviously did reflect on Greene's part a certain indifference to the role of his superior, but then Greene never did respect Lean. He concluded his note:

> In the interest of good personal relations I very much regret the whole tone of your memorandum. It is possible that I am a naturally independent person. Perhaps it is partly due to this that I have been given jobs such as that with NWDR where independence was regarded as an advantage. In any case I feel that even now the advantages need to be carefully weighed against the possible disadvantages.

Though Greene may not have impressed Lean, the first signs of recognition from more august persons came in a letter from Downing Street, asking whether Hugh Carleton-Green (they spelt it wrong) would allow his name to be recommended to the King so that he may be 'graciously pleased to approve that you be appointed an officer of the Order of the British Empire'. The independent-minded head of the propaganda war against the Eastern bloc was pleased to accept.

8

Hugh Greene did much to give the Eastern European Service a firmer backbone in the year that he was there. In particular he made it journalistically sharper and altogether harder hitting, although it was almost impossible for him to know whether he was having any impact. He continued to project the British way of life and to put across with gusto the notion of individual liberty and freedom of conscience.

One morning in the early summer of 1950, Ian Jacob called him into his office. In that clipped, almost abrupt style for which he was by then well-known, he asked, 'Hugh, how would you like to go to Malaya?' Greene remembers two things about the meeting. One, that he had a 'hell of a hangover . . . I came into his office feeling like death.' The other was that he immediately said yes. It eventually emerged that Patrick Gordon Walker, who had worked for Hugh Greene in the German Service and was by 1950 Secretary of State for Commonwealth Relations in the Labour government, had argued to the Secretary of State for the Colonies, Jim Griffiths, that what they needed in Malaya was a psychological warfare expert. Greene, he thought, was just the man.

For Greene it was a leap in the dark, another challenge. It also came at a time when his personal life was going through a period of upheaval. Tatjana Sais had been living with Hugh Greene in London, but now she had decided to resume her career in the German theatre. He needed to escape, to think things through and where better to do that than 12,000 miles away. The situation was analogous to the period immediately before his going to Hamburg. An affair seemed to be over and he craved a new, exacting but exciting job, partly at least as therapy.

As the Second World War ended, the Malayan Communist Party, which had fought the Japanese from its jungle bases, turned its attention to fighting what it regarded as the British imperial presence. For three years the authorities and the MCP existed in open hostility. It was, however, the murder in June 1948 of three European rubber plantation managers which led to the declaration of a full-scale State of Emergency. The British brought full resources to bear— political, military, police and Intelligence—concentrating and coordinating them under the single command of a High Commissioner who had full powers, aided by a Director of Operations.

When Hugh Greene arrived the High Commissioner was Sir Henry Gurney and the Director of Operations in Malaya was Lieutenant General Sir Harold Briggs. Briggs had left the control of propaganda and information to the department of public relations, but he soon realised that the campaign needed intensifying, public morale needed raising, and the local people needed greater inducements to help the authorities with information, with details about where the insurgents were hiding, and what they were up to.

Alex Josey, a rather colourful character, had been working on emergency information but, on his own admission, he had not been very successful. He is convinced that he was removed because he upset the plantation and tin mine owners by suggesting, in some of the material he was putting out, that socialism might be an alternative to the political system which prevailed in Malaya. Josey's departure left a vacuum, hence the request to the British government to provide an officer with experience of propaganda under war conditions. Hugh Greene was the choice and he was seconded for one year to the Federation of Malaya. He arrived in Kuala Lumpur on September 20th, 1950.

He began to travel around the Federation—and for the one and only time in his life he was armed—often with a military escort, talking to people, trying to assess just what the role of propaganda could be. His preliminary study led him to conclude that what was needed were changes both in the organisation of the propaganda machine and in the character of the output. There had been, he felt, an over-reliance on leaflets and on the possibilities of the direct spoken word, whereas the use of broadcasting and films had been largely neglected. Similarly, little use had been made of the propaganda possibilities offered by surrendered bandits or of the detailed intelligence about the terrorists and their organisation available to the police. There was, as he put it in his final report: '. . . too much general exhortation and not enough local detail, too much dwelling on bandit acts of terror (which was only calculated to help the other side) and not enough on the points where the enemy was weak.' There had also, he felt, been too little effort to make sure that what printed material was produced actually reached its intended target.

Greene was always very loyal to, and appreciative of, those he felt deserved it. He went out of his way to make sure that Alex Josey, who had begun to remedy some of these deficiencies even while he was having to operate as a one-man band before being sacked, was reinstated. Greene also had a keen eye for the status of a post and one of the first things he insisted on was changing his own title from Staff Officer (Emergency Information) to Head, Emergency Information Services, and receiving the power to direct and coordinate all propaganda media on behalf of the Director of Operations. He had been dismayed at first with the problems he faced, even if he enjoyed the country. He wrote to his mother in October 1950: 'It is an awful job to find staff to plan for the future and at the same time to do single-handed a job for which by last war's standards one would have employed a dozen or more people. Of course nothing gets done really well. But I continue to find it all great fun.'

He managed eventually to expand the staff to include a Deputy, Eliot Watrous, who came out from the BBC at the end of December 1950, a press officer, a Chinese assistant, chief clerk, telephonist and extra secretarial staff.

In March 1951 the Emergency Information Service moved into a new building which had been specially built for them in the not inappropriately titled Bluff Road. Greene's immediate action was to expand and professionalise the service, to begin to understand the real, as opposed to the assumed, nature of the problem and then to devolve. As Malaya consisted of many separate states and settlements, including Johore, Perak, Selangor, Pahang and Negri Sembilan, he decided that each one would have to have its own emergency information officer with a full-time Chinese assistant, and that to be effective and speedy, the bulk of the propaganda output would have to be divided up into that suitable for each state, and that which would be more effective at district level.

He had three objectives for his work. The first was to 'raise the morale of the civil population and to encourage confidence in government and resistance to the Communists with a view to increasing the flow of information reaching the police'. The second aim was to undermine: '. . . the morale of members of the MRLA [Malayan Liberation Army], the Min Yuen (the Communist underground) and their supporters and to drive a wedge between the leaders and the rank and file with a view to encouraging defection and undermining the determination of the Communists to continue the struggle.' The third was 'to create an awareness of the values of the democratic way of life which is threatened by International Communism'.

The problems and intentions then were not all that different from those in the German Service, in the Eastern European Service, and to a certain extent in NWDR. His initial tactics were also similar to those previous tasks: expansion of resources, a gathering together of able people, a fairly high level of devolution to let them get on with the job they had been employed to do. The difference from his previous experiences was that here the bulk of the population were illiterate, there were four main languages and the military face of the enemy was buried deep in the Malayan jungle.

All the evidence showed that the most potent propaganda weapon was provided by those Communists who surrendered to the police and the army. Surrendered bandits who, through the written and spoken word, explained what had happened to them while in government hands demonstrated to their fellow bandits still in the jungle what they could expect to happen if they themselves surrendered. Letters written by the bandits, explaining their reasons for surrendering and indicating their treatment, were reproduced in their own handwriting in leaflets accompanied by their photos. These were then left on jungle footpaths, in bandit camps and dropped from the air in areas where the Min Yuen were still active. The bandits also made personal appearances in lecture tours in areas where they were known, something which, Greene argued, 'has done more than anything else to undermine the Communist propaganda that surrender means torture and execution'. His methods seemed to produce results and in the first eight months of 1951, 136 bandits surrendered, compared with seventy-four in the same period in 1950.

Greene never believed that propaganda was of itself the cause of the surrender: 'The task of propaganda is to persuade a man that he can safely do what he already secretly wants to do because of disillusionment, grievances or hatred of life in the jungle and to play on those feelings.' He saw the value of having the bandits make the propaganda, since they were of the same race and background as those whom they were addressing. He was especially encouraged to find that captured Min Yuen documents frequently complained that the work of the Min Yuen was being made more difficult by the propaganda activities of such 'traitors and running dogs'.

Greene had a very clear, pragmatic, almost cynical, view of the attitudes of the population: 'In the conditions which existed, and still exist in many parts of the country the only human emotion which can be expected to be stronger than fear among a terrorised population with very little civic consciousness is greed.' It was with this in mind that at the end of 1950 he asked for and obtained approval for big increases in the scale of the rewards offered for information leading to the capture or killing of terrorists, ranging from $60,000 for the Secretary General of the Malayan Communist Party, down to $2,000 for the rank and file. Surrendered bandits were eligible for half these rewards, and later rewards were introduced for the recovery of arms and ammunition, and a thirty per cent increase was introduced for the bringing in of terrorists alive—some of the bandits had developed the habit of only bringing in the head of another bandit, which did not exactly help the possibilities of interrogation.

The main instrument of propaganda used by Greene was the leaflet which contained statements by known leaders or letters written by groups of surrendered bandits or by individuals about their experiences since surrender. Leaflets were also addressed to individual bandit units including intelligence material about the behaviour of leaders, playing on existing strains and stresses. There were also local 'newspapers' aimed at giving members of the MRLA and Min Yuen news of surrenders and killings, 'as well as spicy items about the morals of their leaders'.

Surrendered bandits were used either individually or in teams for word-of-mouth propaganda, but Greene did not feel that this was being especially effective, so in November 1950 he proposed successfully to the War Council that the Malayan film unit should be expanded and that the number of mobile units in the Federation equipped with public address systems and the number of cinema projectors should be increased from twenty-three to fifty-three so that the evil deeds of the communists could be vividly shown on film to the largely illiterate rural population. He was conscious, however, that to try to impart too much information and propaganda at one time could be counterproductive, that entertainment was required as 'jam' to coat the pill. Arrangements were therefore made with MGM for the purchase of the rights for three years of fifty-three feature films, mainly 'Tarzan, Wild West and Knockabout Comedy'.

Broadcasting was the most underdeveloped part of the propaganda campaign, partly because of the number of languages and dialects spoken in the area. Before Greene's arrival, there had been little regular Emergency broadcasting on Radio Malaya, apart from daily news bulletins and some of Alex Josey's Malayan Affairs talks. Now, on November 28th, 1950, Hugh Greene was the subject of a rather grand declaration. The Governor of Singapore and the Officer Administering the Government in the Federation issued a directive making him responsible for all broadcasts concerned with the Emergency 'and the fight against World Communism'. He immediately reappointed Alex Josey Controller of Emergency Broadcasting and in January 1951 the Standing Committee on Finance approved the necessary funds for the staff and equipment of the Community Listening Organisation. The first programme went on the air in Malay, Tamil and four Chinese dialects in February. At the same time Radio Malaya began including regular features and talks on the Emergency. The first broadcast in a weekly series *Spotlight on the Emergency* took place on January 6th, 1951. In that month also, Eliot Watrous took over the writing and broadcasting of the series *This is Communism*, relating broader events in the Communist world to specific events in Malaya. In the summer of 1951 the Broadcasting Department resumed direct responsibility for the Community Listening Programmes under Lloyd Williams and David Lyttle, with every aspect of the Emergency being covered, using various forms, talks, documentary features, radio plays, interviews, and so on.

There was of course the eternally tricky question of news, the particular part of the output of the propaganda services with which Greene, given his background, was bound to be especially concerned. His feeling when he arrived, and after he had had some opportunity to assess the situation, was that the need for security had been allowed to interfere more than was necessary with the provision of news to the public.

Planters complained that they had no idea about the extent of bandit activity in their immediate vicinity. The War Council agreed at the end of November 1950 that in future the names of districts in which incidents occurred would be mentioned, and all possible details given as far as security permitted. When Greene arrived, cooperation between the police, the army and the civil authorities was limited, so he made every effort to strengthen such relationships, since propaganda is an auxiliary weapon which cannot function in a vacuum. When, for example, a very important bandit, Lam Swee, surrendered in June 1950, it was three months before the police informed the Information Services. Greene proceeded to establish weekly meetings with the Director of Intelligence. He also frequently attended meetings of the State and District War Executive Committees to talk about the aims and methods of propaganda, a role which was taken over by Eliot Watrous after his arrival. Greene also ensured that contacts down the line, between the State Emergency information officers and the chief police officer, between district officers and the police and army, at circle and district level, were effective, 'because', he argued, 'local specialisation, speed and sense of urgency are among the essentials for successful propaganda'. He did not overestimate what he could do whilst the government was not winning the war. But as soon as enemy morale really began to break 'propaganda can become the main weapon for hastening the end. The machine to exploit that chance now exists.'

As in Hamburg, Greene inspired a good deal of confidence among the nationals with whom he worked. C. C. Too, recruited by Greene as his chief Chinese assistant and still head of psychological warfare in Malaya today, came to think highly of Greene:

Although he was in this country for only a year, he was one of the most outstanding expatriate officers I have come across . . . His quick and penetrating perception of matters new to him, and his instant grasp of the essentials

133

which provide the basic ingredients for effective counter-measures, have to be seen to be believed. Above all, he was a gentleman who was easy and a pleasure to work with.

It was not all plain sailing for Greene. His wish to improve his links with the army and the police were not initially successful, so he went to Sir Henry Gurney, the High Commissioner, whom he regards now as 'one of the greatest men I've ever met in my life', to say that he was returning to London because the police and army were refusing to allow the propaganda services to offer bandits the chance of surrender and rewards. Gurney immediately straightened matters out, and Greene stayed.

What remains unclear is just what Hugh Greene believed the force of propaganda to be. His work over the previous decade had made him a propagandist of note, and yet one wonders whether he really felt that it made much difference. He seemed to feel that though it was considered important, the word really was not the force; to him the intrinsic interest of the work of the propagandist lay in the intellectual problems it posed and to which solutions had to be found. Alex Josey, who came to know Hugh Greene very well, thought him unemotional if rather earthy in some of his behaviour, but basically 'intellectual'. He did not, Josey felt, have a strategy, rather preferring to deal with problems as they came along. Both men depended much on their enormous respect for Gurney. When Gurney was murdered, he was replaced by General Templer, for whom both felt contempt. Josey commented, 'Templer didn't know the time of day. He created more Communists than he killed.'

Crucially then, Hugh Greene saw his task as an intellectual rather than a moral problem. One colleague recalled how he would consider everything and come up with ingenious solutions, for example suggesting that they cut the grass at the side of the roads in order to give less cover to bandits. He certainly thought that as the basic problems behind the Emergency were political and social, the solutions also had to be political and social. In a piece he wrote in

January 1952 shortly after he had returned home, called 'On Being a Bandit in Malaya', he reviewed the situation in terms which he had first raised in his memo of January 1951:

The jungle of Malaya could soak up division after division of troops like a gigantic sponge. The Communists in Malaya can be dealt with in the long run only by depriving them of their support, and that can be done only by providing the local population, particularly the Chinese, with something to defend, their own land let us say, which they would value more than Communist promises.

One of the British leaders in Malaya once said to me: 'We—the British—have made more Communists out here through our stupidity than all their propagandists put together.' Again, one can understand best what he meant by looking at Malaya through Asian eyes. Wages in Malaya are the highest in South-East Asia (many times higher than in India), more children than ever are going to school, there are fine roads, the health services are good, there is a hard-working and generally honest civil service. True: but there is another side of the picture which our Asian sees. He sees that while fortunes are being made in rubber, Asians are still being admitted to hospital suffering from starvation; while estate managers (Chinese as well as Europeans) are being paid very large bonuses, there is long-drawn-out haggling over the smallest wage increase for rubber workers; while Asian trades-union leaders are risking their lives fighting Communism, European planters, who are risking their lives in the same cause, drive union officials off their estates; while Asians and Eurasians may obtain scholarships to English schools and universities, they are cold-shouldered and not admitted to European clubs, the haunts of their former schoolfellows, when they return to what is, after all, their own country.

He had gone to Malaya to avoid thinking about Tatjana's departure, in almost exactly the same way as he had gone to

Hamburg in order to escape the turmoil of his broken marriage to Helga. Once more history repeated itself. In June 1951 he wrote home to announce that he was becoming engaged. Graham wrote to him: 'Dorothy and I sent you off a telegram of congratulations last night. We really are delighted at the news . . . Now that you are making a break with Tatjana perhaps I can applaud that too without offending you!! I like Elaine a great deal more.' He had met and apparently fallen in love with an American, Elaine Shaplen.

In September, as his time in Malaya was drawing to a close, he was asked by Ian Jacob if he would be the BBC's New York representative. Greene wrote back to say that he was not keen on such an idea. He felt that he had spent too much time out of the country and that it would do him good to stay in England for a change and therefore another overseas posting was not what he was looking for. But he was certain, he told Ian Jacob, that he did not want to return to Bush House; he hoped his job as head of Eastern European Services, which had been left open for him, would be filled by his deputy, George Gretton.

Although Hugh realised that the atmosphere at Bush House was excellent, it was full of people who were in grooves, going nowhere fast. He hated the thought of going back there. It was a backwater in career terms and while he remained surprisingly unclear on just what he did want to do, he was certain that whatever it was, it must be a further step up the ladder.

George Barnes had said that he would like to have Greene in the BBC's Television Service, an idea which did not please William Haley, the Director General, who vetoed it because Greene was, he said, 'a controversial character', and there were enough of those in television.

Greene returned to England at the end of September 1951 with no post, effectively redundant, and no clear view of what he wanted to do. Jacob suggested that it might be wise for him to seek a job with NATO or with one of the Intelligence departments which had been expressing an interest in him. Hugh approached the *Telegraph* first, to see if there were any possibilities there; he was interviewed by Malcolm Muggeridge, then Deputy Editor, as a possible Communist Affairs correspondent, but nothing came of it. He was then interviewed by SIS, but declined their suggestions, on the grounds that they were offering too little money. Operating on the principle of 'better the devil you know' he stayed, albeit in something of a limbo, with the BBC, dawdling away his time on the rather dreary Efficiency Committee.

At the age of forty-one, with a fascinating and highly successful series of jobs behind him, Greene arrived back in London with nothing, suspended, with no real idea of what would come next. Tatjana was back in Germany; Elaine was to be the next Mrs Greene, but Mr Greene, it seemed, was devoid of direction. The one hopeful sign was that Ian Jacob liked him, respected him, and saw that he was too good to be allowed to fester.

9

Ian Jacob had made up his mind that his protégé Hugh
Greene must be properly groomed for high executive position in the BBC. However, if he were to continue to rise in
status and power within the corporation, he had to have a
much clearer understanding of the non-journalistic side. He
had to know how the institution actually functioned.

First Greene was asked to sit on the less than exciting
Efficiency Committee which had been given the brief of
reviewing the general efficiency of the BBC. Then he was
appointed Assistant Controller, Overseas Service as a
breathing space after the exertions of the previous years.
Though this new post was promotion, in reality he found it
more frustrating than running the Eastern European Service, where he had had a good deal of autonomy. But it was
relatively relaxing and afforded opportunities to travel, as it
was concerned more with administering the service than
resolving difficult problems of policy.

The Controller of the Overseas Services, MacAlpine,
whom Greene describes as 'a nice old boy but no good at all',
retained all the authority, leaving very little for Hugh Greene
to exercise. It was not a situation he was used to, since in the
German Service, Hamburg and Malaya, he had been able to
exercise considerable personal power. He had, as he now
sees it, become 'a bit of a dictator', and feels that the period of
frustration under MacAlpine was beneficial, in that it ma-
tured and 'softened' him in his relations with colleagues. He
would also get what he described as 'curious little tasks' from
Ian Jacob, such as going to meet Senator Joe McCarthy's

two investigators, Cohn and Schine, who had brought their witch-hunt to London. Greene did not take such tasks very seriously. When he entered the American Embassy where he was to meet these two unsavoury characters, he was challenged rather aggressively by an American marine to produce his papers. He replied in his most lofty tones: 'In England, my man, one does not have papers', which nearly led to an assault.

Hugh Greene was then sent to New York by Ian Jacob to obtain all the information he could for a report on the possibilities and problems of selling BBC television films to the US. On his return nine days later, Jacob informed Greene that he was to head the investigation into an Overseas TV Service. Hugh was asked to spend about six weeks looking at the setting up and running of such an operation, on the technical possibilities, costs, and whether and when such an enterprise might be expected to become financially self-supporting. He was expressly instructed to focus on talks, documentary or semi-topical programmes, and to avoid 'as far as possible the drama and pure light entertainment fields which are likely to be covered by the commercial organisations making films for television'.

Greene felt that the BBC's only chance of breaking into the American market was if it concentrated on low production costs, novelty, quality, punch, pace and drive, with subjects which made use of England's heritage. He suggested three or four half-hour films dealing with various aspects of the Coronation to begin with, to be made by a new unit of about seventeen people attached to the BBC's television film department at a cost of about £28,000. His report was an impressive job of synthesis of a new, largely unexplored area. He did not attempt to trifle with the philosophical aspects of the implications of the BBC embarking on such a venture. He saw it as a logistical and tactical problem to which he had been asked to provide a solution. His peers were particularly impressed with his findings because they knew he had no previous television experience.

After perusing Greene's report, the Board of Management

argued that if the BBC did not enter the field 'then it must be envisaged, in view of the less developed state of television in other parts of the world, that the American way of life would be the only way of life to be seen on the television screens of other nations'. So they submitted plans to the government's recently announced Committee of Enquiry into the Overseas Information Services under the chairmanship of Lord Drogheda. A further draft was circulated by the Foreign Office to other departments on June 4th, 1952. The paper did not however go forward to the Cabinet and to all intents and purposes they were back where they had been that May.

Throughout these exchanges and developments, Hugh Greene appears as very much the practical man of commerce, the hard-nosed salesman, the man of action rather than ideals. He was always applying commercial psychology, looking for tactical advantages. For him the virtue of the proposed Coronation films was quite simply that they would sell and so would enhance the reputation of the Overseas Film Service, thus in turn making the film service more viable.

He was obviously very much taken with the whole idea of sales and in August 1952 proposed that the BBC establish a central transcription office which would coordinate the sale of BBC television programmes abroad, whether they originated under the Overseas Film Project or from the home television service. He was also actively pursuing new ideas and new projects, and in September 1952 negotiated with representatives from the National Association of Educational Broadcasters (NAEB) in the United States for the BBC to make a series of educational films for them. He was particularly eager to get a quick decision so that the 'extremely efficient and enthusiastic staff which had been assembled to make the Coronation films would not have to be disbanded'. The basic idea was to make thirteen programmes looking at the traces of famous figures, such as Darwin and Wordsworth, in English life today, using documentary and dramatic forms. Not everyone was keen on this idea. It is important to remember that Hugh Greene did not think of the programmes as televisual forms, he did not think conceptually about the relationships of content to form; rather he considered the relationship between such a series of programmes and the enhanced viability of the structure from which they emerged.

Cecil McGivern, the BBC's Controller of Television Programmes, saw it differently. He is an important character in this story, and one to whom we shall return, since he was at the heart of the stirrings of mood and mind within the BBC's television service which were to burst forth with such potency at the end of the decade when Hugh Greene became Director General. To McGivern, a film must have a relationship with a particular audience; it could not succeed if it were just a commercial proposition. To him, Greene's proposed educational NAEB films posed many problems, not least that they would be difficult to make human, warm and compelling and that they would be boring and look phoney if they were not exceptionally well made. It would be necessary, he argued in a note responding to Greene's proposals, '. . . to employ documentary directors and documentary writers of high quality, and not the *usual* film documentary type who can normally do little more than add commentary to visual shots as skilfully as possible, and with as much good lab work as can be afforded.' What was most important, he thought, was that '. . . this type of material is less successful on television than in the cinemas. Television demands more warmth, more intimacy, more humanity than the cinema.' Though he had not yet seen the four Coronation films, which were Hugh Greene's vanguard in the assault on the US market, he was expecting them to be 'rather dry and dead'.

The stirrings here are far more profound than those issues raised by the presence of the Overseas Television Service itself. Note for instance the trilogy of warmth, intimacy, humanity. But what cries out is that such observations were coming from McGivern, not from Greene, whose vision was very different.

By December 1952, the Television Transcription Unit

was formally in existence, and was responsible for the distribution overseas of all complete films and telefilms, whether originally made for the home television service or for overseas.

In January and February 1953 Greene visited Canada and the United States to sell more BBC programmes. In Ottawa he was less than impressed by the BBC agent, Mr Hal Williams, who dealt on their behalf with CBC and the commercial stations, but who, Greene felt, was insufficiently determined in pushing the BBC products. He recommended therefore that the BBC switch to two larger agencies. He was also highly critical of the BBC programmes which the CBC had already re-broadcast, such as a news bulletin and *Radio Newsreel*, largely on the grounds that they insufficiently allowed for local interest.

In the United States he discussed the whole future of radio and television. The American broadcasters argued that radio 'as a major commercial network operation is on the way out', and one broadcaster predicted that 'radio would have to be regarded as a medium for listening to in your car going to work in the morning and going home from work at night'. In Los Angeles Greene asked some CBS people what they intended to do about providing entertainment for housewives who might need some background noise, but would hardly want to be tied to their television sets. He was told, 'That is a point which our programme people are working on at the moment. They are trying to design television programmes which there is no need to look at.'

His mood on the trip was disturbed by what he took to be the frightening and debilitating effect of McCarthyism on free discussion in educational institutions. For him the atmosphere contained disturbing echoes of a time before:

One was often reminded of Germany in 1931–32. It was not that there was any ban on free discussion. But the individual was afraid to take part in it or express his views frankly if he disagreed with those of the present government, not so much because of what might happen to him but because of what might happen in a few years time when such views would be branded as subversive. I was seriously told in Boston, Chicago and San Francisco that the BBC had a very important part to play in keeping alive the tradition of free discussion in the American universities.

The whole trip served to convince him even more of the possibilities of the Overseas Film Project.

Throughout all these efforts to sell the goods of the BBC there was a twinkle in Greene's eye about tactics. The William Morris Agency was obviously keen and pleased to be involved in the enterprise, with illusions which Greene was quick to seize on:

> The William Morris Agency are under the impression that the BBC is all-powerful and that once it is established as a client of theirs it may be able through the British government to do something to protect other foreign enterprises in which they are interested. I did not disillusion them.

A variety of films were being prepared with such titles as 'Comet Over Africa', 'Arctic Mailboat', 'Planning for Discovery' and 'Kingdom in the North'. The key, though, was seen to lie with the films about the Coronation. For the coverage of the Coronation itself, recordings were taken in an operation named 'Pony Express' by helicopter from Alexandra Palace to Heathrow, loaded aboard a Canberra aircraft which crossed the Atlantic to Goose Bay in Labrador, from there by a CF 100 fighter of the RCAF on to Montreal for the CBC, and on by American aircraft to the American networks. By the afternoon, local time, of Coronation day it was estimated that two million Canadians and over eighty-five million people in the United States were watching the coverage of the Coronation. All functioned like a well-organised military operation, which was precisely what was intended, helping to sell BBC programmes projecting Britain.

143

The government, which had been dragging its feet on backing the overseas television venture, may well have been wise to do so, because, by 1954, Hugh Greene had to inform them that 'we are no longer confident of being able to make a financial success of our original plan'. There was a glut of television film material in the US which meant that the chance of recovering any initial expenditure remained slight. At home the emergence of the commercial television companies in 1955, which had not been allowed for in the original thinking, meant that the BBC would find it very difficult to obtain studio space or to engage the necessary technical staff. Greene therefore proposed that the BBC reduce the scale of its ambitions. Ian Jacob, however, still argued that even if there was no possibility of the films making money, '. . . it was clearly better to give the films away if by so doing we ensured their appearance on Canadian and other screens abroad, which was the main object of the exercise, than to drop the whole idea for fear that we might not break even or make a profit'. In other words, there had been a shift from the earlier emphasis on the commercial opportunities offered by the sale of films to a more pronounced, single-minded consideration of their political significance.

What one constantly comes across in the debates and tortuous conscience searching surrounding the question of the transcription service are two different impulses pushing the BBC in different directions. On the one hand its public service, non-commercial tradition led it to the conclusion that it should avoid commercial sponsorship like the plague; on the other, common sense told it that there was money to be made and that sponsorship might be the only practical way of getting BBC programmes shown. Public service broadcasting always faced the dilemma that by trying to increase the audience for programmes which represented the best traditions of the organisation, one might have to 'lighten' them and thus make the whole exercise pointless. In 1953 the Transcription Service Committee agreed that audiences would probably be increased if sponsorships were allowed:

. . . and that that in itself was a good thing, but felt that the material which would reach the increased audience was not of much importance. If the gain of a wider audience for light material was achieved at the cost of reducing the use of our more serious transcriptions, the gain might prove an empty one.'

For Hugh Greene the whole thing was a commercial problem to be solved, and the more Jesuitical discussions around the ethics of sponsorship left him rather cold. Clearly there was a difficulty for the BBC in establishing the proper relationships between popularity and quality. Even if, however, Greene had remained apart from such questions of cultural philosophy, he understood them extremely well. It would not be long before he had to solve the problem of the possible contradiction of mass appeal and a maintenance of public service standards, not just for the BBC's overseas sales, but for its very existence.

Although Hugh Greene had had long talks with Mc-Givern, had discussed the future of television and radio with Americans and Canadians, he still had not grasped many of its subtleties: he had not seen it yet for what it was to become. Others had. McGivern was not the only one to see that the form and style of the product were important, far more important indeed than their ideological impact or commercial viability. One or two people in the BBC, including Peter Dimmock, were keeping a very close, eager, enthusiastic eye on the development of television in the United States.

Peter Dimmock made some interesting comments on the television coverage of the inauguration of President Eisenhower in 1953, and the lessons which could be learned for the Coronation coverage. His observations of the inauguration were part of that process of teasing out the particular techniques of the television form which over the next few years were to lead to a major confrontation between different schools of thought within the BBC, and were laying the basis for the long-term victory of those who thought that television was something more than a visual extension of the élitist

145

fantasy of the Reithian radio. Dimmock wrote of his fascination at the birth of a new art: TV covering major occasions. Techniques which were to become commonplace still retained a wondrous quality. Dimmock wrote to McGivern:

> Presumably you have heard about or seen the teleprompter machine. Please cable me if not as I must try to arrange for a sample machine to be made available in England. It is quite unbelievable how much they increase timing, efficiency, particularly in talks, news and discussion programmes. They are also sometimes used on studio drama shows.

One can see here a slow coalition of forces: the emergent sense of the importance of television as a unique medium, something more than radio with pictures, and the rise of Hugh Greene as an ever more powerful figure within the BBC. In December 1954 he was promoted to Controller of the Overseas Service (COS), with Oliver Whitley taking over as Assistant Controller. As COS, Greene took responsibility for the language services as well as continuing supervision of the Television Transcription Service, whereas Whitley took charge of the English Services, publications, *London Calling*, and the coordination of audience research and publicity. Greene had not, however, been in the senior post very long before he was asked to go to Rhodesia.

He had been invited by Baron Llewellyn, the Governor General of Rhodesia and Nyasaland, to chair a Commission of Inquiry into the future organisation of broadcasting in Rhodesia. The other members of the Commission were Sydney Veats, a retired editor of a Bulawayo paper, George Thornton, a retired colonial official, with Davidson MacDuff Rhind as the secretary to the Commissioner. They were asked to recommend the kind of broadcasting organisation which should be developed in Rhodesia, and in particular the extent to which such an organisation should be independent of the government.

They began their work on April 22nd, 1955 and reported

146

on May 31st. They travelled throughout the Federation and received a wide range of evidence from different groups and individuals. Their recommendations were predictable, given the position and views of the Chairman. They proposed the creation of an independent, statutory Broadcasting Corporation, financed by a licence fee of £1 per listener, controlled by an independent body of governors comprised of non-partisan individuals 'chosen for their ability and standing in the community without regard to race'. They in turn would appoint as chief executive a Director General.

It was, in effect, an attempt to create for Rhodesia and Nyasaland something akin to a BBC. Equally predictable was the long-term failure of the service and its inability to establish anything like political independence. Once more, however, Greene had performed extremely well. At the end of the preparation for the report he wrote to Elaine of his feeling of 'immense but quite pleasurable weariness'. On the evening of May 31st, with the report finally completed, the extent of the effort, of travelling and seeing people, suddenly became apparent. He wrote to Elaine: 'Perhaps it will show the nervous strain this business has involved that when I went to my room I lay down on my bed and cried for quite a long time.'

He had begun to make his mark on the literary world. Graham and Hugh had discussed the possibility of collaborating on a *Spy's Bedside Book*. The talk had gone on between them for years but in October 1955 Graham suggested that they write to Rupert Hart-Davis who agreed to publish. When the book appeared, Herbert threatened both his brothers with a libel action over some reference to him. Hugh's reaction was uncompromising: 'He's a sad character. He'd have been a sounder character if he hadn't been so fundamentally nasty.'

Hugh was happy in the Overseas Service. It provided him with the kind of breathing space he was so eager to obtain. It allowed him to travel, and to achieve some personal and professional satisfaction in his work on the TV Transcription Service and in Rhodesia. He describes the Controller's job as 'one of the nicest jobs in the BBC', because of the travel it entailed.

Running the Overseas Service appealed to his belief in the importance of the Commonwealth, for which he had developed an almost emotional attachment during his spell in Malaya: 'I remember standing on the Beach of Passionate Love and thinking what an awfully small place Europe was and how important the Commonwealth was.'

He left the Overseas Service because once more Jacob intervened, offering him the post of Director of Administration. Initially Hugh had not wanted to accept. He went away for a weekend to Dorset, walked in the countryside, pondered the possibilities and realised that, yes, it was the one job in his life which really frightened him.

He had been interviewed by a sub-committee of the Board of Governors, chaired by the Vice Chairman, Sir Philip Morris, who had asked him if he had any hobbies, to which he replied that he grew roses and was very fond of pruning them. The point registered with the economy-conscious Board, who hoped that he might prune some of the Corporation's costs. In July 1956 Greene was finally appointed and arranged to start in October. Now he would have to be in charge of staff, administration, finance, copyright and industrial relations for the whole of the BBC. 'I used to wake up in the middle of the night thinking, Oh my God, how can I possibly do this job?'

With this appointment he moved one, rather large, step closer to the centre of power: a centre which had been at the heart of a massive cultural gear-change. It is necessary therefore to take a closer look at those changes and in particular to examine the course of the man who was instrumental in changing the Corporation and in grooming Hugh for the succession. Greene would never have ascended to heavenly power without Jacob's ladder.

10

The decade of the 1950s was the decade in which Hugh Greene grew to power and influence in the BBC. Slowly but surely he marked himself out as the most able and dominating influence within a BBC which was undergoing powerful and dramatic changes in its structure, size and sense of purpose. The whole stream of British culture was beginning to move in different directions as the dull, dank and boring days of post-war austerity were replaced by new moods, new needs and new expectations.

No one, however, rises from relative obscurity to control of the world's most prestigious broadcasting organisation without some kind of assistance somewhere along the line. For Hugh Greene the helping hand came, more than once, from the man who, perhaps more than any other, shaped the BBC in the 1950s, Ian Jacob.

Jacob was not an obviously dynamic man. He was quiet, retiring, no big drinker, no great speechmaker, he looked boring and in many ways he was boring. His clipped military manner amused more than it impressed in an age which saw itself increasingly egalitarian, indifferent to a straight-backed soldier with a crease in his trousers. He was also undoubtedly conservative in his political ideas, a fan of Churchill, a remnant of a glorious historical moment but which *was* nevertheless, history. Yet without him Greene would have been nowhere.

To understand Greene and his accomplishments, one has to see the whole canvas on which his career was being drawn, which means that one must see him in the context of the

Jacob years. To understand those, however, one must begin not in 1952 when Jacob became Director General, but with consideration of the thinking of Jacob's own predecessor as Director General, the deeply conservative William Haley, who ran the BBC from 1944 to 1952.

In December 1950, William Haley wrote that broadcasting 'should play its part in bringing about the reign of truth'. Truth was for him a 'living law' against which the broadcasters must measure and judge their work. Truth, its pursuit, its texture, its essence, is a noble quality to seek to attain, but it does really depend on whose truths we are talking about, and for Haley his truths were fashioned in his own image and likeness. When it came to deciding how this truth should be articulated with broadcasting there was, he felt, really only one possible arbiter. If society were constructed of men in majorities and men in minorities, both groups were defined by their essential intolerance, and therefore, broadcasting could 'only be left to those in charge of broadcasting'. What Haley did was to reproduce the cultural assumptions and values of his own life which he presumed to be superior to those of the rest of society, if only because of the virtues of his intellectual and cultural standing.

Haley's is the philosophy of the Christian middle class in Britain which had in its authoritarian, superior, rather precious and precocious Reithian version colonised the BBC. It was a philosophy and way of life which gained its strength from a self-conscious belief in its own superiority and worth. It was also a philosophy and way of life which did not wish to be swamped by the vulgar mass appeal of television. He felt that the nature of the BBC's news and current affairs output reflected the wisdom of British political and parliamentary development. He praised, with astonishing naïveté, what was an intellectual and journalistic Gobi desert, as if it were a garden laid out by Capability Brown.

The narrowness of Haley's social and cultural vision became a threat to the BBC's very existence, for his monstrous complacency infuriated many people who came to resent the BBC's monopoly. Declining audience figures and the advent of ITV encouraged these antimonopolists to query the whole future of public service broadcasting in Britain. The BBC might well be a service whose only interest was the common good, but who decided what that common good actually was?

By the beginning of the 1950s, the traditions which Haley represented were outmoded: it was time for the BBC to forge new links with audiences, to provide programmes which bore some semblance of contemporary relevance to the lives of those who watched and listened. The BBC may have had a mission to preserve excellence, it did not have a mission or a right to be anachronistic.

In June 1952, Haley at long last announced that he was leaving in order to become editor of *The Times*; Ian Jacob then took over to begin to encourage creative development in radio and television, to change the paternalistic image to a more acceptable and popular one, to argue for an alternative channel, to enable the BBC to lose its monopoly with panache and to accept the challenge of commercial television with aplomb. If the growth and excitement of the next decade had a patron saint, he was called St Jake.

Ian Jacob was now fifty-three, short and distinctively boyish in appearance with a slightly naïve air; he had an incisive mind, a retentive memory with a considerable gift for lucid explanation and argument. If the Board of Governors had any doubts about this bright, tough man, it was that he lacked imagination. The Corporation would not fall apart under him, but would it go anywhere?

Jacob's first effort as Director General was to reverse Haley's trend of starving the Corporation, particularly the TV service, of funds and to embark on a ten-year development plan involving the building of new transmitters, the development of the Lime Grove studios and a start on a new television centre. In particular he envisaged the completion of national TV coverage; the provision of an alternative BBC TV service, the development of a colour system, and the expansion of the output of TV programmes from five hours a day to seven. He pointed out that the Corporation needed more money, perhaps with licences of £1 and £3, plus a move to give the BBC the full benefit of the licence, since at that time it only received eighty-five per cent of the revenue. He also told a press conference 'that we have got to develop in TV a news service of the same quality and standard as we have in sound', a comment which was the first shot in a battle that was to rage across the rest of the decade and into the next.

The strengths and weaknesses of the BBC at this time were interrelated. It had a strong organisation, experience, established standards and good staff. Its long-term success had created, however, an inflexibility and complexity of operation, matched by an inhibiting, cloying arrogance which rested on the kudos gained in the war years. It was administered for the most part by nostalgic old men whose rheumy eyes saw only the glories of the past and were largely blind to the problems of the future, although there were those within the BBC who had felt uneasy with its orthodoxies for some time. The staff were also split between the old guard of radio in Broadcasting House, and the TV service at Lime Grove.

Many had already begun to realise, before the advent of commercial competition, that it was impossible for the BBC to fulfil its charter and provide a complete range of broadcasting for fifty million people, 350,000 of whom had TV sets in 1954, with only a single television channel. The public was not a solid block but consisted of listeners and viewers with wide varieties of interests, capabilities, tastes and perceptions. To cover the whole range of broadcasting it would be necessary in Jacob's words, to provide:

> . . . the opportunity for each individual to choose between the best of one kind of programme with which he is familiar, and the best of another kind of programme with which he may be less familiar. In this way a constant opportunity is offered for the widening of experience and the increasing of enjoyment. There should be no lack of entertainment and triviality alongside the more serious and informative, but it should be of a kind which avoids

indecency and does not exploit vulgarity, violence or tawdriness.

The content of the programmes would therefore have to change, but the BBC's charter and other constitutional instruments bound it to inform, educate, entertain, be impartial and to provide a balanced service to minority interests. What Jacob now had to consider was whether they could fulfil these charter obligations, even with two channels, if they lost their monopoly, which was expected to happen in January 1955, with the advent of commercial television, or did the arrival of a competitor and the loss of their monopoly release them from their time-honoured obligations? It was clear that the whole theology of public service broadcasting would have to be re-assessed and re-interpreted as the younger, more radical clerics within the BBC began to question the validity and justification of the neo-Reithian catechism in a changing world.

New choices would shift the audience away from the BBC. If the competition stole the BBC's mass audience by providing popular fare, the Corporation's claim to universality would be undermined. This would in turn undermine the BBC's philosophical foundations of being all things to all men, of being able to appeal to the intellectually and morally exalted along with the tatty mass, as well as its ability to raise revenues as the national instrument of broadcasting. The nightmare of the BBC was precisely that competition would shake it to its intellectual and financial foundations.

Jacob's proposal was that they confront this problem in three ways: that some of their programmes should specifically aim at attracting a mass audience; that the range of programmes attempting this should be greatly broadened as long as the programmes retained 'the highest possible standard of excellence in their own field'; and finally that a second BBC channel 'must be realised as quickly as possible so as to ease the burden thrown on the Service by having to satisfy the Corporation's obligations within so small an output'. Jacob was not going to side-step or ignore the new commercial competition; the BBC needed 'to retain the attention of the mass audience', and therefore must prevent any competition capturing it. It was therefore 'bound to compete'.

To meet the challenge, he asked the governors to develop the television service by introducing television news, expanding the hours to include an earlier start and more on Sunday, improving afternoon programmes and developing the facilities for experiment and training; protecting the BBC's sports coverage as well as its famous parlour games; guaranteeing the fees and work of the best scriptwriters, artists, commentators; improving the salaries of the best staff producers to avoid their being poached by rivals; introducing flexibility into recruitment to ensure that the BBC got 'the best people from the open market'.

The idea of 'the best' tolled out through all his words as Jacob defined this to mean that quality and popularity were not necessarily anathema to each other. Jacob convinced people that the BBC need not be ravished by competition if self-interest and integrity were delicately intertwined, kept in creative tension without snapping. He established a new balancing act for the BBC, demonstrating how to hold the mass of the audience for at least some of the time without departing from a conception of 'the best' whether that be a talk about humanism on radio or a light entertainment programme on TV.

His ideas did not fall on stony ground because many intelligent members of the staff were well aware that the Corporation had begun to drift: that it was in danger of becoming a cultural dinosaur. As Jacob bluntly told the governors, the BBC's efforts to elevate the public taste had given the public indigestion.

Jacob was determined to move right away from traditional commitments and ideas and to give the public genuine choice, abandoning the notion that the audience was there to be improved en bloc and bullied into being cultured. Jacob rejected the old Reithian élitism because he was optimistic that the public, if left to choose, would do so wisely. Moreover he changed official minds so that his views were accepted; and without this new awareness, many other developments which were about to flower in the BBC would not have been possible. The public, the ordinary man, had to be trusted to watch programmes which, while far from being elitist in tone or content, did not betray the sense of professional and moral integrity without which public service broadcasting is meaningless. This shift in the BBC's perception of and relationship with its audience was the core of Jacob's success, upon which Hugh Greene could later build.

But just as Jacob was putting his ideas into action and enthusing the Corporation with his new attitude, ITV began to tempt away key personnel. Haemorrhage was fast and furious: it had to be cauterised before it became fatal. Quickly Jacob asked about 300 men and women in the TV service and engineering division to sign new contracts for three years, in return for which they would receive a salary somewhat in advance of what they would probably have attained by the end of the period. It was a policy decision which reflected 'a choice of evils' devised, as a *Guardian* article described, 'to help staff resist the Siren's song'. It was also recognised by some of those who received the special grade as long overdue, since as a rule the BBC paid miserable wages.

Throughout these middle years of the decade Jacob was telling his staff that the way to defeat ITV, or at least prevent them from defeating the BBC, was to continue to develop competence and to maintain standards. But just what did this notion of 'standards' mean? It had been a difficult enough question to answer in those balmy days when standards had been defined as the broadcasting extension of the cultural values, attitudes and assumptions of high-minded and self-confident gentlemen in Broadcasting House. It became almost unanswerable in the context of the philosophical shift from élitism to a more broadly based humanistic conception of the relationship with the audience. The answer could only lie in practice. Jacob had provided the canvas but the programme-makers had to apply the oils.

The BBC struggled through the 1950s battered but unbowed, sustained by a remarkable level of faith in its own nature, and increasingly armed with its new sense of purpose. There would obviously be a time lag before programme output reflected this, but that something *would* happen was inevitable.

In the summer of 1958 a new offensive appeared on the horizon, a government-sponsored investigation into the future of broadcasting. Immediately Jacob drafted a paper of what he called 'basic propositions' about the BBC and circulated it to all those members of the Corporation who might usefully take part in 'the task of getting the truth of these propositions accepted, particularly by those who guide public opinion and by those who will ultimately have to decide the future development of broadcasting in this country'.

That notion of 'truth', almost brazen in its self-confidence, does explain something of the sheer psychological toughness which the BBC retained. The first of these truths according to Jacob was that the BBC was the founder of *the* concept of public service broadcasting, which was then copied by other societies. Its essence, he observed, is broadcasting by an independent organisation 'which is free from the necessity of bowing to outside pressures and can pursue the single aim of giving the best and most comprehensive programme service to the public'. The two great threats to that service, he argued, were political and commercial pressures and only by maintaining a strong and independent service could the BBC fend off pressures of that nature. At the heart of what he was saying was the idea of a strong and independent BBC.

Precisely because commercial broadcasting was an affront to this almost metaphysical concept of broadcasting, the BBC had to respond to ITV's existence. Another reason it had to respond was that if the BBC became only a service for minorities, some serious questions would be asked about the need for a licence fee. At the same time Jacob also perceived that any organisation would have to consider the likely effect on the morale of its own staff if they were permanently serving a minority audience.

Towards the end of the 1950s, Jacob was beginning to feel quite pleased with himself, as he thought that he had succeeded in maintaining the integrity of the Corporation in the face of competition. The average audience, however, for the BBC at this time was only thirty-five per cent. Curiously, he felt that not only was this sufficient to satisfy the claims of the BBC being a national broadcasting organisation but that they 'would be in grave danger . . . if we had secured a 50:50 average because in doing so we would have made our output indistinguishable from that of the ITV'. He had fallen into the very trap which in many ways he had done more than anyone to destroy, that there was a necessarily negative relationship between quality and a mass audience.

There may indeed have been tucked away in the recesses of his mind a residual, almost Haley-like doubt about TV and its impact on society. There was an incident in Bristol on May 11th, 1955 which led at least one paper, the *Daily Sketch*, to call for his resignation. During a speech he suddenly launched into an attack on TV, arguing that there was too much of it, that people were far too passive when watching it; that it destroyed silence, was half-baked, superficial, and other such ills and evils. On reflection, even he thought that maybe he had gone too far and he formally apologised to his staff over the outburst.

Jacob did not appreciate that, in the final analysis, thirty-five per cent of the audience just would not be good enough to continue to justify the BBC as a national instrument of broadcasting, financed by a licence. But in some ways it was not surprising, since it was to prove nightmarishly difficult for the BBC to hold the attention of fifty per cent of television viewers in the 1960s. Maintaining the best and most comprehensive service and obtaining mass appeal proved to need a tightrope-walker's finesse.

Hugh Greene did walk the tightrope of fifty-fifty when his time came, but he could not have obtained this equal share of

157

the audience if some of the programme developments which enabled him to gain the extra viewers had not already been taking place deep within the recesses of the BBC under Jacob.

It might be asked why, if the BBC saw its role as being a public service system, it was concerned about the problem of the audience? The BBC had always seen itself as 'the national instrument of broadcasting' and therefore even if it did not feel an *obligation* to a mass audience, it did feel the need to appeal to all 'the people' as a collection of minorities who on occasion also exhibited mass taste. Merely to try to serve minorities would, it was felt, over the course of time transform the BBC into a rump service, irrelevant to national life, and above all else the BBC wanted to retain its status as a national institution with all the powers and the responsibilities which went with that status. And why did it have to be a national institution? Because only by being so could it be a public service broadcasting organisation: in short, it had to protect its status in order to protect its identity, in order to protect the things it did, which were programmes of a certain stamp which only it could do—everything revolved around that fundamental self-confidence which bordered on arrogance.

The Haley years had seen the BBC dogged by an outmoded and irrelevant view of the way in which it should carry out its commitments. Ironically it was the emergence of commercial TV and the threat it was seen to pose which created a 'window' through which could flow other ideas, from other men. ITV allowed a new generation of the BBC to begin to alter totally the whole focus and orientation of the Corporation without in any way abandoning the essential commitment to the philosophy of the 'best and brightest'. Jacob's role was to map the broad strategy and then to allow the debates to rage about the programming tactics.

At the end of October 1956, Lindsay Wellington, Director of Sound Broadcasting, asked three of his senior staff—Marriott, Standing and Gillard—to establish a working party to look into the whole future policy of the sound broadcasting service and to assess how that policy might be implemented with fewer and fewer resources. They concluded that the BBC's traditional

> . . . sense of cultural mission is not an inevitable or indeed a natural characteristic of public service broadcasting. It does not derive from the Charter. In indicating that the BBC should disseminate information, education and entertainment, the Charter does not suggest that differing values should be attached to each element, nor that one element should be promoted above another. Nor even that each element should appear in each programme service. All it says is that the three elements should be provided.

At a stroke radio cast aside the whole philosophical structure on which the previous thirty years of the BBC's history had rested. Their reasoning was simple: the BBC was faced with new tasks, if only because it was no longer a monopoly and therefore had

> . . . to earn its existence and esteem alongside commercial broadcasting. It must therefore re-examine the necessities and responsibilities of its situation and adapt its policy and practice accordingly. The result will be recognisably of public service character (for otherwise it would have no title to public funds), but characteristics due to the monopoly alone would disappear. In our view, this would end the paternalism of the present policy. For the future we would root BBC programmes in two qualities—the excellence of the material offered in every category and the skill in adjusting its range for the listeners' free choice. We would substitute 'At your service' for 'This will do you good'.

In effect, listeners' preference was to be a key factor, and the audience was divided up into blocks of different people, with different tastes, different abilities, different interests. The BBC mission was over.

The Board of Management felt ill at ease with this report, the meat was too rich for their stomachs. They huffed and puffed over the radical conclusions even though they made manifest sense, but they sent it to the governors in the end, adding a few provisos. The new generation was now allowed to enlighten, inform and amuse. They did not have to be officious, to patronise. Good broadcasting, it was now accepted, did not have to be serious. Quality was possible without pomposity.

By 1958 matters had progressed even further. The Director of BBC Television, Gerald Beadle, actually wrote:

> We are here to reflect the people, their lives, their perplexities, their humour and their spiritual needs. The current situation of the nation is something we shall fully involve ourselves in. Television, especially non-commercial television, will be very much alive and up to date, not living in an escapist world of old-fashioned thought . . . Above all I hope that we in the BBC will never fall into the error of taking ourselves too seriously. We shall always take our work seriously, but not ourselves.

It ended in words which were precisely the kind that one would have by now expected Hugh Greene to utter: 'Surely it is one of our more important functions in TV to help the human race see the funny side of itself.'

In his speech Beadle had touched on the various elements of the new BBC: the relationship with its mass audience; the commitment to relevance; the examination of contemporary issues of the human condition; the particular area which was to be one of the rawest nerves in the coming years, drama; the commitment to wit and a slight irreverence. It was in essence to be populist, secular, amusing, controversial, and above all, *adult*.

Drama was to explode a few years later. Of much more immediate importance and relevance to these changes was the news and current affairs output. News is always a key part of any large broadcasting organisation, if only because, perhaps more than any other form of broadcasting, it touches the lives of the population by relaying the maxima and minima of their world. Debate about the purpose and direction of any broadcasting organisation therefore tends to be particularly intense and heated in the area of news, and this period of change in the BBC in the late 1950s was no exception.

In this instance, the debate was given particular edge by the fact that the work of the News Division was considered within the BBC as outmoded and reactionary.

The head of News Division was a grim and conservative-minded New Zealander, Tahu Ronald Pearce Hole, who took over in October 1948. One of those who worked closely with him recalls what he describes as Hole's 'extremely rigid concepts of what was news'; of how the only stories which would be used were 'important' stories, of how there was no place for human interest but plenty of place for 'establishment stuff'; of how 'scoops' were frowned upon with no story carried unless it had been checked with more than one other source, such as a news agency.

A popular joke at the time about the conservativeness of the BBC's news was Hole's idea of a lead story on a TV 'newsreel' which would begin with the opening line, 'The Queen Mother yesterday . . .'; it was the Queen Mother because she was fawned on, it was yesterday because they did not know how to process film any faster, and anyhow they had to *confirm* that the Queen Mother had actually done whatever it was she was actually said to be doing, even if they had film of her actually doing it.

Initially Jacob accepted Hole's contention that all news under one director was the most efficient and accurate system, but in January 1955 an incident occurred which gave Jacob cause for worry. At that time, Stephen Bonarjee was Topical Talks Organiser in radio, charged by Ian Jacob with putting on an election results programme, which would begin immediately the polls closed. Bonarjee asked a young political scientist from Cambridge, Noel Annan, to act as their political analyst, and Professor Maurice Kendall,

Professor of Statistics at the University of London, to show them how to use a computer to analyse their results. The problem was how to get the results upon which they could base their judgments.

News Division had a monopoly of results coming in and Hole took the view that Bonarjee's team could not possibly be allowed access to the actual incoming tape service of results: 'We'd asked for a feed from the teleprinters and that was quite impossible (according to Hole) because we might make some ghastly mistake and we weren't responsible journalists and fully trained.'

Ian Jacob was informed that the entire project was being held up because of lack of cooperation by the News Division. On the Friday before the Thursday of the election, he called together the relevant people involved. Hole sent his deputy, Arthur Barker. After hearing Bonarjee's side of the story, Jacob turned to Barker and said, 'Well, why shouldn't they have a supply of News results as they come in?' Barker had no answer. As he stood up to leave, Jacob turned to the assembled group, but with his eyes especially fixed on Hole's surrogate, and said: 'Before this day is out I want this absurd departmental rivalry to cease.' The emissaries who emerged from the News Division, which was then based in Egton House, about fifty yards from Broadcasting House, said that, though they would of course cooperate, it was too late to arrange a direct feed, but that they could lay on a series of runners who would bring copies of the incoming results across to Broadcasting House. It was clearly the beginning of the end of News Division as it was then constituted.

Jacob did not make instant changes but he realised that the whole position of news and current affairs would have to be completely re-organised and with this in mind, as we shall see, he formed a committee to look into the subject.

The most important development in the 1950s was not the emergence of commercial broadcasting, even though that was obviously significant. The key development was the shift from the dominance of radio to the dominance of TV, from the word to the image. This inevitably meant that attitudes to broadcasting were also changed; the old belief, rooted in a traditional view of culture and society, of the differences between high and low, were being re-shaped by the increasing popularity of television. At one level—represented in part by News Division—the battle was between those who believed in vision and those who believed in words. At another, more important level, it was a conflict over the whole relationship between the BBC and the rest of society. That is why News Division's devotion to the imagined beauty and significance of every time the Queen sneezed so appalled all those, like Greene, who brought other, more journalistic and populist values to their task of rendering the world unto itself. That was the real conflict which was raging throughout the 1950s—the traditionalists versus the modernists. The mood of the times meant the inevitable success of the latter, and also guaranteed the success of Hugh Greene. The longer term resolution would equally inevitably be rather different.

11

Hugh Greene's time as Director of Administration is not a period over which one need linger. It was important in his career: it was a way of learning how the BBC functioned as an organisation; but it did not alter any of his views on broadcasting. He was simply there to learn how to administer the machine, not to make programmes, because in Jacob's eye this was the only kind of apprenticeship suitable for the successor to the top job.

In this post Greene was answerable for a variety of departments and units ranging from the influential and important Secretariat to the BBC's Welfare Department; he was also responsible for laying down a policy in all administrative matters. If, however, the post taught him how the BBC functioned, it also taught him the need to improve forms of communication within the organisation. He introduced a fortnightly meeting of all his heads of department and discovered at the first one that the head of buying and the head of programme contracts had never met before. His work brought him into touch with questions of costs, disputes with the trade unions and negotiation of contracts for international agreements through the European Broadcasting Union. In particular he watched, with some dismay, the rise of the new unions of NATKE and the ACTT. The BBC would only recognise one staff union, the Association of Broadcasting Staff, but its decline had brought this practice into question. Greene viewed the ABS as a 'house' union and went out of his way to encourage other members of the BBC's management to establish 'clear contact with the manual staff now attracted by NATKE, with the idea of improving morale and sustaining loyalty to the BBC'. With pride he pointed to one other major triumph: 'For the first time in BBC history an angry correspondent who had been calmed by a letter from Programme Correspondence Section sent a bunch of flowers by way of apology.'

In March 1958 he went to Bad Böll in Germany to speak about the BBC's TV service, about which he was expansive and proud, the beginning of a role which was to become more and more familiar to him in the coming years. He began to flex his muscles to the assembled Germans in an area which was to become ever more important, the presence of commercial TV within the British broadcasting system. He had been asked to speak about the effect of commercial broadcasting on the BBC from a financial, organisational, and programme point of view. On the financial side, the problem was basically that the cost of TV had increased considerably and that was no good thing. When he came to programming, he launched into a robust attack on those who were running the British commercial TV system. (It is, by the way, worth pointing out here that Hugh Greene always refused to call the opposition Independent Television, on the grounds that they were not independent and that it was axiomatic in a psychological war, such as was emerging, that you never, ever named your opponents in a way in which they would wish to be named. He believed in calling a spade a spade; they were commercial and would be declared to be so.)

In particular he attacked their emphasis on mass entertainment at the expense of more serious and important programmes. Then he quoted his colleague Gerald Beadle, the BBC's Director of Television:

I would expect commercial television to go increasingly for well-tried formulae—things which either the BBC or the Americans have devised and built up. It would be very difficult for them to be other than old-fashioned. Commercial television will undoubtedly give pleasure to a very large number of viewers. It will be a faithful servant of industry, and I should not be surprised if it makes a lot of money for its shareholders.

But it would be a mistake to expect it to be a reflection of the advancing tastes and aspirations or of the perplexities of an educated democracy in the making. Such a policy would make for unpredictable audiences and it would almost certainly lower the average audience. In short, it would, I suspect, be bad business for commercial TV.

After observing how the BBC was beginning to claw back some of the audience which it had lost to ITV, Greene exposed one of the raw nerves at the heart of the whole commercial broadcasting system. Most of the people running that system, he said:

> . . . come from the newspaper world or from the entertainment industry. I don't think it would be unfair to say —though there are exceptions—that they are generally not primarily interested in TV as such or in the development of its possibilities. By entering the TV field they are insuring themselves in one way or another against the effects of TV on their major interests; declining newspaper sales and falling attendances at the cinema and theatre.

Within his speech was the kernel of his central thesis, that the BBC existed simply and solely to produce 'good' programmes, whereas ITV existed simply and solely to sell goods, and if good programmes could do that, then fine, but the making of such programmes was not an intrinsic part of its being. As Greene put it:

> Public service broadcasting and television on the other hand only exist to serve the public. This is not a matter for self-congratulation. It is again the nature of the animal. Public service TV can dare to be experimental and adventurous. It can resist pressure groups and ill-informed criticism. It is not tied to a rigid pattern.

It was, to say the least, a fighting speech, certainly not one to expect from the Director of Administration. But then Hugh Greene was back in Germany where he had himself laboured to establish the virtuous structure of the living, creative, responsible, but never safe or dull, public service broadcasting station. Public broadcasting was an idea which was to him simple and clear; there were no moral ambiguities, no problems of definition, no lack of understanding about its qualities when compared to commercial TV. The one was intrinsically good; the other intrinsically bad, and his duty was to praise the one and to damn the other.

As Greene busied himself with the minutiae of the BBC's administration, as well as making the occasional speech, the idea of centralising all control of news and current affairs was forming itself in Jacob's mind.

Jacob therefore set up a committee consisting of McGivern, Hole and Gillard, to be chaired by John Green, which would look into the whole area of current affairs, its editorial control, efficiency and greater liaison between Sound and TV. Jacob was worried that the Corporation was floundering; because of the ways in which it conducted its operations, it was its own worst enemy. He was in a mood for some radical changes, and he hoped for a solution from the members of the committee, two of whom embodied the very problem he was trying to overcome.

The committee received a wide range of papers and interviewed fifty-five members of staff, of whom one was Hugh Greene. He told them that he thought the existing separation between the News Division and the output departments, and in particular television, led to a less than effective service because if one had integrated control beneath an output head, then it was easier to have flexibility and unity within the programme output. Hole's objections would be that if you restructured in this way, then it would threaten the standards of the news. Greene countered by arguing that the solution lay not in any particular structure, 'that the sheet anchor was the professionalism of the staff'.

McGivern, of course, smiled and agreed with him. Greene

expanded further on professionalism and said that BBC training was as important as a journalistic training:

> He had for a number of years been a foreign correspondent. After some years in the BBC he did not dare again to become a journalist, because the BBC had taught him to realise the importance of absolute accuracy, and accuracy was not always required or permitted in newspapers, as in *The Times* in 1939. [Hugh] agreed that News Division was a bit exclusive, and he queried whether the news demands should *always* take priority over other demands, eg. those from programmes.

Having said that, he thought that the TV service should be able to have its own news section: he was asked if that meant he was in favour of Sound having its own section. He said that logically he should be, but was dubious because of the much greater volume of news and of the difficulty of coordinating news and current affairs over the three radio services. He said that he would be in favour of a Controller of Current Affairs straddling Sound and Television, with a Head of News and a Head of Talks under him on either side. Something like this was, in fact, one of the key recommendations of the committee.

In February 1958 the lengthy current affairs report emerged. Tahu Hole disagreed to such an extent that he wrote, as an appendix, an account of his reservations, which is in fact longer than the substantive report. From the point of Hugh Greene's emerging career, the key paragraph was 106, in which they argued that there 'should be a chief assistant to the Director General, with a personal rank of director, who would concern himself exclusively with news and current affairs'. He would be known as the DNCA.

For John Green, the Chairman, the whole exercise had been frustrating because of the open hostility between Hole and McGivern:

> We sat and sat and went round and round every aspect.

We couldn't find any agreement at all on any sort of basis and in the end I don't think Cecil McGivern wrote anything at all, but Frank Gillard and I wrote a report and Tahu wrote a minority report, a book, he was so angry, rather than agree.

John Green believed, until they sat together on the committee, that Hole was the only natural rival to Hugh Greene to succeed Jacob. During those long committee sessions, however, he began to change his mind and conclude that Greene should be the next Director General. John Green felt disappointed that Hole acted as he did.

If only he had not been so intransigent and had listened to me and come halfway to meet me at that time in his attitudes to news and current affairs. If only he'd brought the News Division nearer to Talks Division. You see, he fought me every inch of the way. On the committee we spent a week in Brighton at the Metropole, and we walked up and down the beach for days and days. Now, I'm a very patient man, and I had an approach to Tahu which certainly nobody else in the corporation had by then. Had Tahu compromised one inch, had he yielded the slightest piece to me I could have resolved that position and this I'm certain would have rehabilitated Tahu when the contest came.

His view of Hugh Greene is equally perceptive, equally frank. John Green saw his own world dissolving before his eyes, and it pained him. Hugh Greene saw the same world crumbling and gloried in it, welcomed it, nurtured it:

He let the doors of the BBC open, he let things go through. He's totally insensitive. If he's sensitive it's because it suits his own interests. I think he's got the stuff of which Cromwells are made, his absence of sensitivity doesn't worry him.

It's a fact that he hasn't got it, so he doesn't know what it is, but he does know what he wants in a specific short-term sense, and I regard him as a very dangerous man for that reason. Like all radicals he realised that when the waters were dammed up, kick the bloody thing down, they'll find their own level and they do. That's Hugh Greene. I'm afraid I can't see the world that way. I'm a classicist, I want always to control the waters. I want to create canals—which I think is an equal weakness, but then we are all made of our own weaknesses.

Jacob approached John Green for a recommendation as to who should be the new Director, News and Current Affairs. The obvious candidate was Harman Grisewood, but he had been less than successful as Director of the Spoken Word and Jacob's chief assistant. John Green, therefore, recommended Hugh Greene.

Jacob's reply was, 'How can he be, he's DA?' And I said, 'Well, surely there are masses of people who could be DA, but you've got to have the right person to be DNCA. First of all, you've got to have journalistic knowledge and also what I'd call a political sense, and the DA post doesn't require any of those qualities at all.'

Hugh Greene remembered: 'Jacob again asked me to come and talk to him one evening. One never knew what was going to happen when Jacob asked one to go and talk to him and this time he said to me, "I want you to be Director of News and Current Affairs."' Whereupon Hugh informed the Director General that he had become rather fond of his administrative duties, and that in particular he did not feel that he had actually accomplished the task of convincing administrators that they were there to serve the creative staff and not vice versa. He added that he had made a good start and 'was quite satisfied with myself for once in my life and I wanted to go on with it'.

It had been a relatively quiet time, with little travel other than between the different parts of the BBC in London, and the provinces, which fascinated Hugh by opening up to him a world of which he had known little. One would not have expected him to have enjoyed being Director of Administration, but he did. He was coming to appreciate a sense of orderliness as he grew older; he had slowly learned to savour the logic of the bureaucratic life. This new-found pleasure in organisation, in structure, in getting people to understand their jobs and in encouraging them to do well, is a facet of Hugh Greene's make-up which becomes more apparent at this time.

He asked what Jacob intended to do about Hole. The Director General shocked him by announcing that he had decided to make Hole joint Director of Administration with John Arkell, who would personally take over responsibility for all staff matters.

Greene's appointment to be the new Director of News and Current Affairs, though warmly welcomed, evoked the gloomy comment from William Haley at *The Times*: 'Bush House takes over the BBC.'

On August 18th, 1958, Greene took over the control of all the BBC's news and current affairs output, from topical magazine type programmes to talks and documentaries in both Sound and TV. His job was to impose a sense of order on this output: to landscape the Amazon jungle. He was coming home to the world of journalism which was the only true vocation he had ever had: the streets of Berlin, the midnight deadlines, to be in the centre of an event, which is history in the making, had become part and parcel of his personality. His first important decision was to make Donald Edwards from Bush House the editor of all news. His second, in December, was to commission a report on the state of television news from three young men who worked in the Television service all of whom had exceptional reputations as producers—Ian Atkins, Michael Peacock and Donald Baverstock—the latter two being widely regarded as the rising stars.

Even before they began their investigation, the outcome was predictable since Peacock and Baverstock were about as sympathetic to the ways in which the news service had developed as a South American killer bee to a passing human. Baverstock felt that TV news from the BBC was 'laughably bad', embodying the 'wartime, fake reputation of the BBC'. The significance of the report was to lie precisely in its full-frontal assault on the extant idea of the BBC and in its assertion of the importance of a distinctive TV service to the future of the BBC. It also displayed the contempt which the 'young revolutionaries' of Lime Grove, as the press liked to call them, had for the grey men of News Division. Baverstock in particular felt that the News Division people at this time were really only very ordinary people who had never been pushed, tested or stretched to do other than play safe. He remembered vividly as a young producer meeting Douglas Willis a BBC reporter. Willis had been a lugubrious talker who delighted in quoting somebody in a pub who had said to him, 'Oh, I've heard of you; I always switch you off.' Baverstock had even been a little in awe of Willis and once asked him what he had done before he joined the BBC. Willis had regaled him with a list of newspaper jobs. The young Baverstock had asked, 'Was it promotion each time, more money, variety?' Willis had replied, 'No. No bloody good, that's my trouble.' It had taught Baverstock a lesson about the levels of incompetence and lack of professionalism which lurked in the murkier corners of the Corporation.

Between the end of December 1958 and January 10th, 1959 the group undertook intensive viewing of news programmes, examined scripts and transcripts, examined the scene in the United States and looked at the ITV output. They then visited Alexandra Palace, home of the TV Service, and Egton House, the home of News Division. They constantly emphasised their central point:

> After much thought and analysis, we were forced to conclude that the present system of the integration of Sound and TV News lies at the heart of the trouble. Every time we applied ourselves to analysing a single fault, we were led back to the faults in the present system. As long as

172

people who have little or no first-hand experience of working in TV news continue to control vital aspects of the TV news operation, and as long as editorial decisions have to be arrived at in committee with Sound, then most of the present faults will continue.

In the final words, TV had to have the ability to 'be free to develop a style and methods which are contemporary'. Their conclusions were extensive and devastatingly critical.

This report points to a whole new range of values within programming which were to characterise the 1960s—a more humanistic, egalitarian ethic, looking at, rather than down to the audience, drawing its perspectives from the culture of the common man rather than the expensive and cultivated narrowness of the Broadcasting House mandarin, consciously adopting an anti-establishment stance, animated by a dissatisfaction and restlessness with the old ways. They were redesigning not just the news, but the whole of the Corporation. All in all, the report was a damning indictment of old stuffy ideas which had, in the age of competition, affluence and egalitarianism, about as much relevance as a horse-drawn carriage on a three-lane motorway.

Looking back, Michael Peacock recalled how the constant success of ITV, which was by 1958 having a devastating effect on the BBC's share of the audience, abused his and his colleagues' sense of professional competence: 'What we were confronted with was the constant repetition of professional failure.' Baverstock and Peacock personified the challenge from the middle: the commission to write the news report forced them to articulate their sentiments into a manifesto for radical change. They had received no specific brief from either Cecil McGivern or Hugh Greene, though they knew that the two were basically sympathetic to their ideas; neither, however, had they sought any such instructions.

Greene expressed his warmest thanks for what he described as a 'penetrating and stimulating report', and quickly tackled the criticisms. The intellectual battle had been won. To those working in the News Division, the presence of Greene and Donald Edwards created a new mood, a new atmosphere, as the rigidities of the Hole régime withered beneath the weight of the personalities and the scathing comments of the News Report. As Hugh Greene put it at the time, the trend was

> . . . away from *The Times* to, say, the *Daily Telegraph* or *The Guardian*, with an occasional glance at the more popular dailies. In a family, the father, the mother, son and daughter may each have a favourite paper. The TV news, a family affair, has to please them all.

The most rapid *volte face* occurred in the field of electoral broadcasting. Here the BBC seemed to be following the initiative established by Granada at the Rochdale by-election of 1958, but there is no indication in the Minutes that they were aware of the precedent set by their rivals, although they could not possibly not have noticed and admired.

The BBC's behaviour at election time before 1959 was, to the modern eye, which assumes the prominence of TV in an election in the same way that it assumes sex with marriage, truly amazing. From the moment that Parliament was dissolved to polling day the BBC was, in its own words:

> . . . careful to exclude from its own programmes anything which could fairly be considered likely to influence the elector in recording his vote. This applies to every type of programme from news bulletins to variety programmes. The policy arises directly from the BBC's general obligation to be impartial . . . It has to be recognised that not merely the political talk but the phrasing of a news item or even the political joke of a variety comedian, heard in millions of homes, may be held to have swayed in some way the judgment of the electors. In such matters it is clearly the BBC's duty not merely to be impartial, but also to be seen to be impartial.

At the beginning of 1958 Greene and Grisewood prepared a report for their colleagues on the Board of Management in which they recommended that the General Election campaign should be reported in Sound and TV News 'on the basis of news values' and that 'in spite of the serious misgivings expressed by the parties, reporting on this basis should continue right up to the declaration of results'. The hand of Hugh Greene the journalist is clear in this, particularly in the argument that 'news value' take precedence over 'balance' because 'it is our business as professional journalists to think in these terms every day of the year'. The development was not yet total, since they proposed that no reference be made in programmes to the election itself. It was rather like having a sports programme which did not bother to mention sport. However, the Greene-Grisewood paper provided the basis, with no changes, for Jacob's submission to the board of governors, who proceeded to endorse the plan. Television politics would never be the same again.

As DNCA, Hugh Greene split the organisation of TV and Sound news, revamped election reporting, became principal liaison with No. 10 and the Foreign Office, made decisions about individual programmes and suggested new ideas. He also made it clear that he expected anything which might come within the ambit of his office to be referred to him. One department head informed his producers, 'It is better to refer to DNCA too often than too infrequently. When in doubt, *refer.*'

But the most far-reaching initiative that Greene instigated as he got into his stride as DNCA, was to start a series of weekly meetings for those responsible for news and current affairs: through these meetings he began to shape the whole future direction of the Corporation. He held his first on August 29th, 1958. These soon became the debating chamber of the BBC's journalistic output.

Greene ruled through and influenced by example, making specific suggestions or decisions which had a wide effect on output. For instance he let it be known that a Royal story need not always be given precedence, thus removing much obsequiousness from the whole style of news presentation.

Slowly, imperceptibly, he was beginning to articulate a mood of revolt within the BBC, a call for change, a burning of the old image and the creation of something new. So around such decisions as the treatment of Royalty, legend began to crystalise.

It was widely recognised that this had been precisely Jacob's intention in choosing Greene, if only because he had rejected the only other possible candidate, Harman Grisewood. Kenneth Lamb, a Talks producer at the time, recalls an incident in 1958 when he was working with *Panorama*. On the way back from the United States he stopped off in Bermuda and produced a film which he himself describes as 'a naughty piece' that took a mildly disrespectful look at the three main families on the island. After the broadcast the BBC received a more than normal postbag of complaints and Jacob dispatched Greene to Lime Grove to investigate. When Hugh arrived, the mood was nervous and formal: 'How do you do, DNCA?' 'Fine, thank you, Mr Lamb', and they proceeded into the viewing theatre. The lights went out, and they awaited his reaction. As the lights went up at the end, Greene was beaming. He turned to Lamb and said, 'What's the fuss about?' One more part of the legend was formed as the members of *Panorama* told the tale in bar and corridor and ruefully pondered what might have been said had Harman Grisewood been in the chair. Greene had just thought the Bermudan programme amusing and harmless, if a little cheeky; certainly not something to be stamped on.

By adopting such attitudes, he was winning converts to his side. Lamb, who told this tale, had been one of those within the Talks Department who had had serious initial doubts about the wisdom of the new DNCA post, arguing that it placed TV producers in a difficult position which would in the long run only blunt their ability to work. Yet here was Greene, supporting them in their little wickednesses. 'Why,' they began to say to themselves, 'this chap Greene might even be one of us.'

Greene's sympathies might lie with the programme-makers but they did not own him, as the following incident illustrates. He announced that he wanted much closer liaison between the Foreign Office and Lime Grove where the Talks Department was housed. Precisely why he wanted this close liaison remains unclear, but the very idea worried the people in Lime Grove, on the grounds that it would necessarily entail unfortunate compromises in the way they covered the activities of the Foreign Office.

Kenneth Lamb was asked to put the objections to Hugh Greene after the news and current affairs meeting. Greene listened impassively and at the end merely said, 'But I thought I'd made my decision clear on this.' Lamb manfully tried to re-state the gist of their fears about the problems which might flow from this relationship. Greene stared even harder. The others attending the meeting shuffled in their seats as the temperature dropped, and Greene repeated bluntly, coldly, almost hostilely, 'But I've made my decision.' Lamb returned to Lime Grove with ideas of resignation buzzing in his head. His immediate superior Leonard Miall calmed him down, saying that he himself would not mind going to Foreign Office briefings, and that anyhow the whole idea would die a natural death, which in fact it did. What stayed firmly in Lamb's memory, however, was Hugh Greene's refusal to discuss the issue once he had made up his mind, and the look on his face, like moonlight glinting on a gravestone, which was also becoming part of the legend. His personal authority was being rapidly established, along with a firmness that bordered on ruthlessness.

Another member of TV Talks said:

Hugh was tough enough to cope so that when things went wrong, one was aware of a purposeful, powerful, decisive fellow. He always exuded a sense of power as well as authority. He would sit in his chair, and one had this sense of his personal as well as his corporate authority.

When Charles Curran, the BBC's representative in Canada, heard about a film of Castro's capture of Havana, he offered it to the BBC's TV Talks Department at Lime Grove, only to receive a very dismissive reply. Greene, also in Ottawa at that time, was amazed at this reaction. He told Curran to cable News Division as soon as the film was available and in the meantime ensured that the reaction was more positive. Part of his keen interest in the film may have been due to Graham's interest in Cuba and close links with the Castro forces. In October 1958 they had been discussing the possibilities. Graham wrote to him:

> I discussed the BBC plan for a television picture in Havana and the whole scheme received the support of the mysterious Pedro who is the chief contact of Castro in Havana! Your scheme is thought to be the best, i.e. that you should ask for official permission to interview Battista and the new President after the elections (who will probably be Battista's nominee) and that then one of them should quietly take a plane to Santiago. The trouble is that now the luggage of all passengers to Santiago is searched on arrival, so that you would have to entrust the cameras to a Castro contact and they would be transported underground by the rebels and your man would find them in the mountains on arrival.

Such actions by Hugh Greene were doing wonders for his reputation as tales spread in bars and meetings. The BBC was being stirred, through word of mouth, by story and rumour, into a powerful new force committed to sharper journalism, a more striking and aggressive stance in the coverage of world affairs. The BBC was changing amid the clink of ice and casual conversation, as Greene was demonstrating a forceful authority felt and perceived, if not properly understood, by those around him. He did not need to articulate, to play the orator or the philosopher-king of broadcasting; the force of his influence flowed from him as naturally as water from a spring. When Greene was chairing a meeting, he would listen to the discussion without participating, then at the end he would just say, 'Right, we do this.' He sought information and ideas, but would then make a decision which was his and his alone. He did not seek consensus: his authoritarianism was accepted, as one of his former colleagues observed, 'because of the enormous respect people in the BBC had for his pugnacity and his effective impudence'.

As DNCA, Greene was beginning to create the reputation of a man whose power emanated from his own character, rather than the job he held. He was not just considered a good exponent of journalism within broadcasting, and an able administrator, but was seen as one of the key definers to the outside world of the nature and role of public service broadcasting. In this he was helped by his past successes which gained him access to citadels of power normally reserved for politicians. In a sense, Greene was a politician, a roving advocate of the BBC, talking to heads of state as he wandered the globe organising the Corporation's network of special correspondents.

His years in the German service enabled him to meet Konrad Adenauer, the German Chancellor, in January 1959, in a conversation which moved from broadcasting to off-the-record, political information of importance. On the same trip Greene also held confidential political meetings with Dr Krone, the parliamentary leader of the CDU, with Mende, the leader of the Free Democratic Party, with Erler, the defence expert of the SDP, with Strauss, the Federal Minister of Defence, and with David Bruce, the American Ambassador. He also saw Mikhailov, the First Secretary, and Beburov, the Press Attaché, at the Russian Embassy in East Berlin. In Vienna he had talks with Figl, the Austrian Foreign Minister, (who when he left sent a dozen bottles of Austrian wine to the airport as a farewell present), Chancellor Raab, and various other senior Austrian officials. All these meetings attest to Greene's own personal reputation and show that with him as DNCA, the BBC was treated as if it were a sovereign power which had to be kept informed on official thinking.

By 1959 Jacob felt tired, he felt the need to do something different before he was too old to do anything other than regret that he had done nothing else. On July 11th, 1959, a letter arrived at Hugh Greene's home. Handwritten, in a rather shaky style, it was from the Chairman of the BBC, Sir Arthur fforde, confirming Greene's lunchtime appointment for the following Sunday. The letter gave him the road directions and even contained a rather elaborately scrawled map with the compass points indicated, and the added note, 'Our house is a new villa, the nearest one of three such, all ugly'. Hugh Greene knew that he had been in the running for the post of Director General, even though there had been no formal application procedure and certainly nothing so unseemly as an interview, but he now assumed that fforde, who was a kind and considerate man, was going to tell him that the post was not being offered and was merely trying to make the conditions of that as pleasant as possible.

When Hugh arrived for lunch with his wife, Elaine, fforde immediately told him that the board of governors of the BBC had decided that they would like to appoint him to be the next Director General, provided he was not a Roman Catholic. One or two of the governors, including the national governor for Northern Ireland, had insisted that it was impossible to have a Catholic as a Director General. 'Are you one?' fforde now enquired. Greene was able to assure fforde that he was not, that he would describe himself as 'a respectful agnostic'. fforde replied, 'Well, that's all right. Have a drink, you will be the DG.' Perhaps the most remarkable feature of that story, apart from its undiluted bigotry, was that the BBC did not know whether Hugh Greene was a Catholic or not. Evidently there was some confusion in the governors' minds between Hugh and Graham, who was a convert to Catholicism.

The throne was Hugh's, and he would now be able to define his view of broadcasting and to move the BBC in its direction. He would also clarify the BBC's position vis-à-vis the rest of those institutions which collectively had earned the epithet 'the establishment'. It was a description much in vogue at the time, and had been given a certain sharpness by an article by Henry Fairley in *Encounter*. This suggested that the BBC was a key part of that grouping, and that it was, therefore, committed to its values and its welfare. Greene's task from within the BBC was to engage in a debate with the history of his own organisation. He wished to transform the BBC into what he described as 'the licensed gadfly' of the body politic, shedding once and for all its old pompous establishment aura.

When he spoke in Frankfurt as Director General designate, he quoted Ed Murrow. Radio and television should in the future concern themselves:

> . . . rather more with holding a mirror behind what is going on in contemporary society and I don't care whether what is reflected in the mirror is bigotry, injustice, and intolerance or accomplishment and inspiring achievement. I only want the mirror to be honest, without any curves and held with as steady a hand as may be.

The rest of Greene's speech was equally clear and certain. The BBC was going to change; it was going to be radical; it was going to explore issues which had remained hidden and explore them in ways which had previously only been the practice of the bolder elements within print journalism. It was going to frighten the pants off the establishment, and never again would any journalist be able to say that Auntie BBC was the voice of the status quo, of the great and the good. He said it in tones that were neither harsh nor bitter nor 'radical' sounding. Rather his voice said, 'We are going to do these things together, and my, oh, my, are we going to have fun doing them', and who could argue with that attiude of mind? The revolution was going to be fun.

Someone of Hugh Greene's intellectual calibre would always have been reasonably successful, reasonably comfortable, but without Ian Jacob, Greene would have remained unknown, or only vaguely remembered for his wartime energy, and his Hamburg years. Without the launching pad of the old general he would never have become a major force within the culture. Although it had been ultimately a question for the governors to resolve, Jacob had left them in no doubt that he thought they should appoint Hugh Greene. He knew that

> . . . there were one or two people who thought they ought to have been candidates. I think John Green was one. Harman may have thought he should have been, but nobody but a lunatic would have put him there. I'm terribly fond of him, but he hasn't got the nervous fibre for the top job. It's a very tough business.

Jacob's respect for Hugh Greene, if considerable, stopped well this side of idolatry. He worried that maybe Greene was a bit too tough, a bit too impervious to criticism, a bit too independent and a little too ready to say to hell with pressure. It also worried him that Hugh Greene had no settled convictions:

> Now that may seem a funny thing to say, but I think journalists have tended more and more to become people for whom everything is just fun. No values at all, and this was what I was frightened of. His marital career didn't inspire one with great confidence. In a way this is what carried him over the edge, that he wanted to open up in a way which he regarded as amusing and didn't sufficiently realise that amusement isn't everything and there is a traditional development in these matters which you have to pay more regard to.

To say a man believes in nothing is a major reservation of considerable magnitude. Jacob was not alone in his doubts. Another close colleague observed, more in sadness than in criticism, 'I'm not really sure that Hugh actually believes in anything.'

A questionmark had now entered the minds of those around Hugh Greene who were to watch and work with him as the BBC became a gale within the land. Was this powerful figure soulless? Did he not care what happened, and only care that it amused him? That question was to perch like Jiminy Cricket on the shoulder of the sixties.

12

Hugh had let it be known inside the BBC that he would want to change things. Those who knew him from outside also assumed that the status quo in the BBC was in for a rough ride. His reputation was well established among those chroniclers of the doings of broadcasting who knew him as one of their own. In the *Sunday Pictorial* Malcolm Muggeridge paid glowing tribute to 'our man in the BBC'. Greene, he declared, was by any standards a 'capital choice. He is a man of unusual intelligence and perception . . . tall, whimsical, adventurous, and kindly. His attitude towards the established order is well this side of idolatry.' He called on Greene to rid the BBC of 'the many mandarins who have lingered on from the monopolistic sound broadcasting time', and who he felt were 'repressive, irritating, and muffling in their effect on the BBC'. With a certain bravado and percipience Muggeridge advised Hugh Greene not to 'bother himself about the abounding protests which inevitably would fall round his head'. Muggeridge was calling for indifference to any of those commercial and political pressures which could only harm the work that Greene had to do: 'What a chance for Greene! How devoutly I hope that he makes a great success of it.' *The Star* waxed lyrical about the new Director General who 'does suggest the best kind of uncle—the kind who isn't stuffy, prefers chuckles to a frown; wants his nephews and nieces to treat serious things seriously, but doesn't wish to spoil anybody's fun'. As he took over the Director General's office on the third floor of Broadcasting House, he met with a chorus of delight and approval.

It was widely assumed that his main commitment would

be to protecting news and information from political and commercial pressures on the grounds that these had the effect of 'insulating the audience from realities', in Edward Murrow's phrase—Murrow often crops up in Greene's thinking—producing 'a public incapable of thinking for itself'. One newspaper commented that though such items may have been far from novel, they remained fundamental 'and it is heartening to hear them in the mouth of the Director General elect. Let us hope to see them courageously put into effect by the Director General.' Peter Black in the *Daily Mirror* called it a 'Greene light at the BBC', and the *Manchester Guardian*, in a piece entitled 'High, Wide and Handsome', pointed out how some of Greene's strongest supporters in the BBC were relatively low production staff; he was likely to make the BBC altogether more professional 'and less stuffy'.

If the public expectation was already well formed by the time he took up office, so was his public image. A profile in *The Observer* referred to him as 'a lonely tower of a man', 'an enigma', 'a careerist with private dreams', 'a cold fish'. It was something of a Cromwellian image which lay partly in truth, and partly in a desire for it to be the truth, since it gave him the distance and authority to undertake the task of shaking up an institution which was still a key part of the establishment. Neither was he beyond cultivating a certain image as when he told one newspaper about his journalistic career: 'I wanted to know the truth about the Nazis and to become a reporter seemed to be the best way to do it.' That was nonsense. He drifted almost aimlessly into journalism and *then* developed a career exposing the Nazis. Tactically though, the aimless drifter was less appropriate an image than the tough seeker after truth. Emphasis was, therefore, laid on his journalistic background. His toughness and willingness to fight were quoted with relish in newspapers. A story in the *Express* said:

A tough fight-all-the-way policy against commercial broadcasting is warming up for the men who run BBC radio and TV—direct from Mr Hugh Carleton Greene. He stated emphatically last night: 'I find the idea completely comic that the BBC should sit back and let commercial TV trample all over it. The trouble is that Sir Robert Fraser, the ITA Director General, is beginning to believe his own propaganda about the quality of his programmes and this is dangerous.'

Everywhere it was recognised that Greene embodied a fracture between the *ancien régime* and the new republic, between the old boring commitment to all that was right and proper and a new commitment to something which may not have been right and proper but which got the juices flowing, which quickened the tempo, which, in the symbolism of the street, gave two fingers to the status quo. The fracture was held to be occurring on January 1st, 1960. It had, of course, been building up long before this with those various developments in news and current affairs and in particular the emergence of an unusually bright and energetic generation of Talks producers. Hugh Greene, therefore, was inheriting a development which was well under way.

As he took over on January 1st, 1960, his immediate problem was that in terms of the size of its audience, the BBC had been doing disastrously. At the end of the 1950s its share was down to only twenty-seven per cent. One needs, however, to be careful here in assessing the way in which Greene tackled this disastrous position. The tide had already begun to turn *before* he took up his office; for example, in the first week of January 1960 the BBC's share of the audience was forty-two per cent. To overstate how bad things were was a useful ploy—and Greene always had a deep sense of tactics (if not, some would later claim, of strategy). He never, for example, made a public statement without being aware of what its internal impact might be. Ahead of him lay many complex issues—some of which he perceived with clarity, others which he only vaguely visualised. There would be the committee investigating the future of broadcasting. There would be the vital question of the third TV channel which he was eager that the BBC should be given. His was a policy of 'Lebensraum', since if he had the extra channel, then he could ensure that the BBC both did the kinds of programmes which its public service tradition deemed that it should do, as well as allowing it to get on with the business of competing with the commercial system. There were important financial questions to be faced, not the least of which was to ensure that the BBC got the whole of the licence fee. There were also queries over the BBC's possible commitment to local radio. There was the renewal of the Charter, always an exercise in BBC lobbying at its best, even if no one really believed that it would not be renewed. There were developments in TV in the offing, such as the extension of the transmitter network to try to cover as near as was practically possible the whole of the country; there was colour and the shift from 405 lines to 625. And there would be the final underlining of the rise to prominence of TV with the opening of the new, impressive TV centre.

Those were the issues at the level of building the institution. He knew that it would all be for nought if the institution were not itself a vessel for cultural change and development:

Let's try and put it like this. I spoke about a class attitude in the BBC, that the BBC was tending to appeal to a limited class. I think I was always tending to think in terms of making the BBC appeal to the masses rather than making the BBC appeal to different audiences—that entered into one's thinking but not so much. But I thought it was also tending to appeal to those who were middle aged or elderly and that it should appeal to the young and that meant a big change in its orientation and the sort of programmes that were being done . . . I remember once as one example during that period making a speech in the village hall at Cockfield to the local farmers' club. A young man in his early thirties—an agricultural scientist

—came up to me after the dinner and said he wanted to thank me for what I'd done for the BBC. A few years before the BBC had meant nothing to him whatsoever. Now it seemed to express the thoughts and feelings of his generation, and I thought that that was one of the nicest things that has ever been said to me.

In youth lay a certain innocence and potential. But potential for what? What was it that Hugh Greene was trying to do with the BBC and why did he feel that in youth lay some of the answers?

Through a more 'youthful' approach, he hoped to make the BBC a new moral force within the land. He did not want it to be the voice of the established order but the voice of a new, more youthful order which he felt emerging rather in the way in which the arthritic sense a change in the weather. How this change was to be undertaken was the least articulated idea of all—he needed to find theologians before establishing the church. It had, however, to be accomplished quickly since he was in no mood to hang around waiting for something to happen.

As usual, he moved with an acute eye for the symbolic gesture, and if he could, at the same time ruffle a few aged feathers, well then, that was really all part of the therapy. He began the new era, therefore, not by creation, but by destruction; at a special board meeting on March 14th, 1960 it was agreed that Tahu Hole should leave the BBC.

The Nine O'Clock News on the Home Service had been broadcast every day since October 3rd, 1938 and in its heyday, during the war, had had an audience of twenty million, but by 1960 this was down to less than one million. It was a venerable relic which Greene was in no mood to preserve, so he moved it to ten pm which would make possible an extension of the time for news and current affairs and ease the problems of programme planning in the earlier part of the evening. Pockets of the English middle class, including his brother Herbert, did not like the removal of a familiar landmark: they reacted even more strongly when they realised Greene did not care and might demolish other much-loved monuments as well. But Greene let the shock waves of horror bounce off him. He had begun his reign as he meant to continue, in firm control. Having made these two moves against Hole and the Nine O'Clock News, he could turn his full attention to the Pilkington Inquiry.

The inquiry into the future of radio and TV under the chairmanship of Sir Harry Pilkington was essentially a debate about the idea of broadcasting. Was the concept of public service broadcasting as represented by the BBC still valid? Should there still be a service which was committed only to offering the best and most comprehensive programmes possible or should other factors such as commercial benefit be allowed to intrude?

The Postmaster General made the long-expected announcement of the government's decision to set up this inquiry in the House of Commons on July 13th, 1960. It was something for which the BBC had already been preparing in great detail, and two basic papers which would carry its case were already written. Hugh Greene knew that he would have to spend most of his time in the next two years persuading the Pilkington Committee of the virtues of the public service tradition.

Richard Hoggart, a key member of the Committee, was immensely impressed by Greene's professionalism. It was, said Hoggart, like watching the maestro of one of the world's greatest orchestras conduct, for he knew exactly when and how to use each instrument and involve each player. Much of Greene's work however in shaping the thinking of the Committee was invisible history. At endless dinners and lunches, over drinks at parties, he subtly manoeuvred the conversation to influence those who might possibly themselves influence that thinking. Greene set out to create a climate in which the virtues of the BBC, as opposed to the vices of the commercial opposition, would become received truth in the minds of not just the members of the Pilkington Committee, but anyone at all who might possibly have influence. MPs were lobbied; debates in Parliament were carefully monitored; politicians who might make favourable comments about the BBC were provided with all the material they might need to make the case. One senior politician even provided the BBC with a list of names of MPs he thought they should concentrate on. Nothing, but nothing, was left to chance.

An important part of his strategy was not only to sell the BBC but also to 'unsell' ITV and a great deal of effort as well as gin and tonic was to flow towards that end. The task greatly appealed to Greene's temperament since he was more given to indulging in informal contact and influence than to formal representation. He never had any doubts about the overall tactics of the campaign. He told Reith, 'We must divide this campaign into two stages. First of all, we must get the right report, and then we must see that the report is carried out.'

Greene outlined his ideas to senior management at his very first general liaison meeting on March 30th, 1960 at the newly-opened television centre at White City. Here he sketched out the blueprint for the years to come. He pointed out that a great many people starting from different points of view, including Labour, Liberal and Conservative MPs, and those who had been leading exponents of ITV a few years before, were now anxious to break the commercial monopoly, but the immediate danger here was that the BBC might itself be expected to advertise. He argued that 'if we once went in for advertising, the more successful we were in the commercial field the more dangerous it would be'. He thought that from a severely practical point of view:

> . . . our independence must be based on the rock of the licence revenue, and that once we were driven off that rock, we would be in a very dangerous position. If we were successful in the commercial field there would be inevitable political pressure to deprive us of our licence revenue, gradually, but in the end totally, and we would be reduced to the level of ITV.

He stressed that 'In all our public relations we should maintain our absolutely firm front on this point of our finance, and that we should set as the first objective for the Inquiry the maintenance of the present method of financing the BBC.'

That licence itself, he argued, should be the full proceeds of the £4 currently paid, but presently eaten into by deductions made by the Treasury and the Post Office, which should also rise to £5 to allow the BBC to expand technical developments, and run a second channel.

Greene wanted to use this second channel to plan alternative services to the BBC's own serious programmes; he wished to strangle at birth any suggestion that it should be awarded to a new Authority to use for education, as that, he felt, would be interfering with a service which the BBC already did extremely well. Sensing that there would be proposals for commercial radio, he hedged his bets by announcing that the BBC would now be starting up its own local radio services.

One of Hugh Greene's most potent gifts was his enthusiasm for a fight, for confronting a problem and bringing sheer intelligence to its solution. There were even moments when one could have thought that the fight and the problem to be solved were more important than what it was that was being fought over. Now he tried to inspire his senior executives with the same mood. He was determined that after the big battle was won, the Corporation would emerge properly financed and united. He begged his staff not to be complacent, but to enter the fray with confidence. Everyone must work hard to improve their public relations, to gain friends, to overcome dislike and distrust. 'Too often we appear to be aloof and arrogant. We must give the impression of ourselves as friendly, well-informed and universally intelligent people.' It was a clarion call to arms for the entire Corporation.

Greene himself now set about wooing Lord Reith, who had been the most profound influence on the BBC from its inception until 1938. Reith's vanity was enormous and he resented bitterly those who did not recognise or acknowledge his eminence. Greene knew that to have him with them during the forthcoming inquiry would do the Corporation nothing but good, so he set about soothing Reith's tormented psyche, going out of his way to ask Reith's advice on Pilkington, whilst at the same time making sure that when Reith appeared before the inquiry, or spoke in the House of Lords, he did not veer from the Greene line.

Initially it worked; Greene and Reith became reasonably friendly. On one occasion when Reith had been ill, Hugh and Elaine sent him a greetings telegram. He replied: 'Your greetings telegram last Saturday—I can't tell you how much appreciated it was. I just kept reading it over and over, staring at those so kind and moving words . . . It really is most comforting and encouraging to have such very good friends.'

The relationship did not last, and during the coming years he turned increasingly against Greene. A note in his diary after a lunch with Elaine Greene made it clear what the problem was from his point of view. He had, he said, made it clear to her

. . . that Hugh and I were fundamentally in complete opposition of outlook and attitude. I lead; he follows the crowd in all the disgusting manifestations of the age . . . Without any reservation he gives the public what it wants; I would not, did not and said I wouldn't. I am very annoyed that I even got on to terms with him.

One night Reith telephoned Greene to complain about the cover of the *Radio Times* which showed a comedian. Reith felt this was undignified. He asked, 'Don't you think, Hugh, that dignity is the most important human quality?' Greene replied, with some asperity, 'I'm afraid, John, I do not.' The phone went dead. The relationship was finally over.

Greene was totally clear-headed from the beginning through to the end of the inquiry on what he wanted: maintenance of the licence as the form of revenue; another channel; the go-ahead for colour; the confirmation of the

BBC as the main instrument of broadcasting in the United Kingdom. Defeating the ITA was necessary if only to achieve those aims, but lurking in his mind was also the thrill of besting the opposition in the campaign, and its Director General, Robert Fraser.

As Greene warmed to the fight, he lured others in to help him. Arthur fforde, his chairman, sent the Pilkington Committee a hand-written note, pointing out that the BBC originated eighty per cent of its own programmes, a higher proportion than any other broadcasting organisation in the world. Figures were produced that demonstrated the BBC's superior cost-effectiveness in programmes per listener/viewer. An intelligence paper on 'The Effect of Commercial TV on the Gathering of Provincial and Local News' was prepared, even though the man who prepared it had to put in his covering note to Hugh Greene: 'I have made the best I can of the case against commercial TV and, although we certainly have a point, I do not think that it is a very strong one.'

Timing was always very important in Hugh Greene's mind, finding exactly the right moment to send in a paper, write a letter, make a speech, see an MP. On one occasion when the Director of Administration was asking for more time to complete two papers, Greene replied that he should stick to the agreed timetable and added, 'Better B-plus this month, than A-plus later on'.

Hugh Greene saw it as his personal duty to take the case of the BBC into the public domain. He is not a naturally good public speaker, but he was determined to remove the battle from the corridors of Broadcasting House, away from committee rooms, away from the Pilkington Committee itself, and into the lecture theatre. There he developed the theme of the BBC as a complete entity greater than the sum of its various parts. He did not ask for a third channel or a new local broadcasting system because of what they represented in themselves, but because they were one more way of allowing the BBC to fulfil its moral and social purpose. A society, he implied, was like an organism which needed to be sustained, to be cultivated and allowed to develop; thus, if its people needed health, then they would be given medicine; if they needed to develop the mind, then they would be given education; if they needed culture, then they would be given the BBC. As Greene described it:

> The history of broadcasting is part of our social and institutional growth . . . Now broadcasting can safely boast that it is the most public of all services. The essence of it, as its very name implies, is to convey to the public material which would otherwise be restricted. The ideal of using broadcasting for the benefit of the whole community —rather than for the interest of any group or class— appealed strongly to those who established broadcasting in this country.

The BBC, he argued, should be all things to all men: if they want music, it shall be provided; if they want information, drama, light entertainment, discussion, emotion, to be stretched intellectually, to enjoy sport, anything that one could think of, then the BBC was, literally, constituted to offer it, but not just to offer, but to offer *the best*. He told a Canadian audience that the BBC '. . . has to concern itself with the whole of life in Britain, with the popular and the unpopular . . . People must turn to the BBC to find what they want, whatever it is.' At the same time he did not want to create the impression that the BBC had ceased to develop; that month he told another meeting that 'we are in a mood for expansion'.

On a later occasion he added, 'It would be a sad thing for mankind if the music of the spheres turned out to be no more than the jangling of cash registers.' Wherever he was going, from civic reception to political meeting, he made the same points: the need to stop the spread of commercial broadcasting and to support public broadcasting. Running within that key theme were the arguments for a new channel, for radio and for colour: and geared towards the provision of good, and therefore public service broadcasting. It was a role, moreover, which he was clearly enjoying. He told a meeting of Conservative MPs in a revealing moment: 'Perhaps a certain spice has been added to life; perhaps I am enjoying making this speech more because I have got something to attack.' The more that attack could succeed, the more likely he was to be able to convince opinion inside and outside the Committee that the BBC was worth defending. He was not suggesting that it should be defended simply because it existed but because only that particular form of broadcasting organisation with that particular set of principles could offer something far more valuable than all the stocks and shares so carefully accumulated by all those gentlemen who formed his opposition. The BBC could offer *truth*, a quality which the old journalist in him treasured above all else.

His finest exposition, however, did not take place at home but in the lion's den itself. In November 1961 he addressed NBC's anniversary dinner in New York. It was an invitation which had filled NBC executives with trepidation as to what he might say to the assembled body of the great and the good in America. They feared that he might strengthen the hands of those who were pressing for increased control of the network.

Greene described the 'true purpose of the BBC' as being

... concerned with the whole of life. The broadcaster opens a window on the world and for many, especially for the young, it is a window opened for the first time. If those who look out, with the eyes we have given them, see only the familiar, the comfortable, the reassuring, then surely we have failed, for the world is not like that. If we ensure that only the ugly, the bestial, the violent and the tawdry appear before them, then just as surely we have failed, for the world is not like that either.

He continued:

The new age of broadcasting which lies before us should not stand in the service of governments, political parties, big business or sectional interests. It should stand to my

195

mind in the service of truth or the nearest to the truth one can get, and it is important to remember that there is artistic truth as well as the hard factual truth with which events should be presented.

During the period of the Pilkington Inquiry, Hugh Greene had constantly to clarify his view of broadcasting. He had never been an especially reflective person, but he did have a number of sharply defined beliefs about the nature of culture and the kinds of values which should prevail. He was now having to articulate those values in a way which reflected his conception of the relationship between the BBC and the rest of society.

Richard Hoggart, who had always concerned himself closely with the cultural impact of broadcasting, was well aware of the danger of a mass culture which was 'too damned nice, a bland, muted, processed, institutionalised decency, a suburban limbo in which nothing ever happens and the grit has gone out of life'. It was a widespread fear, and Hugh Greene now had to persuade the Committee that the BBC would avoid the quicksands of mass taste, and also put some of that 'grit' back into the national life. He had to steer a delicate middle course between giving the people what they wanted and Reithian paternalism. What he wished to convey was faith in all those individuals who possessed a wide range of different interests but who from time to time exhibited mass taste. He quoted with pride the one million people who had listened to a Bach Promenade Concert and the four million who had watched Sir Mortimer Wheeler's series on archaeology.

Greene was turning the popular image of the BBC as an élitist channel on its head. 'Democracy rests in the last resort on faith in the plain man. The cynicism that provides a flow of trivial entertainment for the masses while despising it and them'—and here he had in mind Norman Collins—'is very close to the political cynicism which regards them as dupes to be manipulated or fooled.' In his argument he had to establish a balance between the BBC's need to maintain a certain cultural dignity and eminence within broadcasting, without its becoming distanced from the bulk of the society. Television, he argued, must provide a platform for 'men of culture' and thereby 'make a common culture part of the common good'. He invoked Matthew Arnold's 'men of culture' as 'the true apostles of equality'. The great men of culture, he said, are those who have had

> . . . a passion for diffusing, for making prevail, for carrying from one end of society to the other the best knowledge, the best ideas of their time, who have laboured to divest knowledge of all that is harsh, uncouth, difficult, abstract, professional, exclusive; to humanise it, to make it efficient outside the clique of the cultivated and learned, yet still remaining the best knowledge and thought of the time, and a true source therefore of sweetness and light.

It was a new view of an old idea, a democratised and humanised version of the missionary role of the BBC to bring 'sweetness and light' to people not because they needed it, but because without quite having realised it they in effect wanted it. Hence his rhetorical question: 'How many of the British public would have asked in 1945 for programmes on archaeology?'

The Pilkington Committee's report, published on June 27th, 1962, was an almost total vindication of broadcasting as seen by the BBC. Public service values were praised, commercial values seriously questioned. The BBC had gained support for almost everything it wanted: a new channel, colour, a switch to 625 lines, maintenance of the licence fee as the source of revenue, the development of sound broadcasting, and confirmation that it remained the main instrument of broadcasting in the country. These were recommended by the Committee in a package of structural and psychological developments which left the BBC probably stronger and more prestigious than at any time in its history.

Whatever happened from now on, the battle had been

won. The report was there, and nobody was going to be able to ignore it or laugh it off however much some of the competitors might try to do so. Nothing was ever going to be the same again in broadcasting in Britain, particularly with ITV. Greene admitted that he had rather enjoyed the sessions with Pilkington. He had been told that Sir Ivone Kirkpatrick, the Chairman of the ITA, and Sir Robert Fraser, had not. 'One had been, as Lord Reith would perhaps have liked to say, stretched. But it had been in many ways fun.'

The public reaction by the BBC was studiously and deliberately reserved. The governors had issued a press statement which 'welcomed' the report and looked forward to being empowered to carry out the recommendations at the earliest possible date. Privately Hugh Greene pointed out that the public squeals of horror from ITV could only be to the advantage of the BBC, which preserved its dignity with its relative silence. He was not above trying to make matters worse for ITV by giving their childish gestures more publicity; he personally ensured that there would be cameras at a party to be held by Peter Cadbury, a leading ITV figure, at which he had announced he would burn a huge copy of the report.

Pilkington was a sweet, sweet victory, but it did open up an era of expansion and development for which someone had to pay. In the White Paper following Pilkington, the government accepted its 'responsibility' to see that the BBC would secure sufficient income to finance adequate services, including more hours for sound, a second TV channel, a start to colour, Welsh and Scottish television, and more adult education TV programmes. The only major development which the BBC had pushed for but which the government, at least for the time being, had rejected was local broadcasting. The actual size of the licence that would pay for this ambitious programme remained an open question, in fact a tricky question in which both sides were jockeying for the most favourable positions. The BBC's own estimates of how much they would need had in fact changed and they had told the government that they would want the full proceeds from a £5 licence.

Greene exhibited a certain clever pragmatism at this point. One of the main grievances of the BBC had always been that it paid an excise tax on the licence. Greene saw the opportunity to get this removed and, at the same time, to be seen to be doing the government a favour. He informed them that he understood that though the BBC actually needed a £5 licence, he was well aware of the 'hard facts of the political world we live in' and that of course the government would find it difficult to increase what the public had to pay just before an election. He said that the BBC could get by until April 1st, 1965 with £4, provided that the excise tax was surrendered by the government and they had the £4 licence from April 1st, 1963. What he managed to get was the £4 from October 1st, 1963. In practice this meant that the BBC could not pay all its services out of the licence revenue, and therefore would have to use its borrowing powers, as well as making cuts. It was, he told the liaison meeting, going to be a very difficult time financially, with far more rigid administration and a careful look at new projects: 'This was not a happy situation. But there we were and there we would be for some time to come, at least until after the General Election that would probably not take place before the autumn of 1964.' The two bright points were that the excise tax had finally gone, and revenues from such things as publications and TV enterprises were increasing.

One important feature of the BBC which came to the fore during the Pilkington Inquiry was its inherent tendency to expand in order to defend the home base, as well as to propagate itself. The second channel, colour, local radio, external broadcasting, adult education—all reflected this basic tendency. For Greene they were developments in his 'war' strategy and as such were highly successful elements. The problem would lie in the future when this tendency to expand would lead the BBC to overstretch itself.

The BBC's licence and agreement were debated in the House on January 14th, 1964. The Royal Charter was approved by the Privy Council on February 26th. The Pilkington era was finally over, and Greene had won a considerable victory. The BBC was assured of its traditional independence in programme matters and day-to-day administration. Government powers remained reserve powers. The fundamental position of the BBC remained unchanged. Most important of all, as far as Greene was concerned, nothing had been written into the Charter and licence about broadcasting standards.

Greene and the BBC now felt keen to exercise a new-found strength and confidence. There was only one way to do that and that was in the programmes. The process had already begun before the ordeal of the committee of inquiry was over, but now they could really get their teeth into the problem of making the BBC not just a prestigious institution within the land, but also an intellectual and moral force that articulated the sentiments of change which were beginning to swirl in Britain as the age of affluence came pounding in.

13

The most creative and energetic people in the BBC at the end of the 'fifties were Cecil McGivern and Donald Baverstock. Cecil McGivern had been made television programme director in 1947, whereupon he had developed a single-minded passion to involve himself in every aspect of this branch of broadcasting. He watched and commented on every programme: ruthless, clear, involved, prickly but respected, he was determined to force programme makers under him to come to grips with quality. From the first he recognised that television was a separate activity, unique to itself: it was not radio with pictures. Its audience too was special.

The average figure who sat at home in front of his TV set should not be seen as an object for commercial exploitation, nor as a hopeless cultural ignoramus. Rather he should be treated with respect; he might be wracked with worries and doubts, but he was a warm-hearted human being who wished to be enlightened and entertained; someone of little knowledge but great understanding.

McGivern was also most anxious that those who worked in his department should stand on their own feet: it was not for them to run whimpering to others to make decisions for them, they must take their own risks, shoulder responsibility for their own ideas, judge for themselves, for they *were* the BBC. They, the production staff, were the strength of the BBC, not the part-time governors at the top: they should not defer to those above them in the hierarchy all the time as though senior people had a monopoly on wisdom. If the BBC was functioning properly, then ideas, purpose, commitment and policy should be flowing upwards from them, not downwards from above.

Donald Baverstock had joined the BBC in 1949. For four years he had worked in the general overseas service and then in 1954 he had joined the television talks department. His memories of this time are episodic, little vignettes which in the mind's eye capture the process of change. He recalls the influence of American TV and bringing back copies of Mort Sahl's records from the United States. He remembers, too, an occasion when a young couple came to his flat for dinner. They were very impressed that Baverstock worked for the BBC and met famous people. How marvellous it must be, they cooed, to know the stars. 'Well, actually it wasn't', Baverstock replied, and when asked about Gilbert Harding he informed the lady that the great man did his broadcasts while he sat on the toilet. With a cry of certainty, she yelled 'I knew it'. Baverstock linked that little anecdote to one heard of Macmillan in White's Club saying of Selwyn Lloyd, 'He's just a middle-class lawyer'. 'That', said Baverstock with force and passion, 'was the truth'. With that rising self-confidence then arose the idea that their programmes would unearth the prosaic truths about great men, would take nothing at face value, would probe and inquire.

The press reports are full of descriptions of Baverstock as dynamic, aggressive, unpredictable, a cross between a Welsh bard and fairground boxing-booth fighter. One account of him from the time quotes him as saying 'who wants to be liked anyway?' Another report said that, 'he doesn't attempt to conceal an essential scorn for the reactionary, establishmentarian roots of the Corporation'. He was the genuine pugnacious but exciting lad from the provinces, with his Welsh roots, a father—whom he adored—who ran a small grocer's shop, and a love for his homeland which always seems to overcome those who are hell-bent on leaving it.

For much of the fifties, children's programmes had ended at 6 pm and the rest of the schedules had not started until 7.30 pm. It was known as the 'toddlers' truce' because that was when mums were meant to put the children of the nation to bed. Following the emergence of ITV, programmes were started again at 7 pm with news and newsreel to 7.15. This therefore left 15 minutes to fill before the evening's programmes proper began. McGivern had the idea that they would have a daily televised edition of *The Archers* from Birmingham. Having seen the pilots shortly before it was due to be broadcast he decided that it had not worked. He turned to Leonard Miall, the Head of TV Talks, and told him to fill the fifteen-minute slot which was going begging. The only snag was that there were no resources to speak of, apart from a tiny presentation studio in Lime Grove from which continuity announcements and the weather were broadcast. The form of the filler-programme almost determined itself, it had to be interviews. The man charged with producing it was Donald Baverstock.

Shortly before, Baverstock had seen a programme about the differences between the north and south of England by someone he had not heard of before, Jacqueline McKenzie. He was struck by the amusing but perceptive way she captured the northern mood. It stayed in his mind. At the same time he had read a brilliant take-off by Alan Brien in the *Observer* of the producer of 'What's My Line'. He thought to himself 'Crikey, it's the *New Yorker* style, humorous reports, not overdoing it.' A wisp of suggestion then back to the sober style.

Baverstock's new programme went out five nights a week, was called *Highlights* and had Jacqueline McKenzie in it. He now learned a great deal about finding people and stories quickly and portraying them attractively. It was a great success and when the end came to 'toddlers' truce' in 1956 it was inevitable that Baverstock's considerable talent would be harnessed to produce the programme that would fill the gap.

The BBC had always been eager to talk at the public but never with them. What Baverstock now had in mind was a series of episodic, amusing half-hour 'conversations' about people, their prejudices, their characters, their behaviour and their longings which would encourage viewers to think 'I'm not like that' or 'there but for the Grace of God go I . . .'

By the end of December 1956 the idea had crystallised into a forty-five minute, five nights a week programme called *Tonight*, produced by Baverstock and assisted by a new young man, Alasdair Milne, which set out to appeal to the 'captives' in their armchairs, to those moving about on household affairs or those who had just walked through the front door. With short, varied items you could either sit through it all, or dip into it occasionally to see what was on offer.

Tonight was very successful, attracting fifty per cent of the viewing audience. It, therefore, became the key to the BBC's nightly battle to beat ITV. As important, however, was that its success was not at the expense of quality: it brought prestige and goodwill. Baverstock and his colleagues had begun to rethink the nature of their relationship with the audience and in so doing had not had to betray the public service tradition. There was no Faustian bargain in Baverstock's story as yet.

Baverstock ran *Tonight* first as a producer and then, as it grew, as editor, until the beginning of 1961. He was then made Assistant Controller TV Programmes, with Alasdair Milne taking over the editorship of *Tonight*. As these two stars continued to rise, McGivern had gone into a steep and pitiful decline. He had begun to prevaricate hopelessly; he drank too much; he became only a shadow. On December 5th, 1960, he went on sick leave; on January 25th, 1961, his post of Deputy Director of Television Broadcasting was abolished, and he was placed on 'special writing assignment'. On March 3rd, 1961, he retired prematurely. Not long afterwards he was burnt to death at home, a terrible end to a fascinating career.

His departure was followed in the spring of 1962 by a series of other changes that signalled to many of his colleagues a ruthless side to Hugh Greene's character. On May 17th, 1962, the BBC announced that Leonard Miall would no longer be running Talks: Grace Wyndham Goldie would replace him. The following day it was announced that Milne had been promoted to Assistant Head of Talks (Current Affairs) Huw Wheldon to Assistant Head of Talks (General); Tony Jay to Editor of *Tonight* and Humphrey Burton as Editor of *Monitor*.

What really disturbed many people was the manner of Miall's going. Out of the blue he received a letter from Hugh Greene saying that he would no longer be running Talks, that the only position open to him would be Controller, Scotland. Miall was dumbfounded. He turned to various people for advice, and the consensus was that he should go to Kenneth Adam who was known to have 'a soft centre', to have the decision rescinded. It worked and an alternative was found for Miall, but the event had gone through the corridors of the BBC like a chilly wind, reminding people that Hugh Greene was not all twinkling eyes and liberal-mindedness.

The truth of the matter was that Hugh Greene felt the need for a change in Talks, wanted to know more of what was happening, and could make the move without himself injecting any emotion into it—teeth had to be pulled, and if there was no anaesthetic then that was just too bad. It certainly made sense tactically for him to want to be better informed since TV Talks had emerged as the vanguard in his efforts to transform the public image and purpose of the BBC.

Greene might not have been directly involved in programming but this did not mean that he was unimportant. Indeed, he was crucial. If Baverstock and his cohorts were to be able to beat the nation around the head with their wit, irreverence and occasional truths, then they needed the support from above, even if the form of that support was to allow them to get on with whatever it was they wished to do. Hugh Greene was precisely the right kind of person to have as the chief executive at this moment. Indeed, this moment is inconceivable without him. He was skilled in letting it be seen that he welcomed the ideas and plans of Baverstock and his colleagues, that his nature had its own element of mischief allied to a combative robustness and the instincts of a journalist.

In 1960 the Cambridge Footlights produced a lively cabaret at the Lyceum Theatre, Edinburgh, called *Beyond the Fringe* with Jonathan Miller, Dudley Moore, Peter Cook and Alan Bennett. They did not see themselves engaged in satire, in exposing folly and vice but rather desired to 'remind people by the shock of recognition of how absurd things are'. The main butts were established figures and institutions, including the Royal Family, the Prime Minister, the Church, and politicians. Peter Cook then went on to open a restaurant in Soho called The Establishment which had a nightly performance of sketches attacking the government, bureaucracy and the rich. The mood of the times was teasing and ebullient, and the rhythms emerging from *Beyond the Fringe* and *The Establishment* were inevitably reflected in the mood inside the post-Pilkington era BBC.

In February 1962 Ned Sherrin of Talks suggested a new programme which would be 'aware, pointed, irreverent, fundamentally serious, intelligently witty, outspoken in the proper sense of the word, and would provide an opportunity for saying things worth saying'. It would, he said, necessarily be an irritant, and if they were going to make people scratch, the object of the programme would be to give them something worth scratching. He specifically likened the programme to some of the features of *Beyond the Fringe*, the Establishment Club, American satirical shows, and ad-lib comedians such as Mike Nichols and Elaine May.

He proposed a number of different 'satirical sketches' to be built around a nucleus of actors and script-writers, held together by a presenter or anchor man capable of spontaneous comedy. The budget was to work out at £2,035 per programme.

By the summer of 1962 this new programme had been scheduled for eleven pm to midnight on Saturdays and the title had become *That Was the Week That Was*. Editorial responsibility had been given to Alasdair Milne. He was asked to regard his supervision of the programme 'as an absolute priority over all his other duties'. In cases of doubt about policy or taste he was to refer to Baverstock, who nevertheless was acutely aware of the need not to over-control the programme's development. He told Stuart Hood, Controller of BBC TV:

> I shall continue to take as much of a personal interest in this programme as I can, though as you will understand, as Assistant Controller of Programmes, my role cannot be other than passive or even negative. Producers rightly have to put the creation of their programmes as their first and dominant responsibility. In my position I have to be concerned first with the interests of the service. This is a role which I cannot exercise through detailed interference without inhibiting the producers and sterilising their creative drive.

Hugh Greene had not been party to any of the discussions about the programme. He had merely hinted at one point that he would like a fairly close eye kept on proceedings—hence Baverstock's role in overall supervision. Of what it would be like, he had absolutely no idea. On the opening night he just sat at home and waited. By the time midnight came he was delighted. It particularly amused him when the press, who were astounded by it all, rang up the Postmaster General, Reginald Bevins, to discover his reaction. Rather incautiously he replied, 'I'm going to do something about it', a sentiment which was quoted in the press. On arriving at his office he found on his desk a very short note from Harold Macmillan, the Prime Minister, which merely said, 'Oh, no you're not'.

As the weeks went by, *TW3* grew in fame and importance. It had been assumed that the audience would be about two million. To everyone's amazement the audience began to grow. By the beginning of 1963 it was six and a half million with an appreciation which, according to the BBC's own audience research figures, was extremely high. The great British public was not only watching it but loving it and to their astonishment, even in the first weeks, Sherrin, Baverstock, Milne, Goldie and Greene found themselves with a huge 'hit' on their hands. They also had the making of a legend.

Although *TW3* was only broadcast on thirty-seven occasions between November 1962 and December 1963, it had a remarkable impact, stamping its character on the early years of the decade as if they were hot wax and as if it were the seal. Hugh Greene relished the programme and the success, but he quickly realised the problems. Even by the fifth episode he suggested in passing that perhaps they should lay off the Lord Chancellor for a while. Even in its infancy, the programme's 'sacred indignation' was beginning to get a reaction. There were complaints. Much disquiet was expressed by the governors and by senior members of the Conservative party. There were also signs of internal strain within the BBC. Whether this was an emerging failure of nerve or a real sense of professional concern with the programme is now almost impossible to decide. The truth is actually a cocktail of the two as the programme was beginning to get into the bloodstream of both the nation and the institution.

On January 14th, 1963, Baverstock wrote to Milne about the previous Saturday's programme. It was, he said, 'the worst yet'. Several items should never have been included; another was 'unimaginative and took an obvious, predictable line' in which the item was reduced to no more than a set of obscene gestures. On another item about Lord Hailsham he commented that it 'swiped at the government with less precision that we would expect from ill-educated local labour ward politicians'. Of particular annoyance to Baverstock was that the programme had overrun twenty minutes. Had that been cut, then, he suggested, not only would they have saved money but they would also have had less time

> to suggest to the audience that behind the programme that attacks other people's standards there are only glib cheap-jack values. This is the point that worries me most. If we are asked, 'By what right do these people attack as they

do', we have to be able to point to the programme and say, 'By the right of the programme's fair-mindedness, its quality, its style, and the consistency of its own values.' Judging last Saturday's programme, I for one cannot make this defence.

Having discussed the programme, Baverstock then cracked the whip in the direction of Ned Sherrin. He instructed Milne to inform him that the BBC's restrictions on the use of swear words, blue jokes and obscene gestures applied to *TW3* as to all other programmes. He was henceforth to consult with Milne in all matters of programme content, in detail and with complete candour. Sherrin had to be made to recognise, Baverstock continued, that all editorial control rested not with himself as producer but with Milne.

Although the programme at this stage was less than two months old, its indignation, which had been held by Baverstock to be one of its major forces, was beginning to give some people indigestion. Its critical, intelligent edge created antagonism and controversy. The particular programme which Baverstock had attacked so viciously, also contained an item called 'Consumer Report on Religion' in which David Frost described each of the main religions as if they were goods on offer. Inevitably it aroused strong criticism. In a note to Kenneth Lamb, the BBC's Head of Religious TV, Milne explained that the whole idea had been to attack the increasingly familiar tones of progressive clergy who sought to promote their beliefs by using secular values and methods. Lamb returned the memo with a brief hand-written note appended to it saying, 'Not that it should never be done, but it should be done better.'

TW3 was receiving enormous coverage in the press. Its performers were now stars, though if justice had been done as much fame and credit should have been given to the writers. But complaints were increasing from those who felt that, as part of the established order, they were being intellectually and morally lashed for offences which they only half understood. Hugh Greene, watching still from the heady heights of the Director General's office, remained cautiously supportive. On January 23rd, 1963 he sent a message: 'tell them I take my hat off to them', but added in passing (what may well have been the real point of the message) that they should perhaps 'lay off George Brown' for the time being.

Greene was indeed bursting with pride at the way things were going. On February 15th he broadcast on the German station, Sender Freies Berlin:

> At the end of last year we embarked on an entirely new venture. This is a satirical review of the events of the week placed late on Saturday evening. It has bite and pungency and spares neither institutions nor persons, neither Prime Minister nor bishop—nor courtier. We thought that it would probably attract a minority audience of about one million. Now after a couple of months, it has a regular audience of seven million and is probably the most talked about programme ever produced in Britain. I am not boasting if I say that there is nothing like it in the world because that is what the American magazine, *Time*, said.
>
> So you see that in a competitive situation we have not stuck to time-honoured formulas, or tried to match programme for programme in an effort to achieve the largest audience. We have tried instead to provide something for everybody. Our programmes have been lively, controversial and demanding, and we have tried consistently to find out what people want by means of bold experiment. I think I can safely say that this policy is a responsible one and that it is helping our country to adjust itself honestly and without illusion to the facts of its position in the world today.

He told his German audience also about Donald Baverstock and Michael Peacock, who had just been promoted. He pointed out that they were thirty-eight and thirty-three, 'young, alive, and full of ideas, and so is the service they represent'. He ended with some words of advice to his

German listeners and particularly the broadcasters among them, words which were in fact his credo of broadcasting:

> Maintain your standards; aim at the highest professionalism and technical expertise; keep your range of programming wide and try to provide everything for somebody and something for everybody; be adventurous and experimental; be bold; try always to keep one jump ahead; don't compromise with politicians or advertisers or vested interests; get the best people and give them the chance and don't be afraid to make mistakes because if you make no mistakes you will be dull and that is the worst sin of all.

This trip also revealed another facet of Hugh Greene's personality. Charles Wheeler, the BBC's Berlin representative, had written to say that the Germans were planning to take him to see *My Fair Lady*. Appalled at the thought, Greene wrote back saying that he would much prefer a night on the town and a visit to a political cabaret.

Greene's German speech was typical of the kind of statement he was making wherever he went. In New York, Montreal, Warsaw, Berlin, Prague, Paris, Washington, and many other cities the message was always the same: the dignity, virtues and record of the BBC, and above all the prime virtue of public service broadcasting. *TW3* was always heralded as the very essence of that virtue.

By the time the first series of *TW3* had ended on April 27th, 1963 the image of the BBC which Greene and others had been struggling to alter had finally been changed. The 'old Auntie' image of the BBC had been kicked out, and it was fashionable now to praise the Corporation's bold, original TV programmes. The comments were ostensibly about the whole of the BBC but in fact were essentially about this one programme. The rest of the schedule could not be called wildly exciting or radical. Preceding *TW3* on Saturday night, for example, were *Juke Box Jury*, *Dixon of Dock Green*, an old film and sport. Sunday would consist of another old movie, religion, *The Billy Cotton Show*, or *The Black and White Minstrels*.

These may all have been good and worthy programmes of their type, but they hardly added up to a creative hurricane. The truth of the matter was that in a brilliant manoeuvre, which was half intuitive, half planned, in openly supporting *TW3* and praising it as the kind of programme he wanted, Hugh Greene had transformed the image of the BBC with just forty-five minutes of television a week. In doing so, he lit the fuse which several years later was to explode. Therein lay the paradox: success entailed what amounted to an act of self-destruction.

14

The working through of that paradox lay in the future. In the short term praise was being heaped on the programme. The board of governors formally recorded their congratulations to the TV service on the introduction of what they described as 'an important programme' in which they had taken a continuing interest and 'which had their support throughout'. The Vice Chairman had written separately to Kenneth Adam describing the final programme of the first series as 'brilliant'. Far more important, however, was the caveat to the governors' praise. They wanted to hear in some detail from Alasdair Milne the plans for the next series. Adam commented in a note on April 30th:

> It is, I think, an inevitable part of the support that we have had from above for this highly controversial programme that a constructive interest should be taken in its future. I mention this now because I think it important that Alasdair Milne should realise that he is likely to be asked to undertake a rather stricter responsibility when it returns, and Ned Sherrin and those others most intimately concerned must also be aware of this.

He sent a further note to Hood on the same theme, headed 'A phrase from fforde'. At the governors' meeting, in which support had been expressed for the programme, fforde had made an observation which had not been minuted: 'It would be a pity to spoil the ship for a ha 'porth of dirt.' Adam added that it 'does, I think, sum up nicely the obscenity point'.

The difficulty with fforde's point was that the 'rudeness' of the programme was the vessel for its irreverence and was, therefore, far more important than just being a 'ha'porth of dirt'. Neither was there any evidence that the vast bulk of those ten million viewers particularly minded what Adam had cared to call 'obscenity'. Indeed, one suspects that it had much to do with their watching the programme. The programme had been successful precisely because its raw wit was beginning to lance a number of social boils. That was why it had been created in the beginning and why Hugh Greene personally supported it, so that it could look at the world with a sceptical eye and become part of the examination of this island now. At times its sketches were brilliantly witty pieces of investigative journalism. It mercilessly attacked the policies of the pompous and the powerful. No one with his head above the social parapet was safe.

The approach and style were exactly what Greene wanted from the BBC. He told the Commonwealth Broadcasting Conference in May 1963:

We have become more outspoken and freer in our handling of controversial political and social subjects. We think it is an important part of our duty to enquire, to question authority rather than to accept it, to ask in fact whether the Emperor has any clothes. I have no doubt that strong institutions flourish in an atmosphere of free public discussion and criticism.

A comment such as that was aimed at internal consumption within the BBC as much as by the conference. It was a firm reminder to everyone that the Director General thought things were just fine, that the ship was sailing in exactly the right direction with a speed and force unparalleled in its history, and that there was no need for any more tar. Greene was, of course, absolutely right. Never had the BBC quite the presence within the culture as it had at the beginning of the decade. He had come to power just at the moment at which he could guarantee its success by allowing the ship to continue plotting the same course. Somewhere over the horizon, however, was the inevitable iceberg.

The governors remained worried and asked Stuart Hood and Kenneth Adam to appear before them on July 4th, to discuss future editorial control of the programme. Hood and Adam promised them that measures would be taken to prevent the return of smut, that the Deity would be spared in the future, and that attacks on mere mortals would also 'have to be properly chosen as to target and judicious in execution'. Certainly its very success in becoming both popular and the essence of the BBC's contemporary image, had frightened many people inside the Corporation. An unstated assumption was growing in these spring and summer months of 1963: it was almost inconceivable that the programme could survive, since it would prove to be just too potent and heavy a brew for the sober establishment body of the governors.

The problem of standards and morality which *TW3* had raised was suddenly sharpened on Sunday, July 14th, 1963. In a programme series called *This Nation Tomorrow*, a number of people spoke on the theme of 'Sex and Family Life'. One of them was Dr Alex Comfort, a multi-talented character with radical views on sex, which he had expressed most recently in a book called *Sex in Society*. In the programme he spoke freely of young people's use of contraceptives and described the chivalrous boy as one who went to meet his girlfriend armed with a rubber. He also proposed that the institution of marriage was only propped up by adultery and that chastity was no more of a virtue than malnutrition. His words dropped like bombs into the laps of the Sunday viewing audience, one of whom was a Midland housewife, Mary Whitehouse. The following day the typical newspaper headline was 'TV Talk on Sex Starts Storm'.

In the mind of Sir Arthur fforde, the Chairman of the BBC, *TW3* and the Comfort programme fused together, causing him considerable anxiety.

The second series of *TW3* began on September 28th, 1963, and was due to run until April 1964. On the Monday morning after the first programme there were fifty-nine telephone calls of criticism, none of praise, forty-one letters of criticism and five of praise. The complaints ranged from bad taste, anti-Catholicism and distress to Jews, dullness, vulgarity, smut, infantilism, boredom, dreariness. More worrying for the BBC, however, was that a number of MPs began to write to complain. The edition of October 19th evoked a storm of protest, with 599 phone calls and 310 letters of complaint. The part of the item which annoyed most was Frost's closing remark: 'And so there is the choice for the electorate: on the one hand Lord Home—on the other hand, Mr Harold Wilson. Dull Alec versus Smart-Alec.' Greene, himself, had approved the item before transmission, much to the joy of the script-writer, Christopher Booker, and the angst of the governors.

On October 10th, 1963 the Board 'expressed anxiety' about the ability of the programme to survive a long run. It was, they said, dull, lacking in new ideas. They did not mention anything of its alleged unsettling immorality or political controversy. Greene refused to be drawn on its future, saying that its 'survival value' was too early to assess, though he did agree that it should be kept under review. At this meeting fforde was an ally to Greene and argued that while he hoped that the blue jokes would disappear he also hoped that it would survive at the level of its best achievements.

The very existence of the programme was now being called into question, for the governors feared that Greene had lost control. Even angrier than the governors were the General Advisory Council, that large body of men and women from all walks of life who ostensibly existed to keep the BBC in touch with grassroots opinion. They did not care for the values now being depicted on BBC television, and said so.

On October 23rd, 1963 the row boiled over at a meeting attended by fforde and Greene. One of the GAC members attacked the programme for being offensive, undergraduate, potentially venomous, increasingly humourless and creating too many difficulties. It was produced, he added, by young

216

Hugh, aged 3 months with his mother

Graham, aged 9 and Hugh, aged 3

Sitting: Graham, Herbert, Molly with Elisabeth on her lap.
Standing: Raymond and Hugh. *c.* 1917/1918

Elisabeth, Molly, Graham, Aunt Nora (always known as Aunt
Nono) and Hugh at Bacton, Norfolk, summer 1920

men 'who were permanently out of their depth' and who were using the opportunity to vent their spleen. It was, he said, 'not helpful to the image of the BBC'.

A prominent member of the Council, Sir Hugh Linstead, said that 'in recent months, or even in the past year or two, something sour had overtaken the BBC at the core'. The Bishop of Manchester, another GAC member, also waded in with the suggestion that an occasional glance into the gutter or the dustbin could be a useful and sanitary operation, but if one did this continuously it could be dangerous to the life and morale of the nation.

Once more fforde came to Hugh Greene's assistance. He said that *TW3* 'reminded one of one's own experiences at school, where one sometimes knew in one's heart that the most promising person in the whole place was the problem child'.

Greene had a problem, which was in part of his own making. He had openly and actively encouraged *TW3*. In a characteristic letter on October 4th, 1963 to Sir Wavell Wakefield, MP, about a constituent's complaint, Greene said that 'at its best the programme was on the side of liberty, honesty, sanity, and tolerance and against their evil opposites'. There were at this stage no doubts, no anxieties, no worry lines to be seen in the BBC's public face. In private they all too readily appeared. *TW3*'s very success had laid a minefield through which Greene and his colleagues had to walk.

Greene went to unusual lengths to try to ensure that the programme did not blow up in his face. He had all but taken over editorial control as the production staff talked with him on the phone before each programme about editorial problems. Similarly, *TW3* was the only issue on which he would systematically go round the Board of Management asking each member what they had felt about the previous Saturday's programme. The reactions would vary from outright dislike to worries about its moral content, to positive pleasure and, in the case of Kenneth Adam, joy that it was no longer his problem now that Greene had taken control. A residual feeling among some members of the Board of Management, which was very much behind Greene on most of his programme policy, was that the production team of *TW3* were exploiting his tolerant nature.

As the programme grew in fame and controversy it began to colour the whole of the image of the BBC. Greene's tricky task was to tread a very fine line between not being seen to be withdrawing his support, but all the while pointing out that it was still only one fish in a very big pond. He told the General Advisory Council that they should remember the way in which *TW3* was balanced by the more sober reality of *Panorama*, *Gallery*, and *Tonight*. Seeing it in that way, he suggested, might eventually reduce to a proper size something which had 'loomed too large'. That it loomed too large was largely his doing, since he had fed the flames constantly.

In the minds of the General Advisory Council, *TW3* had come to symbolise all that they felt was wrong with the BBC. Drama, religious and current affairs programmes were also castigated, they were all too cynical, negative and destructive. Where was the BBC's moral responsibility to the rest of society? Was the BBC, asked Lord Strang, offering what it promised in the inscription at the entrance to Broadcasting House, 'whatsoever things are beautiful, and honest, and of good report'?

It was an intelligent, bruising but reactionary assault by the GAC on some of the central tenets of Greene's BBC. Greene tried to defend himself by playing down the programme's actual importance and suggesting that perhaps the whole thing had become one great red herring. Interestingly enough, fforde's defence both of the programme and those issues of principle which it had raised was much tougher than Hugh Greene's. He told the members of the Council that '. . . there must be throughout the Corporation, and largely existed already, a sense of involvement in the human situation, a sense of responsibility to it and a sense of historical perspective . . .'

The arguments of the members of the GAC had cut very deep. Their reservations found agreement both among the board of governors and among some senior executives. John Arkell, the Director of Administration, in a note to Greene placed the blame firmly at the feet of Sherrin who, he said, had misused the freedom which Greene's policy had allowed him and every other producer. In reality there were many layers of editorial control—Milne, Goldie, Baverstock, Hood, Adam, Greene. Indeed the programme was so swathed in layers of control that it was in imminent danger of being mummified. What Arkell was really opposing was the theory of 'the untrammelled freedom of the producer' with the role of the layers above being to cushion the pressure from outside. If this were BBC policy, he added in an acid aside, then the TV Service was being run by a staff with an average age of twenty-seven. Who, he was asking, was in charge?

Despite all the criticism which was being heaped upon Greene, *TW3* and the BBC in general, and despite the occasional gaffe, it could not be said that those twenty-seven-year-olds had betrayed the Director General's trust. They had done precisely what he had implied that he wanted them to do; they had placed the BBC at the very heart of Britain in the 1960s. They had demonstrated with great skill and wit that broadcasting did not just have to be the amplifier of orthodox thoughts, that it could have a separate presence within the community. That was all that Hugh Greene had been asking.

When the second series started in October 1963, Greene remained optimistic, proud and combative, despite growing opposition. He wrote to Tatjana:

I think this is one of the most difficult years I have ever had. Things had been going too well in the previous 3 years, but 1963 has been the year of criticism and of quite bitter attacks on the sorts of things I've been trying to do. But I've survived this far and I expect I shall go on surviving.

The board of governors and the GAC had now begun to feel that the young men *were* betraying the trust implicit in their freedom, because the questions they were asking and the values they were assuming were utterly different from those of these august bodies.

On November 17th came the bombshell. The BBC announced that production of *TW3* would end on December 28th, 1963. The reason given was that 1964 would inevitably be an election year, and that in that context it would be extremely difficult to maintain the political content of the programme. The announcement came as a great surprise to almost everyone—including those who had attacked the programme. The reaction to this decision from the audience was immediate and hostile, with 700 letters protesting at the decision and 200 letters praising it.

The fact that 1964 would be an election year had been known for a long time. Nowhere in the weeks and months of debate about the programme had the political dimension been central. In some ways *TW3* had had a remarkably easy ride from politicians, and there had been nothing in the way of warning shots across the bows about the coming election from any of the major parties. The debate had been over-whelmingly about the moral and ideological stance of the programme, of Hugh Greene and of the BBC.

The Director General had become increasingly worried about the attitudes of the board of governors and in particu-lar of the attitude of Sir James Duff, the Vice Chairman. Duff was coming close to resigning over the issue of the pro-gramme. A very upright and forceful character, he had made it increasingly clear that either he or *TW3* would go. Greene's anxiety was that if Duff went there would be a wholescale collapse of the governors and a severe weaken-ing of the Corporation. It was not a prospect he was pre-pared to contemplate.

At the beginning of November Greene had been in bed with flu. With time to think he decided that the threat to the stability of the governors was too great and that therefore the programme would have to come off. When he informed the governors of his decision, there was an audible sigh of relief around the table. Arthur fforde, who had also been ill and who had taken no part in the decision, wrote to Greene: 'I do feel that you and the TV Service have a hard task on your hands and offer my sympathies.'

The election year was more than just a convenient excuse but not much more. It was agreed at the Board of Management that Greene was withdrawing the programme '. . . because it had become a symbol. It could not be expected to continue if the string of control were drawn any tighter. It could not expect to go on being as good as it had been unless it created a periodical uproar.' He had lost some of his earlier faith in the production staff of *TW3*, and referred to their curious innocence of judgment, including Alasdair Milne, and their inability to see what constituted a dirty joke.

Throughout all the discussions there had been frequent references to the Pilkington Committee's argument that broadcasting could not be neutral in relation to the moral standards of society. The expressions of sorrow, Hugh Greene said, coming from old friends, demanded that the BBC re-examine itself and its output with humility and consider the question of its relationship to the moral standards of society. It did not take a prophet to see that the moral standards that the BBC would have to reflect would be those of Sir James Duff and his ilk, rather than the majority of the ten million or so regular viewers of *TW3*.

The dimensions and nature of the battle were well caught in an editorial in the *Northern Echo* on September 30th. It argued that *TW3* had been sucked into the centre of a debate which had been taking place in Britain for several centuries. It was:

> . . . the argument between the Cavaliers and the Round-heads, between those who believe in the liberty of the individual in matters sexual, spiritual and artistic, and those who warn that in certain instances this liberty may corrupt . . . *TW3* is a radical, angry programme that seeks to liberate us from cant . . .

TW3 had blazed a trail: it opened up the possibility of political humour on TV; it signalled new kinds of language, thought and wit. This created the cultural and creative space within which *Steptoe and Son*, and *Till Death Us Do Part* could prosper. It had also raised questions of standards and taste, the role of the governors and their relationship with Greene, the position of the producer, and of the future of Greene's ideas about broadcasting. There was no doubt that Greene simply enjoyed the programme for its wit, its risqué jokes, its satire, its attacks on the establishment, its sheer youthful naughtiness. If, however, he was unable to keep going one single programme that was an astonishing critical and popular success, how on earth could he ever expect to win along a broad front? He could not.

Whatever the legacy of *TW3*, whatever Hugh Greene's final failure to support the programme in the face of pressure from Duff, he had allowed the programme to happen in the first place. He had nurtured it, at first from a distance, then close in. He had given its producers confidence, he had been courageous and had demonstrated the potential of public service broadcasting when given its head. Other programmes would later be measured against *TW3* and, on the whole, found wanting.

The essence of the situation was that after Pilkington, led by someone such as Greene, but confronted by a reactionary establishment, the BBC was faced with a paradox: to achieve one part of its purpose it had to allow freedom to the creative individual; in so doing it evoked the reaction that it had *other* social and moral responsibilities which necessarily meant the imposition of controls on that creative talent.

Controversy and change were not the monopoly of current affairs under Hugh Greene. An important assumption of Greene's was that the real job of examining the soul of society belongs not to the journalist, but to the writer. If there is pain or flaw in the body, then it is the dramatist who can best describe it and, through description, heal. But drama cannot do this if it is dogged by the hypocrisy that bedevils so much else in television, that good lies are better than disagreeable truths. Inevitably dramatists would be seen to be ideologically out of step with consensus politics.

What began to worry the board of governors, almost as soon as Hugh Greene had become Director General, was that the only view television dramatists had of life was of its pain and sores, its misery, its seediness, its evil. Where, voices began to ask, was the other side of the coin. At a governors' meeting on January 14th, 1960, Arthur fforde 'suggested'—a word loaded with menace when it is uttered from such exalted heights—that in its drama the BBC was allowing itself 'a little too much freedom where manners and morals were concerned'. He agreed that there could be no directive on such questions and that, as Greene had persuaded him, 'no imposed censorship was practicable or desirable'. If fforde did not wish to offer any strict definition, he did offer an appropriate metaphor: 'The ship was sailing with the wind free, and we could afford to haul in the sheets a bit and use a little more rudder.'

Two weeks later Kenneth Adam was complaining to the staff of TV Drama that 'the volume of criticism' of the plays on Sunday had increased and that 'it cannot be ignored, and ought not to be invited again'. A year later he was still arguing that both critics and public were tired 'of the tendency of contemporary drama to follow a line of misery and despair', and his rather improbable solution was a competition for comedy writers. The complaint was being heard more and more: too little joy, too much misery.

Hugh Greene himself was not too perturbed by this. He demanded that the BBC's TV Drama output should be revitalised by bringing in the man who was then the most successful person in British TV drama, Sydney Newman of ABC.

Newman had been born in Canada and began his professional life as a graphic artist. He then went on to produce films for the National Film Board of Canada, to become head of drama at CBC and then ABC, where he produced a highly successful series of plays every Sunday night, under the generic title *Armchair Theatre*, which attracted audiences of over fifteen million and were frequently in the Top Ten. They were the drama of the doorstep, for they examined the turning points of a society undergoing change; they looked too at such subject as strikes, misfits, and the working class; very different to the BBC's rather old-fashioned drawing-room comedies.

Greene believed that if this success in conjuring up plays which were both critically and popularly acclaimed could be transferred to the BBC, then they would become a potent weapon in the BBC's fight back against ITV.

Newman joined the BBC in December 1962. Greene then left him almost totally to his own devices, merely saying:

You've managed to collect writers like Harold Pinter, Alun Owen, Clive Exton, and Bill Naughton for your Armchair Theatre. They got their start on BBC Radio. I want you to get them back—and find all the new ones you can so that we can reinstate the BBC's reputation as the home of the best original playwrights in the country.

Newman himself observed later that he had come to Britain '. . . at a crucial time in 1958 when the seeds of *Look Back in Anger* were beginning to flower. I am proud that I played some part in the recognition that the working man was a fit subject for drama, and not just a comic foil in a play on middle class manners.' He described his job as 'sprinkling humus on the manure of dramatic production', and himself as a 'creative midwife'.

It did not take Newman particularly long to become dispirited with the staff he had inherited. They were just 'too bloody old'. The problem was how he would get rid of them and bring in new blood. The solution was provided by the emergence of BBC 2 which allowed him to extend his staff by forty per cent. He divided his department into series, serials and single plays and promoted young people like Ken Loach, brought in Tony Garnett and Roger Smith, recruited old friends from ABC and found new writers like Dennis Potter.

The shift in emphasis which this created was more than a move from the drawing room to the kitchen; it was a bus ride across town to the council estates and working-class slums, to peroxide hair, bags under the eyes, to real and meta-phorical violence, bad language and, above all, to manifest sexuality. The epitome of these developments was to be a series of plays contained under the generic title of *The Wednesday Play*, which were started by New-man in 1964 and which were a systematic effort to connect with real issues and real people. The problem was that the inevitable themes of violence, language and sex seemed to be the sum total of the lives of real people, some of whom did not like the image and equally inevitably began to pro-test.

Even before Newman had arrived, however, one of the issues with which he would have to deal had reared its head in a particularly sharp and, to Greene, especially annoying way. On September 11th, 1962 the BBC offered a TV adaptation of Graham Greene's novel *Stamboul Train*. The Director General and his brother were not best pleased with the production and said so in a rather forceful way. He wrote to Stuard Hood that:

> . . . the prolongation of the seduction scene was entirely wasteful and unnecessary. There have been a great many letters complaining of our recent plays and their preoc-cupation with what might be described as 'sex in the raw'. It is perfectly possible to defend scenes of this kind in late night plays when they are essential to the author's pur-pose. It is impossible to defend the treatment which titillates. It is essential that producers should be able to distinguish between the permissible and the impermiss-ible, or we shall lose the right to treat those subjects in adult fashion.

Arthur fforde's attitude was once more basically firm and supportive of the producer. In a reply to a viewer who had complained about *Stamboul Train*, he said:

225

You ask me to use my influence against the repetition of this sort of thing [the subject of sex] . . . influence is the right word. I felt when I was Headmaster of Rugby the same as I did when I was a boy there, that there is a kind of discipline which *can* prevent not only the wrong thing happening but anything happening. I feel that I have a responsibility for ensuring that producers in general have as large a sense of freedom for enterprise as they can be given if the programmes are to be lively. The obverse of this, of course, is that every so often someone makes a complete error of judgment, but I feel that is a risk that has to be taken.

Stamboul Train, along with a number of other plays, such as *The Weather in the Streets*, shown on August 20th, 1962, and *Summer Storm*, shown on August 24th, led to efforts to tighten up editorial control and in particular to ensure that the judgment of the individual producer was not the sole determinant.

The Chairman basically accepted Hugh Greene's idea that one had to give producers their head and that mistakes were, in fact, a sign of health, not of decay but this did not prevent senior management from engaging in the creative guidance of producers and seeking to minimise those mistakes. That certainly made sense since the BBC under fforde and Greene was trying to be adventurous and lively, not masochistic and self-destructive.

The difficulty which arose in 1962, however, and which began to loom large in drama, was that guidance to protect the integrity and professionalism of the output, became restraint for the sake of allaying the wrath of a conservative strand within British culture.

In October 1963 Newman was forced to send a stiff memo to the senior staff in Drama Group:

There is a directorial trend in our Group that's getting to be a bit of a bore. I am referring to scenes of men and women, married and unmarried, legitimate and illicit, who are found lying in bed together. Such a scene was in 'First Night's' *Guilty* last Sunday, *Maigret* last night, and 'Festival's' *The Duel* has one tonight. Complaints have come in. Viewers are pretty resilient about accepting such scenes, but a minority of the audience finds them offensive and some go as far as to say that they encourage immorality. While it is possible to explain away the occasional scene, when they turn up in rapid succession as they seem to be doing now, we are going to get into dead trouble. This is especially bad when such scenes are interpreted as being put into the show 'just for kicks' or to achieve an audience-getting opening.

Now no one wants to say 'thou shalt never show a man and a woman in bed together', so please let's be sensible about the whole question of sexual relations; otherwise somebody will be reduced to making such a commandment . . .

It was a memo as much written for Greene's eyes—Adam passed a copy on to him—as for Newman's employees. Greene was the immediate lightning rod for the reactions of the governors, and therefore needed to be able to reassure them that all was under control.

As criticism grew about TV drama from the BBC's own Advisory Council, as well as in letters of complaint, it became perfectly clear that the output of Newman's department was applying pressure along the fault line which divided, and continues to divide, British society. On the one hand were those who felt his drama was dealing with an area of life which was fresh, vital, troubled, perhaps alienated, certainly in need of understanding. On the other were those who believed that this area represented no more than the dregs of society and who were offended by its values, coarseness, sex, language, by its very difference. Through the intervention of Greene and Newman, the English shires had met Wigan pier, and the experience was not to the former's liking.

Obviously the problem of this collision of cultures would

not go away. Following a play called *Say Nothing* in February 1964, the governors' view of Newman and his department's output was becoming so aggressive that Adam suggested to Hood that he vet every single play.

Some of the governors had told Greene that not only was this particular play, *Say Nothing*, beyond the bounds of what was permissible on TV, but that in general there was 'something amiss' with current TV play policy. The immediate problem for both Newman and Greene was that producers in the Drama Department did not seem especially to care about any instructions from above. Adam was even becoming embarrassed about having to complain to Newman so much, with a fear that he might come to be seen as a narrow-minded prude: 'I am continually let down by directors whose obsession with a single act outruns prudence and taste.'

His problems, however, were only just beginning; the new series of single plays was due to start on October 28th, 1964 under a title, *The Wednesday Play*, which had been devised by Greene and Adam on the grounds that it was more neutral than the likes of *First Night* and *Festival*. With such powerful offerings as *Cathy Come Home*, this series emphasised the BBC's new reputation for dealing with a raw and difficult issues. It also further affirmed in some minds that Greene's BBC was out of control and desperately in need of a restraining hand. Newman himself described them as being 'gutsy, spontaneous, contemporary—plays that concentrated mainly on the here and now . . . our changing times'. He added, either bravely or naïvely:

It is one of those key series in which 'broadcasting must be most willing to make mistakes; or if it does not, it will make no discoveries' [Pilkington]. Mistakes draw criticism. Discoveries are uncomfortable. Both compel controversy. So on occasion does 'The Wednesday Play'. It would be surprising and disappointing if it did not.

The emergence of a revitalised and powerful TV drama did not meet raptures of applause from everyone within the Corporation. Members of current TV programmes became increasingly anxious that the plays, with their contemporary social and political issues, were treading on territory which was rightly the domain of news and current affairs. In this conflict can be seen some of the real genius of Hugh Greene. He had an intuitive ability not merely to stimulate and allow new ideas, but also to disturb the very forms of television. Thus, *TW3*, which had originally been thought of as an entertainment programme, was moved over to current affairs. Drama addressed issues which were clearly of concern to current affairs. In so doing, a tension was created between Tom Sloan, Head of Light Entertainment, Newman as Head of Drama, and Grace Wyndham Goldie as Head of Current Affairs output. The tension flowed in large part from Hugh Greene's tendency to show a lack of respect for existing patterns of programming and a great respect for a good idea. This may not have ensured inter-departmental harmony, but it did tend to guarantee creative development.

The BBC's attitude to drama production had, with considerable courage, raised the making of a mistake to the level of principle. Despite all the anxieties of the governors, the BBC retained a healthy concern with examining the confusion of values, the perplexities and ethical dilemmas of post-Suez British culture; it was concerned with breathing some life into the ethical and moral vacuum, which had emerged as the old order decayed, and a new one was undergoing a difficult birth. Because of Greene's inspiration, the Corporation had placed itself at the heart of a swirling culture. It did not ape or merely reflect, but led; not in any prescriptive sense of saying 'we should go this way or that', but by being the one force which could give visibility, clarity and coherence to new questions of value which so many, especially the young, were posing. That was, in essence, Hugh Greene's wish for the BBC and for Britain: know thyself. It went back to a desire to be honest about social, political and human truths. It went back to his feelings in

Berlin and, even earlier, at school, that a culture as much as an individual could so readily, and dangerously, live a lie. There was a revealing comment which he made at this time at a staff management course at Uplands near High Wycombe. He was asked what were his core beliefs:

My so-called central core would tend to be political and social rather than religious. My attitude in the Civil War, for instance? I'd have been an unhappy supporter of the King—or a Leveller. A core of scepticism and curiosity is just as important as a core of belief. At heart, I think I may be just a Berlin correspondent who wants to find out what is happening in the next street. To ask questions rather than enhance. I admit that this scepticism may indeed be a great lack in myself . . . The time may come when a very different type of person will have to carry on.

If he had a view of the creative and journalistic responsibilities of the BBC, did he have an equally developed view of its responsibilities to the audience? He *was* concerned about violence on TV, especially in children's programmes. He was certainly personally far more concerned with that than he was with sex on television, but then he passionately abhorred violence and was rather keen on sex. At this time, in 1964, his two boys by Elaine, Timothy and Christopher, were still young, and their viewing of Westerns, for example, occasionally caused him great concern. On more than one occasion he raised questions about *The Lone Ranger*, *Bronco*, and *Laramie*. One of his first acts when he came into office was to insist that a code of practice on violence in programmes be drawn up.

Codes or no codes, there were sections of the population who would never be happy. They were those sections for which the work of Hugh Greene's BBC was too rich a meal, too painful, too embarrassing, too threatening. On the morning of July 31st, 1963, Arthur fforde found on his desk a note from his secretary:

A Mrs Whitehouse phoned. She was extremely forceful and wants very much to come and see you 'about a very personal matter' ... She is in London for a Moral Rearmament Conference! She is a schoolteacher. So it looks as if she simply wants to talk with you further about the morals and standards, etc. of the BBC and its programmes.

fforde declined the offer to see her, but Greene began to take an interest in her activities. He saw a report of the inaugural meeting of the 'Clean Up TV' Campaign on May 5th, 1964 in Birmingham Town Hall. The report is a straightforward account of the arguments put forward by Whitehouse and her co-founder Norah Buckland, arguments with which we are by now familiar. *TW3* was attacked in particular, and Mary Whitehouse also said: 'We are told that the dramatists are portraying real life, but why concentrate on the kitchen sink when there are so many pleasant sitting rooms? We want plays that can be viewed by the entire family—plays that are wholesome.'

What caught Hugh Greene's eye, however, was that outside in the foyer, MRA literature was being distributed. That did it, as far as he was concerned. In the inter-war years, the evangelical Oxford Group, which became MRA in 1938, was thought by many people to have extreme right wing, and possibly neo-fascist, tendencies. Whitehouse herself, as it turned out, had been heavily involved with the group.

Greene saw Whitehouse as dangerous to freedom, tolerance and adventure:

I thought that Mrs Whitehouse was the sort of person who would have been at home in Nazi Germany or at home in Communist Russia. And that is the sort of thing which through all my early experience I have learnt to hate. I saw Mrs Whitehouse as a sign of an unattractive degree of filthy madness in this country as shown later in such things as the National Front. Even though I am sure that

Mrs Whitehouse herself would disown the National Front, they would tend to approve of her.

To Roy Shaw, who had written suggesting that they do a counter-assault on what he described as 'dark forces', Hugh Greene replied: 'One has the feeling that people who would be the potential supporters of a Nazi régime in this country have found a focus in Mrs Whitehouse, even if she is not as bad as all that.' He declined the suggestion of a programme about her on the grounds that she thrived on such publicity.

Equally, Mrs Whitehouse was no fan of Hugh Greene. In her personal demonology he was Old Nick himself: she observed that 'If you were to ask me to name the one man who more than anybody else has been responsible for the moral collapse in this country I would name Greene'. She believed that he self-consciously, and with great cunning, set out to use his position in the BBC to attack and undermine authority, the family, Parliament, the police, the Church.

Major changes were taking place in British society in the 1960s: Greene and Whitehouse epitomised two areas where controversy over change was strong. He wished to modernise a national cultural institution; she wished to reassert old-fashioned Christian values which she felt were losing their grip. The conflict between them was fought out in a series of symbolic battles over attitudes to be taken towards sex and violence. There was no possibility of compromise, no common ground. She wanted broadcasting to be used for moral uplift: he wanted it to scan the national mood.

But it would be wrong if this suggested that Greene was issuing fighting orders or influencing programmes in depth, for that was not Greene's style. He liked to nudge things along through indirect asides. Two programmes he was personally responsible for putting on the air were *Perry Mason* and *Songs of Praise*. He was tipped off about the former while having drinks with Ian Fleming who had seen the series in America. Greene discovered that both the BBC and ITV programme buyers had turned down the series. He asked to see an edition, loved it, and issued instructions that the whole series should be bought. The latter emerged from a conversation with Megan Lloyd George. Both of these programmes became considerable popular successes, but they hardly reflect the image of a gung-ho Director General laying waste to traditional values.

Greene's public image was that of a radical liberal executive. It was that image which was creating the storms of criticism which broke from time to time. Greene was nevertheless determined to press on. This could be seen in the continuing success and support for *Steptoe and Son*, which had begun in June 1962, and which, despite its allegedly foul language, drew huge audiences. It was also evidenced in the promised reappearance on November 13th, 1964 of the successor to *That Was The Week That Was*, which was to be called *Not So Much A Programme, More A Way Of Life*. Donald Baverstock recalls being summoned to a governors' meeting to discuss this new project. It was made clear to him that the governors hoped that it would not cause them the problems which its illustrious predecessor had. They then wished him well. On the way out Baverstock thanked them for their time and added with intended sarcasm: 'You can rest assured that the brakes are firmly on. All we need to do now is invent the engine.'

Four weeks after the demise of *TW3* and while drama was still causing controversy, on January 29th, 1964 Arthur fforde, the Chairman of the BBC, had retired. His had been a quiet public presence, almost subdued, always leaving the limelight to his Director General. These really had been Hugh Greene's years, and yet a chief executive of the BBC needs to have a working relationship with his Chairman if only because the latter embodies the total constitutional power and authority of the organisation. For Hugh Greene, fforde had been a supporter, an advocate, a friend. With the departure of fforde, who had guided and defended him, the era of Pilkington came to an end. The BBC was no longer under scrutiny; approved, licensed and chartered anew, it stood proud and powerful under Greene.

On his last day in office, fforde and Greene went to pay a

farewell visit to Rab Butler, to talk about possible candidates for the new Chairman. During the course of the discussion, Hugh Greene was delighted to hear Arthur fforde say that it was most important to have someone who would work well with Hugh, which was music to his ears. They set off back together in a taxi which would go first to the BBC and then on to the railway station to take fforde away from the BBC for ever. When they arrived at Broadcasting House, Hugh Greene got out and waved the taxi away. His face was streaked with tears. fforde was one of the few men whom Hugh Greene had ever come to love: he would be lonely without him. The Chairman had been an enormous support for this licensed gadfly, this *enfant terrible*, who had excited the BBC and its audience in ways which had never happened before. As Greene well knew, it could not have happened without fforde. This quiet reflective man, probably the greatest Chairman the BBC ever had, is an important, even key part of the history of these early years, and his departure marked the beginning of the end of the so-called Greene years.

fforde's attitude was an important reason why these first three or four years were so successful for the BBC in general and for Hugh Greene in particular. On the face of it the Greene-fforde partnership was an implausible one. On the one hand, the agnostic journalist; on the other, the deeply religious ex-public school headmaster. Perhaps even more paradoxical is that this deeply religious man was actively leading and encouraging an organisation which was increasingly under attack from different directions for being irreligious, radical, a disruptive force within the community.

An important clue to his thinking, and therefore an important clue to the nature of these years, lies in a strange little booklet which fforde produced in 1963. It was called 'What is Broadcasting About?' and was printed privately in an edition of 400. In this he tried to develop a theological context for what was happening within the BBC. The booklet is on first reading impenetrably obscure. On second reading what becomes clear is that it is fforde's attempt to justify the way in which the BBC had moved under Hugh Greene, and to harmonise its emergent agnostic and humanistic ethos with a more ancient view of the nature of religious experience.

In his pamphlet fforde made it clear that he welcomed change as long as it was not mindless change: 'By its nature broadcasting must be in a constant and sensitive relationship with the moral condition of society.' That moral condition was undergoing an important change as standards which had been for so long, for so many people, successful route maps, were being re-drafted, something which, however, he thought was 'not in itself regrettable'. What concerned him was whether or not the standards which would replace them were worthy, even if they were secular rather than religious.

fforde's concern is slap bang in the middle of the haunting debate which has formed the core of Western thought this century: can one develop and live by a humanistic philosophy which is of its nature not dependent on, or sustained by, an external deified source of authority?

fforde felt that the moral establishment had failed society and that perhaps broadcasting was one way in which that failure could be rectified. He was, of course, aware that the BBC was, and would continue to be, increasingly under siege. That was a result of its impact, but so long as the BBC retained its integrity, then in his eyes it need not worry. It must however maintain the correct balance between social responsibilities and creative freedom. Perhaps the single most powerful explanation why he was such a keen supporter of Hugh Greene was that he believed that it:

. . . is of cardinal importance that everyone in a position of responsibility should be ready to set himself or herself the duty of assuring, to those creative members of the BBC staff, who must take the daily, hourly, and even instantaneous decisions . . . that measure of freedom, independence and élan without which the arts do not flourish.

235

Greene had never really developed any particularly close and binding attachments. There were friends but not really very close friends. What he seems to have searched for in people was not so much friendship as someone to respect and to love, perhaps in the way that one respects or loves a parent. In talking to people who know him, it is not, on the whole, the intensity of the relationship which is commented upon, but the lack of intensity. If one goes down the roll call of his friends and acquaintances, it is almost impossible to find someone for whom he really cared, other than, at certain moments, for his wives.

That is why the sight of Hugh Greene outside Broadcasting House with a tear-streaked face was so extraordinary. Such a reaction to the departure of someone who was not a lover was almost unknown to him. He himself did not and does not know what the roots of that affection-cum-love for fforde actually were. At one level it was undoubtedly the sheer sense of calm and confidence which fforde extended. It was not just respect for fforde which mattered; it was the sense of belonging and deep friendship which fforde's manner and personality had been able to create in Hugh Greene. It was also a relationship which coincided with good years, and the departure of the Chairman may have sounded off an alarm bell in some recess of the mind. fforde had been a great support, but he was also attractive because he represented an emotional stability and certainty which Hugh Greene lacked. At the time of fforde's departure Hugh Greene's second marriage was not prospering, and so he was faced once more with domestic insecurity, and all the problems which would flow from having two young boys to care for. fforde was the opposite: calm, deeply religious, and therefore morally certain, dignified with the utmost rectitude but, most of all, happily and securely married. The nuances of the relationship had never been visible, his departure brought them to the surface—hence the tears on the pavement.

While a successor to fforde was being sought by the government, the temporary Chairman was Sir James Duff.

The press was now full of stories of how the government was looking for a new strong man who would be able to curb Greene. Hugh was not, however, totally out of favour, and on January 1st, 1964 it was announced that he had been made a Knight Commander of St Michael and St George. The *Evening Standard* welcomed the award: 'He is a man of fine character, and good judgment and is well capable of defending himself against the inevitable attack which his bold policies have incurred. There has been a revolution in broadcasting and TV since he took over in 1960.'

Rumours, however, were rife that the government was out to stop him being an effective, powerful Director General. On March 3rd, 1964 the *Daily Express* carried a report that the government felt that he was 'substantially too big for his dainty boots', and that he was responsible for allowing 'much of the sex, sin and sadism' which they were alleging had crept into the BBC's output. The Postmaster General, Reg Bevins, and his assistant Ray Mawby, the report continued, were looking for someone who would 'cut him down to size . . . a tough tycoon who can take over the Chairmanship of the BBC's Board of Governors next summer and wrest some of the levers back from Sir Hugh'. Other newspapers carried headlines such as 'Curbing Greene's Power', and 'Chairman of Stature for the BBC Sought'. *The Guardian* suggested that the aim was to have an executive chairman with the Director General's office becoming mainly administrative.

Before Greene's arrival, the Director General had left detailed concern to his deputies and had fulfilled the role of umpire, maintaining a certain elevated detachment from the daily grind of making programme decisions. But Greene, as an old journalist with an obvious wish to be seen to be closely involved with news, current affairs and new ventures such as *TW3*, had eschewed such an Olympian stance. Instead, he had abolished his old post of DNCA and split the supervision of news and current affairs into two parts: one chaired by a subordinate ENCA, and the other, more powerful, section, in which important policy decisions were discussed, chaired

237

by himself. As a result, by 1964 the role of umpire was now more likely to fall upon the governors.

This may not have mattered under fforde but, at the beginning of April 1964, it was announced that the new chairman of the BBC would be Lord Normanbrook, former secretary to the Cabinet and head of the civil service. In party terms he was a neutral mandarin and therefore not someone whose appointment would cause a row. He was, however, like most of the governors, intellectually and personally very different from his Director General. Greene was the gadfly, Normanbrook the tough, independent man whose life had been devoted to serving the state.

15

The arrival of Lord Normanbrook as the new chairman of the BBC in the middle of Hugh Greene's term of office is perhaps a good moment to look at some of Greene's attitudes after five years as Director General. In particular it might be opportune to single out the main question facing Greene and the BBC, which the various controversies of the first four years had sharply illustrated: what should be the balance between the need for creative freedom and a wider social responsibility.

On a snowy morning in Rome on February 9th, 1965 he tried to resolve the dilemma in a speech entitled 'The Conscience of the Programme Director.'

It was an odd, rather amusing occasion. He arrived in Rome on the 8th. On the morning of the 9th, he drew the curtains of his hotel room to find Rome blanketed with a thick duvet of snow. In the night the city had had its heaviest snowfall for two centuries. The hall in which he was to address the International Catholic Association for Radio and TV was half an hour's drive away. His car failed to turn up and he was taken there by a private taxi driver. The journey was not helped by the fact that the Rome authorities had decided that it would be a good idea to clear the snow by hosing the streets down with water. The car slithered and lurched to its destination, and he was an hour late. This did not matter greatly since the only other person there was—a blessing—the barman. Greene sat down to await his hosts and audience, and comforted himself with large amounts of coffee liberally laced with brandy. Eventually the audience drifted in until the hall was filled with a throng of priests from around the globe. It was suggested, after more coffee and brandy, that he should start. Alas, the interpreters were not there. A wait. More liquid nourishment. The interpreters arrived. Hugh Greene stood up to deliver his address. He had been speaking for about a minute when the lights went out, and the interpreting equipment fell silent. Candles were produced and he proceeded to deliver the rest of the speech without an interpreter in the candlelight and the aroma of liquor, much to the annoyance of the French priests who thought it was all a plot against the glory of France.

The idea for the address had been Father Agnellus Andrews', the BBC's Roman Catholic adviser. The major task of preparing the preliminary draft had been given to another Catholic, Charles Curran, the Secretary of the BBC, with assistance from Kenneth Lamb. He began by saying that the duty of the broadcaster was to examine views and opinions within society from a position of healthy scepticism, and to do so from a position of freedom from the state. How, he asked, was 'freedom' interpreted and used:

We do not see this freedom as total licence. We have (and believe strongly in) editorial control. Producers of individual programmes are not simply allowed to do whatever they like. Lines must be drawn somewhere.

But, in an operation as diverse in its output as broadcasting, the only sure way of exercising control—here we come to one of my most strongly held personal convictions—is to proceed by persuasion and not by written directives; by encouraging the programme staff immediately responsible to apply their judgment to particular problems, within a framework of general guidance arising from the continuing discussion of individual programmes by themselves, by their seniors and, when necessary, by the board of governors. In my view there is nothing to be achieved by coercion or censorship, whether from inside the Corporation or from outside—nothing, that is, except the frustration of creative people who can achieve far more by positive stimulation of their ideas in an atmosphere of freedom.

We have to resist attempts at censorship. As Professor Hoggart has noted recently, these attempts at censorship come not merely from what he describes as the old 'Guardians' (senior clergy, writers of leading articles in newspapers, presidents of national voluntary organisations) who like to think of themselves as upholders of cultural standards although, in many cases, they lack the qualities of intellect and imagination to justify that claim.

The attempts at censorship come nowadays also from groups—Hoggart calls them the 'new Populists', one might call them the 'new Puritans'—which do not claim to be 'Guardians' but claim to speak for 'ordinary, decent people' and claim to be 'forced to take a stand against' what they arbitrarily call unnecessary dirt, gratuitous sex, excessive violence—and so on. These 'new Populists' will attack whatever does not underwrite a set of prior assumptions, assumptions which are anti-intellectual and unimaginative. Superficially this seems to be and likes to think of itself as a 'grass-roots' movement. In practice it can threaten a dangerous form of censorship—censorship which works by causing artists and writers not to take risks, not to undertake those adventures of the spirit which must be at the heart of every truly new creative work.

Such a censorship to my mind is the more to be condemned when we remember that, historically, the greatest risks have attached to the maintenance of what is right and honourable and true. Truth for ever on the scaffold, wrong for ever on the throne . . .

I believe that broadcasters have a duty not to be diverted by arguments in favour of what is, in fact, disguised censorship. I believe we have a duty to take account of the changes in society, to be ahead of public opinion, rather than always to wait upon it. I believe that great broadcasting organisations, with their immense powers of patronage for writers and artists, should not neglect to cultivate young writers who may, by many, be considered 'too advanced' or 'shocking'.

To Greene, therefore, the need to foster and protect creativity was paramount, overriding any responsibility to his audience. He could not, of course, forget the argument that broadcasting had access to every home, to an audience of all ages and varying degrees of sophistication. But responsibility for deciding what they watched belonged to the audience not to the BBC: programmes must be planned on the assumption that the audience was capable of reasonable behaviour, the exercise of intelligence and choice. He then added, or rather Curran had included in the draft for him:

> If the audience is to be considered as it really is—as a series of individual minds (each with its own claim to enlightenment, each of different capacity and interests) and not as that statistical abstraction the 'mass' audience —then it would seem to me that no subject—no subject whatever—can be excluded from the range of broadcasting simply for being what it is. The questions which we must face are those of identifying the times and the circumstances in which we may expect to find the intended audiences for a given programme.

Of the last two sentences Curran thought he was getting 'very near to the edge of what Hugh would accept—he thought it was too conformist by committing him too far towards a specific discipline.' Charles Curran specifically mentioned drafting one of the most quoted paragraphs:

> Relevance is the key—relevance to the audience, and to the tide of opinion in society. Outrage is wrong. Shock may be good. Provocation can be healthy and indeed socially imperative. These are issues to which the broadcaster must apply his conscience. But treatment of the subject, once chosen, demands the most careful assessment of the reasonable limits of tolerance in the audience,

if there is any likelihood of these limits being tested by the manner of presentation of the material. As I have said, however, no subject is (for me) excluded simply for what it is.

The original Curran draft read: 'shock may not be good'. Hugh Greene eliminated the 'not'.

Everything he was proposing rested, he continued, on the need to be 'truly independent' because without that one could not be truthful, accurate, impartial. Journalists were important because they were vessels of truth and without truth lay evil and repression. At such moments his mind slipped back to the Berlin years. There lay an abominable truth resting on a bedrock of deceit and self-delusion.

Truth for him was like an endangered species that one needed not only to try to breed, but where necessary to protect. He had talked of impartiality, but there were in his mind—and here the memory of Berlin came bursting in —certain moral truths about which one could not be impartial without risking their ultimate obliteration:

> But although in the day-to-day issues of public life the BBC does try to attain the highest standards of impartiality, there are some respects in which it is not neutral, unbiased or impartial. That is, where there are clashes for and against the basic moral values—truthfulness, justice, freedom, compassion, tolerance.
>
> Nor do I believe that we should be impartial about certain things like racialism, or extreme forms of political belief. Being too good 'democrats' in these matters could open the way to the destruction of democracy itself. I believe a healthy democracy does not evade decisions about what it can never allow if it is to survive.

These two paragraphs were his and his alone. In fact, Curran, who was playing such a vital role, profoundly disagreed with Greene's sentiments here.

The message was clear and courageous: if one did not have

an atmosphere of freedom and tolerance within which producers could work, then one would have a deathbed for
culture.

The speech received wide coverage. In particular,
Greene's words were specifically attacked by the General
Assembly of the Church of Scotland, on the grounds that it
espoused a decadent morality and was therefore a threat to
'democracy and society'. In March two MPs, James Dance
and Sir Leslie Thomas, called on Greene to resign. Mary
Whitehouse was becoming more and more vocal and well
known in her condemnation of Greene. In June there was a
headline in *The Telegraph* 'BBC attacked by "Fed-up" Tory
MPs'.

What had really miffed his opponents, however, was his
bold claim that any broadcasting organisation worth its salt
had to be allowed to make mistakes. Most people spend their
lives explaining away their mistakes—they did not happen,
they will not happen again, they were a momentary lapse.
The ego of the ordinary man finds it difficult to accept that he
has made a mistake. To do so would be to chip away at an
already fragile psyche. There was a further twist in the screw
for Greene's opponents. They were miffed, not just because
he had said that the BBC must be allowed to make what,
after the event, were recognised as mistakes. They wanted
him to accept something which was far more exacting—that
the BBC would not make what other people, judging before
the event, would regard as mistakes. The problem with that
in the first instance lay in the very real moral difficulty of
trying to mould the decisions of one's own conscience
according to the dictates of another's prescriptions. The
second was the more overtly practical problem of establishing any agreed set of standards.

'Standards' it could be argued could be derived from
common sense, that assumed accumulation of the wisdom of
ages. The problem here was that common sense itself, by its
nature, was constantly changing. It was also shot through
with contradictions and profound vagueness. If there was no
growth, no change, no development of thought, then this

244

cumulative wisdom would become no more than a codifica-
tion of precedent—and all precedent in the end becomes
hide-bound. It takes, therefore, a deliberate break with the
past to restore innovation to its proper place. Hugh Greene
told a meeting at Kings' College on the December 3rd, 1965:

> If nobody is pursuing new thoughts, if nobody is breaking
> yesterday's precedents, because they do not suit today's
> needs, then common sense will soon cease to mean any-
> thing worthwhile. It is not, in these terms, a useful stan-
> dard of judgment for broadcasters, because it derives
> entirely from what is already being done. It has no aspira-
> tion for the future, no forward-looking perspective.

Hugh Greene viewed broadcasting as a process of trial and
error, in which the broadcaster moved out from the heartland of his society while drawing his purpose, ideas and
strength from that heartland. Successfully achieved—even
via its 'mistakes'—it tugs that heartland along with it.
Where a programme practice threatened harm, that then
was the point where one drew the line and changed or
inhibited that practice.

As an example of what he called 'the wrong subject for the
time', he refused to allow *Panorama* to do a constituency
survey of Smethwick during the run up to the General
Election of 1964 because it could not have been accomplished without raising the question of immigration, which
he felt was damaging to the public interest.

His view of the nature of 'mistakes' was clear and powerful:

> Mistakes are never justified. They may be excusable. The
> circumstances which give rise to them may be understand-
> able. And the motives which lead to those circumstances
> may be laudable. But error in itself is something to regret.
> The pride which we take in our freedom to make an
> occasional mistake is grounded in the claim that our
> mistakes are made in the course of our efforts to broaden

the range of artistic experience, or to stretch the boundaries of thought and perception, either for ourselves or for our audiences.

In this philosophically prudent year of the new chairmanship, 1965, one sees Hugh Greene grappling with the key problem: how does one envisage, let alone define, the moral responsibility of an abstract notion such as broadcasting culture. An old adage said, 'A public corporation has neither a bottom to kick nor a conscience to prick.' In *The Listener* in September 1965 Christopher Driver wrote: 'A duty is something which one is not bound to perform except in some moral sense. One consults one's conscience, not a rule book, before deciding where one's duty lies, and whether or not to perform it. The BBC does not have duties because it is far too amorphous to have a conscience.' If the BBC were not a person, except in the legal sense of being a Corporate person, then it could have no personal conscience. How then would it select its moral imperatives?

The Corporation, however, did have flesh and blood in the form of the governors who, in law, were the BBC. They in turn employed another person, the Director General. Wherever the search was for a conscience and for a set of moral imperatives, for a way of making decisions that were not piecemeal but rooted in some coherent set of thoughts, it became inevitable that the well from which these would be drawn would be the individual and collective conscience of the governors plus the Director General. The extent of tension and dynamic within the BBC would thus depend upon the gap in thought between the Director General and the governors.

It was constitutionally perfectly proper for policy and programme decisions to come occasionally from the governors for they were there to be made use of; the Director General was expected to draw upon their maturity, wisdom and judgment as 'trustees of the public interest'.

But snags would arise when a Director General wished to 'broaden the range of artistic experience' or 'stretch the boundaries of thought and perception' in a way in which the governors disapproved. If the governors said they did not want such programmes they would be in head-on collision with their own Director General. What would happen then? Even if the governors tried to make no moral judgments, but let a hundred flowers bloom for a while, might they not be tempted in the end to insist upon weeding the garden?

Hugh Greene was well aware of the dangers of such a clash with his governing body: it was to avoid such disagreement that he had withdrawn *TW3*. Indeed, it was central to his whole view of the BBC that there should be an atmosphere of trust and confidence between the DG and the board. But he was equally ready to do battle over his right to let his programme producers experiment with daring. A confrontation therefore looked inevitable.

Under Arthur fforde there had been problems over specific programme decisions but the general atmosphere of trust and confidence had been good. Now Greene had to build up a new relationship with another personality at the very moment when he felt ebullient, experienced and firmly in the saddle.

Given Greene's recognition of the power of the governing board, it had already occurred to him, not surprisingly, that he might be able to influence its composition. In January 1961 he wrote to the BBC's Controller, Midland Region:

When I was in Birmingham I mentioned the possibility that we might be interested in suggestions from you for possible Labour ladies for the board of governors. I should now like to ask you definitely to get down to this and consider whether you have any good candidates. What one would ideally want would be a sensible, intelligent, down-to-earth person with working class roots and preferably a trades union background. The absence of bees in bonnets would be an advantage.

On July 1st, 1962, Dame Anne Godwin, former Chairwoman of the TUC, was appointed. On another occasion he wrote to Sir John Nicholls in the Foreign Office suggesting that both he and Normanbrook thought Ralph Murray's nomination would be an excellent idea: 'Unfortunately we don't choose our own governors, but we are sometimes consulted. If you managed to get Ralph Murray's name fed into the Foreign Office machine and we were asked about it, we should give it warm support. It is very much better that the original suggestion should come from you.' This was written in July, 1966. Sir Ralph Murray became a governor on October 1st, 1967.

To have some governors on his side was a great help if it came to a vote of confidence, but much more important was to be on good terms with Normanbrook. Greene kept in close touch with him through regular weekly meetings. Their offices were linked by a secretarial pool which they shared and Normanbrook went out of his way to tell Greene of anything important which was said. Greene, in his turn, endeavoured to be as open as possible with the governors, even if this might be to his detriment. At one governors' meeting he was just completing his report, when his secretary came with a note. This confirmed that an interview had been arranged with Baldur von Schirach, the former Nazi Youth leader who had just been released from Spandau. Greene did not regard this as a matter for the board even though he himself rather looked forward to hearing Schirach. He decided that he would inform them in case they also wished to watch it. All hell broke loose, as several governors, including Normanbrook, protested vehemently at the idea. Two possible allies of Greene, Lusty and Glanmor Williams, were absent. Normanbrook then did something which was very unusual; he took a head count. A majority were in favour of the item being scrapped. The governors, to Greene's horror, fury and amazement had spoken, and von Schirach would not be appearing on the BBC. He had the painful task of telling the programme people that the interview was off—pain which was increased by the protocol that prevented him from informing them that it had been the governors' decision and not his. The follow-

Fancy dress party: Graham standing second from left, Hugh second from right. In background Molly, mother, father and Raymond, with cousins at The Hall. *c.* 1915

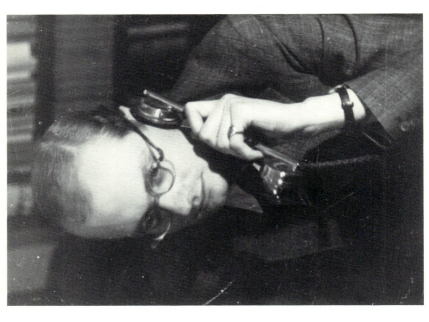

Berlin Press Card when Chief Correspondent of
The Daily Telegraph

Telephoning in Berlin office in Unter den Linden

ing day he informed Normanbrook that he had never been as close to resignation in his life. He felt especially grieved because he had thought that the interview would have been worthwhile despite his own passionate feelings against Nazism. Normanbrook was phlegmatic and merely said—demonstrating his own powerful personality—'It's your own bloody fault, you shouldn't have mentioned it.'

It was a rare moment of discord, if not a rare moment of the governors exerting their authority. The head counting was most unusual. Hugh Greene could recall only two occasions under fforde when a vote had been taken: on proposals that starting prices should be given on TV when they were covering races, and that liquor advertisements should be allowed in the *Radio Times* as well as *The Listener*, where they already appeared. On both occasions two governors had been opposed to changes in the policy and fforde, even though the majority was in favour of change, had said, 'Two against is too many.' Later, when one of the two dissenting governors had left, the issue was raised once more, a vote taken and only one was now against. fforde extended his aphorism of several months back when he observed, 'One against is too few'. The policies were therefore changed in a rather startling, if now seemingly trivial, example of the lengths to which the governors went to maintain their sense of cohesiveness.

Greene believed that it was essential that the governors remember that they were governors and not the executive; that 'to use the definition of the functions of the monarchy' they should be mainly advising, encouraging and warning, and not interfering. It was especially important—and here he says he always felt totally supported by fforde and Normanbrook—that the board should not see programmes before they went out; their duties, and it was very much in the BBC tradition, must be retrospective. This made sense because if they did view programmes which were then broadcast and became the source of controversy, they would possibly have to sit in judgment on their own decision. That in turn could well lead to an embarrassing situation in which the problematic logic of their position became transparent and was called into question.

Normanbrook himself had begun to consider this relationship between the governors and the DG as soon as he took office. In a lecture which he gave in 1965, he argued that the ultimate level of decisions 'even executive decisions on matters of first importance' lay with the board of governors, and in certain instances, with the Chairman acting under the authority vested in him by the board. He added an important caveat to this however, when he said that this was the ultimate point of reference; in practice it was very difficult to say where the making of policy ended and its execution began. He also admitted that the control which the governors exercise 'is mainly by retrospective review—by comment, whether praise or blame, after the event'. Such a system was, he said, the only viable and wise way in which the governors could work.

Soon after taking office, Normanbrook began to be increasingly worried about Hugh Greene's impact on those outside the Corporation. There is absolutely no evidence to suggest personal animosity, nor is there any sign of a desire to remove Greene in any way, but Normanbrook clearly feared that forces of antagonism were building up against Greene which might eventually become overwhelming.

Many of Greene's senior colleagues also began to think that Hugh Greene was creating too many waves. Rocking the boat might not have been too dangerous on the placid waters of the Macmillan lake, but in the rather choppier waters of the Wilson years it could drown them all. Charles Curran was Secretary to the BBC at this time and welcomed Greene's robust defence of the BBC's independence, but he felt that this could have been achieved without the problems which seemed to follow in the DG's wake. Curran admired Greene's anti-establishment impishness but was worried by his lack of concern for outside groups and his belief that the job of the BBC was to tread on toes.

Shortly before he died, Curran described what he termed

Hugh Greene's 'freewheeling and not particularly caring' attitude towards his job. He also observed that Normanbrook took this view and had made it clear to Curran that he thought Greene should go. Normanbrook apparently offered three grounds for this: Greene was becoming tired; he no longer especially 'cared'; and he had an excessive attachment to libertarianism. By 1966 Normanbrook, according to Curran, had decided that Hugh Greene should be removed 'but he wanted to have it done with dignity and without Hugh Greene losing face'. His problem was to find the right circumstances. These circumstances emerged, with black irony, on Normanbrook's own death.

It must be stated that there is absolutely no hard evidence that Normanbrook actually held these views: indeed Hugh Greene himself strongly denies this. There is however another piece of evidence: Glanmor Williams had just been appointed national governor for Wales in 1965, and he recalled that at one of the first dinners he attended, other governors heatedly argued that the BBC had become too extreme, that it had lost its sense of responsibility and that Greene had lost control of 'his wildmen'. Some of Greene's most senior colleagues working within Broadcasting House argue that if Normanbrook had not died in 1967 then a conflict would inevitably have arisen between the two men. That Greene did not recognise the trend of the Chairman's thinking was, again according to Curran, entirely predictable 'even if Normanbrook had dropped a hint, Hugh probably wouldn't have realised it, and this was because of a kind of self-deception rooted in the fact that he couldn't afford to recognise it—quite literally'. Curran was implying here that Greene could not leave the BBC for financial reasons. Greene certainly had the education of his two children from his marriage to Elaine, Christopher and Timothy, to consider. In 1964 he had also bought a house in the country, at Cockfield in Suffolk. His income was therefore well stretched, but it would be wrong to emphasise this as a major problem.

Far more significant was the emergence of Normanbrook

as a strong-willed and determined Chairman. Nothing better demonstrates this than the decision to ban *The War Game*.

Peter Watkins had already made a brilliant debut with *Culloden*. In the autumn of 1963, whilst he was working in the documentary section of Talks under Huw Wheldon, he asked if he might make an imaginative reconstruction of the impact of a nuclear attack on Britain. Wheldon commended this idea to Kenneth Adam, Director of BBC Television: 'Other factors apart I am anxious to keep Watkins; and to do so I must certainly let him get this film out of his system'. He went on to say that he had already discussed the project several times with Grace Wyndham Goldie 'who thinks that the film should be made, on the grounds that, so long as there is no security risk and the facts are authentic, the people should be trusted with the truth'. Wheldon was, he said, not making the recommendation without 'the greatest anxiety' and admitted that anyhow the decision about the programme could only be made once they had had a chance to see it.

Eventually the Chairman decided, most unusually, to take soundings in Whitehall and to consult various civil servants before making any recommendations. He feared that showing the film on TV might damage the national interest, might have a significant effect on public attitudes towards the policy of the nuclear deterrent and might inadvertently be considered by some to seem as if the BBC was lending support to CND.

Some time between November 5th and 24th a basic decision not to show the film crystallised, as 'the effect of the film has been judged by the BBC to be too horrifying for the medium of broadcast.' It is impossible to discover who made the specific decision or what the exact arguments were because no written records of the decision itself, or who made it, exist. But there is no question that the decision was a BBC one and that Normanbrook was closely involved.

Hugh Greene undoubtedly thought the programme chillingly horrific. He also saw which way the wind was blowing from Normanbrook's office. It was clearly not worth Greene's while to go to the wall in confrontation with the Chairman over a programme which, though brilliant, made him doubt whether the national psyche would stand the experience. Therefore he said, no, we will not show this film and I have decided that because I consider it too horrific, as do many of my colleagues. He put forward the most publicly acceptable reason for doing something which he knew he would, given the Chairman's attitudes, have had to do anyway. The situation parallels closely the end of *TW3*, when it was announced publicly by the BBC that the programme was being removed because of the forthcoming election when in fact the true reason was that given the attitudes of certain governors it was becoming more trouble than it was worth.

To many eyes the decision not to show *The War Game* was unfortunate; it was an issue over which Hugh Greene should have fought. Tactically, to ban it may well have been the right thing to do. Strategically it was wrong, not only because it negated an important debate, but because it illustrated the way in which an interventionist Chairman could shape the direction of the BBC and prevail over a Director General who on other occasions had shown himself wonderfully supportive of the purpose of public service broadcasting—the provision of the best programmes available which did not pander to partial political interests and viewpoints. It also demonstrated the enormous problems which arise when a talented member of staff of a public service organisation focuses his abilities in the direction of difficult, contemporary, social and political issues. He is immediately placed at the juncture of the broadcasting world and the political world. Unfortunately for Watkins the two worlds met during Normanbrook's chairmanship on the third floor of Broadcasting House: the Greeks were already within the walls.

There were other developments in 1965 which suggested that Greene's ·BBC was changing, and not for the better.

Once more they concerned the Welsh wizard, Donald Baverstock.

Baverstock had been promoted to Chief of Programmes BBC1 in January 1963; he had, therefore, overseen years of success and controversy. *Steptoe, TW3, Z Cars*, drama were all hugely successful, and highly controversial. Something, however, had begun to go wrong with the audience ratings, and by the end of 1964, ITV once more seemed to be gaining the upper hand. In charge of the mercurial Baverstock was a man the *Observer* described as 'an individualist, with a reflective and profound mind, who likes to do things on his own,' Stuart Hood, the Controller of Programmes, TV.

Throughout 1964 divisions and tensions had begun to emerge in Television Centre. There was a power struggle which centred round the personalities of Donald Baverstock and the men who were in charge of the most important output departments, Sydney Newman, Head of Drama, and Tom Sloan, Head of Light Entertainment. Sloan had been a vociferous critic of *TW3*. He also represented that area of TV which Baverstock, with his more didactic, journalistic, quizzical background, held in some contempt.

Baverstock was an impatient man, full of ideas, who tended to collide with those who stood in his way. Newman and Sloan were not going to be bullied by anyone. Hood was caught in the middle and desperately tried to assert his authority and restore some sense of peace. It was clearly too much and in June 1964 Hood resigned. The immediate pretext was a row over who should control adult educational TV. The reality seems to have been the broader problem of controlling the barons of TV. One morning Hood slipped a note under the door of Kenneth Adam, the Director of TV, and slipped out of the BBC—a sad gesture, much regretted by Greene, from a man whose career he had done so much to further.

Greene decided that Adam would take on the duties which Hood had previously done until a suitable replacement could be found. The net effect of this was to create further tensions between Baverstock, Newman and Sloan by removing any kind of buffer between them. This was exacerbated when Baverstock, conscious of BBC 1's falling audience, wanted to switch the emphasis of drama from the rather difficult single play to serials. Newman was not having that, he went to Kenneth Adam to say that he could not work with Baverstock; he would rather leave. Suddenly at the beginning of 1965 Greene was faced with what was widely referred to as 'the Baverstock problem'. To add to Greene's troubles, BBC 2 had had a disastrous start and something clearly had to be done to change its fortunes.

A solution which would have made sense would have been to swop Baverstock and Peacock around because BBC 2 required inventiveness, drive and innovation if it was to make its mark. Baverstock had more of those qualities than anyone else in broadcasting. Peacock would also have been more suited to the needs of BBC 1. But what was also beginning to occur to Greene and Adam was that the man for the job of Controller of Programmes was Huw Wheldon. However, Wheldon informed them that he would only be interested if Baverstock was looked after. The problem was that Baverstock refused to move over to BBC 2, seeing it as an insult to be asked to take over the ailing, junior partner.

At the end of February, Greene called Baverstock into his office and offered him three options: he could head a new unit, working directly to Wheldon, which would devise ideas for programmes; he could run the Paris office, or he could go on a trip around the world. The options were the BBC's version of exit.

On February 25th the news broke that Baverstock—who at the time was on holiday in France, thinking through the options—had lost his job as Chief of Programmes, BBC 1. The news also broke that Wheldon would be the new Controller of Programmes, TV.

On his return Baverstock informed Greene that he would be resigning from the BBC. With him went Alasdair Milne, who was very tired from the years with *Tonight* and *TW3*, and who also felt that Baverstock had been badly treated. Milne rightly felt that things had begun to go wrong for Baverstock when he left the world of Talks, where he had been among friends whose very presence sharpened his intellectual contribution and muted his combative character.

Certainly the aggressively questioning world of Talks suited Baverstock. The more pragmatic, political world of institutional politics did not, and that really was something Hugh Greene should have seen. Baverstock's gift was not executive but creative. He had an uncanny ability to devise programmes which engaged both serious and popular applause. With *Tonight*, *TW3*, and *Not So Much* he was crafting programmes of great impact and he was doing it from within himself. He had cascades of ideas of his own and he stimulated others. All the while he demanded respect not of, but for, the audience. His ambition outgrew him, however, and within the great producer burned a desire to be an impresario. Maybe it was the challenge, the desire to do something new as well as he had done the producer's job. In this hubris lay his destruction. Hugh Greene might have prevented this had he understood Baverstock better. He liked and respected Baverstock, and maybe that had affected his judgment. Even after Baverstock had left the BBC, Greene always hoped that he would return.

On one occasion he was in favour of his being brought back as Controller, Wales. This was immediately opposed by John Arkell, the Director of Administration, who believed it would be disastrous for the staff of BBC Wales. Arkell was angry and disappointed with Greene about this and saw it as a rather unprincipled move on his part. The appointment was to be made by a small committee of the governors, chaired by the national governor for Wales, Glanmor Williams, with Hugh Greene in attendance. Baverstock had understood from the overture, which had been made to him by Hugh Greene, that he was being offered the job, and that his invitation to Broadcasting House was merely to confirm the appointment. He arrived to see other candidates being ushered in and out. He was furious. Greene says of the interview that followed:

I have never seen a man kill himself in the way that Baverstock did. Glanmor Williams put to Baverstock the sort of questions which, if you were Controller Wales, you might expect that a mayor in Wales, or some local official, would put. Baverstock just got absolutely impatient, saying that he thought it was ridiculous that anybody should ask him this sort of question. Killed himself stone dead.

Baverstock epitomised attitudes which had thrust their way to the surface in the first years of the 1960s. He was, if you like, the leaven in the bread or, some would argue, the catalyst in the explosion. He embodied and articulated, as no one else, the assumptions and values by which Hugh Greene's BBC was defined. As much as anyone, he had defined the importance of the creative questioning role of the producer which in turn had created the mood that coloured these years. Baverstock was in at the heart of the process in which the BBC, in Dr Johnson's words, was being 'blown about by every wind of criticism'.

In the wake of successful programmes, controversy stalked the BBC. The latest grandchild of *TW3*, *BBC3*, caused a major row when on November 13th, 1965, Kenneth Tynan uttered the word 'fuck' for the very first time on British TV. It was not a first which the Chairman, the governors or indeed anyone else welcomed. The phone lines were jammed. Letters poured in and there were four motions tabled in the Commons attacking the BBC. Nineteen sixty-five was also the year the BBC broadcast *Up the Junction*, in which an abortion scene was heavily attacked by some viewers. Greene wrote in reply to one correspondent:

The purpose of the playwright in writing this play, and ours in screening it, was to show the ugliness and suffering to which loose-living and stealing can lead, and to portray characters who, despite this ugliness, are vital human beings. The purpose of [the abortion scene] was to convey some of the tragic consequences which can arise from promiscuity. The billing of this programme in the *Radio Times* gave quite clear advance warning of the nature of the play, for those who did not wish to have the themes brought home to them on the screen.

Steptoe and Son also came in for attacks from viewers, particularly over the language used. Again in reply to a complaint Greene offered a stout defence: 'So far as the language is concerned, the leading characters are engaged in a rag and bone business, and this is naturally somewhat earthy in character. If the dialogue had been purged of all coarseness, it would simply not have rung true . . . the BBC has to try and cater for all tastes.' The most powerful argument he could deploy to support *Steptoe* was a very practical one, that each week over twenty-one million people watched and loved it.

The general tone of the attack on programming was familiar: 'low standards', 'coarse taste', 'foul language', 'vulgarity', 'a planned campaign of dirt and sex', that the Corporation was 'at the mercy of a small band of men with lavatory minds'.

But the year was not totally taken up with arguments about standards. There were moments of great pleasure for Greene, most usually when he was travelling abroad, and particularly because he had for two or three years been seeing more of Tatjana, despite his still being married to Elaine.

Africa he loved. The pace was slower; parties and receptions abounded. In October he was in Nigeria attending the Commonwealth Broadcasting Conference. He held the Conference in high estimation both because he was firmly committed to the idea of a Commonwealth and because he recognised and was deeply proud of the BBC's importance to other public service broadcasting stations. Most of all, he just enjoyed himself. On his way back he stayed in Freetown, Sierra Leone. From there he wrote to Tatjana:

Last night some of the funniest incidents of this whole tour happened when I was having a late night drink in the City

Hotel, scene of many of the scenes in *The Heart of the Matter*. An earnest and rather drunk Sierra Leonean got into conversation with me and told me how dangerous it was to do jig-jig—you can guess what that is—more than three times a week. I assured him that he was wrong. I failed to convince him. As I was walking back from the hotel, accompanied on the way by this sad acquaintance, I was accosted by another African who asked me if I was an American sailor. I said no, I was an English airman. 'But,' he objected, 'you have international movements.' 'That,' I said, 'comes from dancing the high life.' And I asked him what he would have done if I had been an American sailor. 'I would have told you stories of Freetown life,' he said sadly and faded away into the shadows.

On another occasion he was in Ghana. After dinner in his hotel he set off to his room. He wrote to Tatjana:

I must have looked dejected from the back because a chap came running after me and said that the Director of Administration invited me to a drink. The DA is also the hereditary chief of a group of about 20,000 people. At an earlier dinner party his rather attractive little wife had been telling me about his functions. He said that I looked depressed and started talking about how sad it was to sleep alone, with which I heartily agreed. Meanwhile his wife sat and watched me with a secret smile. As he went on with the subject in a roundabout way, I suddenly thought, 'Good God, he's going to offer me his wife. It's probably a deadly insult to refuse, what on earth shall I do'. It wasn't that. He snapped his fingers for a minion and whispered something to him. In a couple of minutes the minion returned with two very obvious hotel tarts. My chief said grandly, 'These are my subjects, do with them what you will.' This offer was possible to decline gracefully, and I proceeded to my lonely bed.

There were other more obviously gloomy moments. He had become worried about the BBC's financial position. When he addressed his senior executives on the financial problems facing the Corporation and urged them to avoid profligacy, the details of the meeting were leaked to the *Daily Mirror* which had a double-page spread attacking waste in Greene's BBC. He wrote to Tatjana that the *Mirror* had launched 'a very violent and possibly damaging attack on me. I've never felt so sick and dispirited, partly because it means treachery somewhere. But of course I have to pretend to be gay and undisturbed.'

However, a piece in the *Television Mail* on December 31st, 1965, argued that his achievements had taken three forms. First, he had 'shown his belief that TV is for people and the people for TV'. Second, 'he has immeasurably widened the scope of TV as a communication medium. He has given TV the same rights as the contemporary press and other media to discuss any subject under the sun without shifty evasion and falsely modest circumlocution.' Third, 'he has done much to invalidate the case for censorship'. In short, and despite *The War Game* decision, Greene had declared that the BBC, indeed any broadcasting organisation, should be an effectively autonomous force within society, subject to moral and philosophical demands, not political and institutional constraints. That was the source of the wind of change and almost inevitably, to use a biblical phrase, 'after the wind an earthquake'.

16

Since the creation of radio and television, politicians have been nervous about the potential of broadcasting to influence their lives. It worries them, makes them itch and feel uncomfortable. It was inevitable that the more people watched television, the greater would be the politicians' anxiety. In the first part of the decade opposition to Greene had come from conservative forces who felt that he was actively undermining a moral order. As the second half of the decade progressed, the main concern came increasingly from the Labour party which felt that he and the BBC were a threat to the power and position of the Labour government.

In his time Greene had voted for all three of the main political parties, but he drew a very clear distinction between Fascism, which he considered to be innately evil, and Communism which he thought was not, though he saw that the tenets of Communism might be used for what appeared to be evil purposes. Under him, therefore, the BBC was never impartial about racism or Fascism but was equivocal over Communism. Two incidents will serve to illustrate the way in which this worked.

There had for many years been a running battle between the BBC and the Communist party of Great Britain over air time during elections. The BBC had claimed that the reason for their exclusion was simply that they did not put up enough candidates. The CPGB claimed that the real reason was that their views were unpalatable to the British political establishment. In February 1964 there were to be elections for the Greater London Council. The initial idea had been

that the BBC would organise a series of hustings programmes in which candidates of the various parties would put
forward their policies. The programmes never happened,
and John Gollan, the General Secretary of the CPGB, was
later to claim that the reason that the hustings programme
had not gone ahead was because it would have given an
opportunity to the Communist party to put forward its
policies. He was absolutely correct.

Two internal memos reveal the thinking inside the BBC:

> DG has ruled that there should be no Greater London
> Election Hustings. I hear that the reason for this is anxiety
> about the position of the Communists. The Labour party
> feel that it is possible that the Communists may contest
> some of the elections, and they do not wish to appear on
> the same platform with them. As you will remember, John
> Harris and Clive Bradley [Wilson associates] said that
> they would wish to refer any decision about these hustings
> in relation to Communist candidates back to Headquar-
> ters and presumably this view is the result of the expres-
> sion of Mr Wilson's decision to DG who had accepted it.

Hugh Greene himself wrote to a member of the Labour
party: 'This time the Communists are contesting so many
seats that they, too, would have had to be represented. We
had discussions with Mr Herbert Bowden about the problem
this created, and he entirely agreed with our decision not to
go ahead with that particular project.'

A small anecdote which adds much to the whole flavour of
the relationship with the Communist party can be added.
On March 18th, 1964, John Gollan and thirty-five prospective Communist party parliamentary candidates turned up
at the BBC to complain about the Corporation's refusal to
give the party air time and to hand in a petition. The BBC
note of the confrontation states: 'Before the meeting Sergeant
Piper and Detective Cheetham, Special Branch, called and
asked if we would kindly let them have a copy of the petition.
Arrangements in hand to do this. After the meeting Inspec-

tor Hodgson, Special Branch, called and was given details of the notes I took.'

There was a similar incident on the other end of the political spectrum. Greene had had a particularly deep hatred of Fascism since his Berlin days. It was a bitter taste which just stayed in his mouth, and he had no wish that the airwaves should be used to further Fascism one jot.

On November 16th, 1961 a by-election was due in the Moss Side Division of Manchester. The constituency had a high level of black and Irish immigrants. One of the candidates, Hesketh, was standing for the Mosleyite Fascist organisation British Union, on a platform which demanded the control of Black immigration. It was widely expected that race riots would ensue. BBC North Region wanted to cover the election with a special programme in which all the candidates would appear. They sought Greene's opinion on whether it would be permissible for a Fascist to appear before a BBC camera and microphones? What should they do if the other candidates refused to appear? What would be the BBC's liability if comments on such a programme led to racial disturbances? Should they organise a wider discussion on immigration and racial disturbances?

Greene replied:

I do not think that it would be *advisable* for a Fascist to appear before a BBC microphone in a BBC television studio. I do not think that we should lend ourselves in this way to the dissemination of Fascist doctrines, and it could lead in the present day world to serious misrepresentation, not only in this country but in Africa and Asia. That means that we should not mount a programme in which the candidates appeared in a studio to be questioned or to make statements. I can, however, see no objection to a programme in which a political reporter did a filmed report on the constituency and the main issues at the by-election. In such a report there could be brief camera coverage of the different candidates speaking at election meetings. In this way, it seems to me we could provide an interesting programme, meet our obligations under the Representation of the People Act and at the same time avoid the necessity of a Fascist candidate appearing in a BBC studio.

It was probably this as much as anything else which laid the basis for the idea that there was an absolute ban on Oswald Mosley ever appearing on the BBC while Greene was DG. No such ban existed. Apart from anything else, such specific ruling was not the way Greene liked to work. It would, however, have needed an extremely good reason to persuade Greene that an appearance by Mosley was justified.

Greene sat foursquare in the moral and intellectual centre ground of liberal democratic society. He would have no truck with anything which potentially challenged its central assumptions or threatened the political and social forms of that moral order. To defend it, he was tough and deter- mined, and where necessary Machiavellian. There is no doubt that his real hatred was for the Fascists. Equally there is no doubt that when a paper came on to his desk such as this one about the Moss Side election, he gazed at it and some- where in the more distant parts of his memory he could hear the tinkle of breaking glass on Kristallnacht and see the gaunt faces of the destroyed in a camp called Dachau. At that level his moral sense was sharp, straightforward and certain: never again.

The real political battle of Greene's tenure was not, however, fought over extremes of political belief but in the middle ground, with one man, Harold Wilson.

Wilson was determined to make good use of TV during the 1964 election and in particular to dominate the campaign personally. Clive Bradley, who advised Wilson on broad- casting affairs during the 1964 election, recalls how on one occasion he went to a studio where Wilson was to be interviewed by Robert McKenzie. To his horror he discov- ered that the set for the interview was a large desk *behind* which would sit McKenzie and *in front of* which would be Wilson, like a schoolboy being interrogated by a headmaster. Bradley refused to let Wilson continue under these conditions; it was only after a furious row with the producer and the intervention of the Head of Talks, Grace Wyndham Goldie, that the situation was resolved and the desk removed. A trivial incident in itself, but it does indicate the very great attention paid to detail in the effort to project Wilson in the most favourable way.

If, however, the intention from within the Labour party was to 'use' TV as much as it could to its own advantage, TV, which was just beginning to find its journalistic legs, was not about to be 'used' without a fight. There was also a psychological shock awaiting Labour politicians as first the promise and then the reality of power loomed large. In the long years in opposition they had established friendly relations with many TV journalists and executives: Christian names were used and they dined with each other frequently. They had come to assume that all this meant plenty of supportive money in the TV-relations' bank account. When, however, they came to cash the cheque in the years of power after 1964, to their horror, it bounced.

Greene cannot recall the first time that he met Wilson, but he did welcome his victory. Two days before voting he had written to Tatjana Sais: 'I have to keep my political opinions a dead secret, but I don't mind saying to you that I long for a Labour victory. I've never before felt so intensely about an election. It looks as if it will be all right, but one can't be sure.' Greene undoubtedly met Wilson socially in the months after he became party leader but no clear memory remains. The first time that Greene really felt the force of Wilson's presence was during the 1964 election campaign itself. After the dissolution of Parliament, the BBC introduced for the first time a series of programmes called *Election Forum* in which the leaders of the three main parties would appear separately and be faced with questions sent in by the public. It was a way round the problem of senior political figures refusing to agree to televised debates. After the first performances Wilson was to be heard complaining that the treatment meted out to him had been much tougher than that to Alec Douglas Home and Jo Grimond. His own people did not agree and were very pleased with his performance. It was, however, a little pointer to the emerging sensitivity of the Labour leader.

After Wilson's appearance on *Election Forum*, he was seen huddled in the corner of the studio in an intense discussion with his broadcasting adviser, Clive Bradley. It was assumed that he was discussing whether or not the questions put to him had been too hostile. In fact, his mind was on something very different. The cameraman whom Bradley had been using in the campaign had previously worked for a public relations firm which had been involved in events in Katanga. He had just informed Bradley that the same firm had approached him once more with a view to his flying to the Yemen to shoot a night parachute landing. This seemed to confirm in Wilson and Bradley's minds a rumour that the Tory government might create some kind of war situation there in order to rally popular feeling behind it in the closing days of the campaign. Wilson took the rumour seriously enough to lodge a letter with the Governor of the Bank of England, explaining his understanding of the plan, to be released should such an event happen.

At the traditional pre-election meeting of the Leader of the House, the Labour and the Conservative parties, and the Director Generals of the BBC and the ITA, to discuss the broadcasting provisions for the election, Wilson had been horrified to learn that the BBC had scheduled a repeat showing of *Steptoe and Son* for the early evening of election night. He felt, probably rightly, that this would have a disproportionate influence on Labour voters and could possibly, therefore, lose him the election. He explained his problem to a clearly very sympathetic Greene, who offered to shift *Steptoe* to nine pm when the polls would be closed. The Labour leader was overjoyed and said, 'Thank you very much, Hugh, that will be worth a dozen or more seats to me.' In the light of the eventual four-seat majority which the Labour party obtained, the manoeuvre is perhaps one of the most important pieces of re-scheduling ever done.

It certainly augured well for the future, and in correspondence it was all 'Dear Harold' and 'Dear Hugh'. But how long would it be before the assertive journalistic instincts of Greene's BBC and the prickly fears of Wilson would collide? There should have been considerable affinity between the liberally progressive Greene and the social democratic, egalitarian Wilson: this obviously lay behind Greene's hopes that Wilson would win the election. In reality, however, there was bound to be conflict between those who controlled access to the national mind, the broadcasters, and those who wanted to make sure that that control was exercised in their favour, the politicians.

In some ways the most difficult kind of political pressure which any Director General has to deal with is where an appeal is made by the government to 'the national interest'. He has to decide whether what is at stake *is* the national interest or whether it is no more than party interest. The BBC Russian Service was planning to broadcast extracts from Svetlana Alliluyeva's *Letters to a Friend*, a move not especially guaranteed to find favour with the gentlemen in the Kremlin, when the Foreign Secretary, George Brown, was on a visit to Moscow. Hugh Greene received a call from the Cabinet Office asking if the broadcast could be postponed. Greene explained that this would not be easy to do since a good deal of publicity had been given to it already and that, therefore, he did not see how he could possibly accede to the request. A few hours later he had a further call from the Secretary to the Cabinet saying that he was speaking on behalf of the Prime Minister who wished to put it very seriously to Greene that it would be against the national interest to go ahead with the broadcast. Gromyko had informed George Brown that if the programme went ahead the talks would be called off. In this instance Greene complied with the government's request about the broadcast, but only to a postponement for forty-eight hours until Brown had finished.

In 1965 George Brown wished to present the details of his National Plan. He argued that it was an issue of national interest which should be aired in a ministerial broadcast. Ministerial broadcasts were governed by an aide-mémoire dating back to 1947 in which the BBC and the government agreed that these broadcasts should be non-controversial. If the Ministerial material was controversial, then the Leader of the Opposition would have the right to claim a reply. In the first instance this would be done through an approach to the government's Chief Whip. If the government agreed that it had been controversial, then the BBC arranged for air time for the reply. If the government denied that the broadcast had been controversial, then it was left to the discretion of the BBC. Greene had decided even before the event that Brown's broadcast could not possibly be non-controversial, that it could not, therefore, be a Ministerial broadcast and that arrangements should be made in advance for the Conservatives to reply.

Wilson and Brown argued that the issue was of interest to the whole nation, and that it was not controversial. They were furious with Greene's view and accused him of bending the rules and the terms of the aide-mémoire. In the end Greene had his way and both Labour and Conservatives were given air time. The fact that this situation had occurred, however, worried Greene to such an extent that he was determined to tighten up the aide-mémoire to ensure that it could not happen again. Nevertheless, he knew that the incident had badly soured the relationship between himself and the Prime Minister. Many years later Wilson said during a conversation in a BBC television programme that Greene had been quite right in the line he had taken.

Relations that year were made even worse by difficulties which arose at the Labour Party Conference at the end of September 1965. Wilson was apparently furious about an interview between Robin Day and Clive Jenkins. His point was that Jenkins could in no way be regarded as a representative of the Conference. He summoned, therefore, the senior BBC current affairs executive present in Blackpool, John Grist, and gave him what was widely reported as a dressing down. There then followed another row about whether George Brown had been unfairly interviewed by Robin Day. A further row erupted between Grist and Wilson, who, as he left the room, was said to be quivering with fury. He became even angrier when the BBC leaked the story to the *Daily Mail*. Wilson recalls it now as no more than an argument.

On October 3rd *The Sunday Times* carried a piece headlined 'Curb Threat to the BBC' and referred to rumour of a Wilson plan to impose some sort of supervision on the BBC. It also referred to a Labour plan to monitor the BBC coverage of the Conservative Party Conference to see if there was any bias. The following day *The Times* spoke of how Wilson had 'warned Mr Grist to mend his ways, or the government would have to think about bringing the BBC under tighter discipline'. On October 7th, *The Guardian* said the Labour party was denying that it was angry with the coverage of the Conference. Rather, the piece said, obviously on information from within Transport House, they were angry about the BBC refusal to allow Brown to launch his National Plan in a Ministerial broadcast without a counterstatement from Ian Macleod for the Tories. The article observed: 'Ministers go out of their way to pay tribute to the impeccable impartiality of Independent TV in dealing with Ministers. However, they left no doubt that they are very angry indeed with the BBC.'

Ted Short, who as Chief Whip for a time during this period, was a principal channel for liaison between Greene and Wilson, argues that one has to see such rows against the backdrop of a tense parliamentary situation. The Wilson government had a tiny majority, first of four and then of three. It made them acutely sensitive about their treatment on TV and both ITV and the BBC found themselves having to walk gingerly through the minefield laid by Harold Wilson's paranoid fears of conspiracy. Ted Short, always a close friend and ally of Wilson, has argued that 'Harold is innately insecure. He's got to be assured about his security all the time.' Harold Wilson now wanted journalists to treat him with all the dignity his office of Prime Minister demanded, but he had been chummy with them for too long. To them he was still Harold: they could not suddenly be made to be respectful to him, if he did not gain their respect.

Throughout these events and the realisation that the new Prime Minister was not going to be anywhere near as accommodating as Macmillan had been, Greene had remained calm, slowly letting tempers cool. Ted Short recalls: 'He was always relaxed. He had this marvellous charm of manner, this smile of his, which charmed all kinds of people throughout his life. I think he was the ideal Director General to deal with that kind of Prime Minister.' Equally some of the professionals within the Labour party thought highly of Greene's performance: 'He handled politicians well, maintained his integrity, listened and would be open-minded about other people's arguments.'

On April 1st, 1966, Harold Wilson sat aboard the train from Liverpool to London. He was heading back to Downing Street after another general election, secure in the knowledge that he would have a massively increased majority for the next Parliament. It was a moment of triumph for him and his party. Wilson, however, was disgruntled; he thought that he had been badly treated throughout the campaign by a BBC which was openly biased against the Labour party. He felt in particular that the central phalanx of the BBC's political staff, Paul Fox, Head of Current Affairs, John Grist, Assistant Head, and interviewers Ian Trethowan, Robin Day and Robert McKenzie all had a conscious or unconscious predilection against committed left-wing politics. He had a particular distaste for Robert McKenzie.

It rankled that the BBC news coverage during the run up to the election refused to refer to him as the Prime Minister, instead using the description Leader of the Labour Party. What really hurt, however, was what he believed to be the differential treatment of himself and Heath. A confrontation between the two men had been suggested but neither of them wished for a gladiatorial contest; Heath, because he knew that Wilson could be a superb debater, and Wilson, because it was widely assumed that the person most likely to benefit from these confrontations was the lesser-known figure.

Heath however was manoeuvred by one interviewer into saying that he would be willing to debate with Wilson if it could be arranged. This did not mean that he especially wanted to debate, rather that he did not wish to be seen to be avoiding doing so. Wilson takes up the story:

> The BBC were pressing me and making news items of my refusal. It then became clear that somebody in the BBC was working very closely with Tory Central Office and with Heath. They kept varying the conditions to make it more acceptable to him. Heath knew that he was going to lose the election anyway and this was the one thing that might have swung it, if I had said something daft and he had got on top. I travelled up overnight on the sleeper to Liverpool, and I was going to do my nomination in my constituency, get my forms in. I arrived at the Adelphi and was having breakfast and had the 8 o'clock news on. They'd put a new proposition to Heath who was leaving Liverpool the previous night; they did not put it to me, and then they announced that agreement had been reached with all concerned, which meant that I had to say that it hadn't and they admitted that it was a mistake. But of course the story was running all day. It was a disgraceful thing and so we complained about it.

Wilson's office complained on a number of occasions to Hugh Greene. Clearly the people in Lime Grove were eager for a confrontation. Their eagerness, however, led them to treat Wilson in a particularly unfortunate way, which Greene now admits was both discourteous and tactically wrong. There is no evidence that Wilson felt any particular animosity towards Greene: just that 'there were one or two warrior earls at lower levels who more or less conditioned the kings's policies.'

Wilson's immediate revenge was short and sharp. The BBC had requisitioned a whole carriage on the train which they knew Wilson would be taking back to London. They had worked for a month to set up the first ever live interview in Britain from a train. The problem, and here the BBC people responsible exhibited stupid arrogance, was that they had not informed Wilson till the night before that they wished to do the interview. 'Not with me, you won't,' Wilson replied, and the interviewer and producer sat forlornly and Prime Ministerless in their special moving studio. Wilson observed, 'They hadn't properly approached me, not till the night before. They announced I'd do it, but after all this business about the Heath interview and all the rest of it I was damned if I was going to give them one.' Wilson rubbed salt into the wound by giving an interview to an ITV crew who were also on the train. The interview done, the film was handed out of the window at Crewe for transmission to London; the BBC had been upstaged, and Wilson had his revenge.

Greene agrees that the cavalier way in which Wilson had been approached was utterly wrong. Again it was a situation which Greene had not created but which he would have to try to resolve. Undoubtedly this was a low point in their relations and left him with a good deal to worry about. He suggested that he and Normanbrook go to see Wilson to talk things over, to see if the Prime Minister's concern with the BBC could not be soothed.

Wilson agreed to see them and suggested that when they arrived at No 10, they went in by the side door from Whitehall rather than the front door, since he did not want reporters to speculate on the reason for their visit. They sat in the Cabinet room with Wilson and Herbert Bowden, the Lord President of the Council. The Prime Minister went back to the troubles of the previous year and began to list a whole series of grievances he felt against the BBC. Greene and Normanbrook put their case and as they did so, Bowden occasionally chirped in with 'You know, Prime Minister, they are quite right,' which made Greene think, 'My dear boy, you won't be there much longer'. Normanbrook told Wilson that the mistake he had made had been to deal with low-level people such as John Grist. In any future situations he re-commended that he deal only with the Chairman or the DG.

The whole episode had alarmed Greene. Even he agreed with some of the complaints which Wilson had made, and in particular felt that Wilson should have been accorded the respect due to his Prime Ministerial office; but Hugh had seen something in the man which he not only disliked but which in a strange way frightened him. He saw a suspicious man who believed that conspiracies abounded to trap and to destroy him. The row over the 1966 election was really the end of their relationship and quite deliberately he hardly saw Wilson after: 'I was very glad not to see too much of him. I think it is dangerous to see too much of a man like that.' He told Tatjana of his own feelings about the election: 'I would never vote Conservative. I have too much of a sense of the past to vote for the party of Munich and Suez. I have seen too much of Wilson's behaviour in this campaign, but all the same I voted Labour however reluctantly. So I lay my reputation for impartiality in your hands.' In April he told her of what he regarded as Wilson's hostile attitude to the BBC: 'I fear that a small man who I thought had some elements of greatness is going to show himself smaller and smaller as his power increases. I hope I am wrong, but if I am right the next few years are going to be very difficult indeed. But I have not lost my taste for a fight.'

Greene effectively stopped trying to get through to Wilson, to persuade him that there was no conspiracy in the BBC against him. Instead he communicated through the Whip's Office, the Postmaster General and the Lord President of the Council. That he should do so was probably inevitable. Nevertheless, it was a mistake because Wilson remained enormously important to the future of the BBC and, rightly or wrongly, he did believe that, while Greene may have been reasonable enough in his policies, he had unleashed unreasonable men below him. Wilson was determined to put paid to the power of the 'barons' with whom he had to argue in smoke-filled rooms in Blackpool. To do that he would have to deal with Greene.

There were other members of the Labour government who also wished to change the BBC. On May 24th, 1965

Wedgwood Benn, the Postmaster General, proposed to the Cabinet's Broadcasting Committee that the government ought to ensure that any expansion of the BBC's programme output was financed by advertising, not by an increase in the licence fee. The proposal apparently found favour with the Cabinet Committee, and indeed the suggestion seemed to be that the BBC should *in principle* allow advertising on TV and in its Light Programme on radio. Greene and the board of governors were greatly alarmed when news of these proposals was leaked in February 1966. In that month a meeting took place between Fulton (who was acting as Chairman of the governors during Normanbrook's absence through illness), Hugh Greene, Harold Wilson, Herbert Bowden, the Lord President of the Council and Wedgwood Benn. At least one researcher believes that the BBC's case was helped by Fulton having been Wilson's tutor at Oxford. Whatever the reason, after this meeting the idea of the BBC taking advertising was effectively shelved.

At this meeting Wilson also raised the question of a possible University of the Air and how to finance it. The idea caught Greene's attention and when Lord Goodman later approached him to see if the BBC would help, Greene readily agreed. He prepared a detailed memo on the costing for such a service, which was appended to Goodman's report to Wilson. Both these people acknowledge that without Greene's enthusiasm and cooperation—against, it must be said, a good deal of internal opposition—the idea which became the Open University would have been still-born.

In January 1966 Benn was replaced as Postmaster General by Edward Short, who was immediately under pressure to take action against 'pirate' radio stations broadcasting pop music from ships anchored in international waters. The pirate programmes were highly popular with young people who much preferred their style and presentation to what they regarded as the staid, boring BBC. Short approached Greene to suggest that the BBC openly face this challenge. Greene was agreeable and therefore in the same month Short tabled the Marine Offences Bill to abolish the pirates. In

274

December the government published a White Paper on Broadcasting which ruled out advertising as a source of revenue for the Corporation, and gave the go-ahead to start a local radio service.

Greene was delighted and felt that he had obtained everything he wanted. It had been his most important formal victory since Pilkington. Normanbrook, however, told him that it was all a bit too good and that from here on they should watch their backs. Greene saw no point in worrying and replied that if you set out to fight a battle, you do not go for half a victory. The victory had made him feel very good.

The Short-Greene relationship had been productive, and both men came to see the other as sensible and cooperative. In return for government backing in the White Paper, the BBC now agreed to re-structure completely its radio output, to allow for the creation of a national pop music channel which would fill the gap left by the demise of the pirates. The new structure of Radio 1 (popular music); Radio 2 (light music and entertainment); Radio 3 ('highbrow' music and drama); and Radio 4 (news, current affairs, features) reflected finally and totally the recognition of the main cultural strata within British society.

As the decade progressed, Greene would have liked the BBC to expand further, but it was increasingly short of money. In April 1963 they had been awarded a £4 licence fee rather than the £5 they had requested. In April 1965 they received £5 instead of £6, for the financial year 1964–65 the deficit went from £3.2 million to £7.4 million, and the bank overdraft increased from £0.9 million to £6.1 million. They had the right to borrow up to £10 million only. Greene did not let financial problems overwhelm him, but he could see that a growing overdraft would put them at the government's mercy, for they alone could fix the amount of the licence fee.

Greene remained remarkably unconcerned with all the fuss throughout the conflicts with Benn and Wilson. Asked that autumn which events had done the greatest service to the BBC in the past year, his reply was so forthright that he

275

did not allow it to be minuted. In his own notes for this reply he had written, 'The greatest service to the BBC was the resignation of Frank Cousins, and the chain reaction of Cabinet changes that followed.' Those changes paved the way for Short becoming Postmaster General. He also pointed to the usefulness of what he described as 'our tiff with the Prime Minister', since that proved beyond doubt that the BBC was independent of the political parties. The 'tiff' was, of course, the election row.

He was feeling confident and assertive. At the same meeting, when one of the assembled executives asked if he felt it was possible to have satire without lapses of judgment, Greene immediately complained that the problem with the existing satire show, a seventh son of *TW3*, *The Late Show*, was that 'it is a bore, perhaps because there are too few lapses of judgment. Lapses of judgment are inevitable in satire programmes.'

His assertiveness spilled over into his relationships with the political parties. Richard Crossman from 1966 to 1968 was Lord President of the Council and Leader of the House of Commons. As such he was involved in negotiating with Hugh Greene on the Broadcasting Committee which decided the number and timing of the party political broadcasts. At the meeting in January 1967, which was also attended by the leaders of the Tories and Liberals, as well as by the Director General of the ITA, Greene had proposed minor changes. Heath and Thorpe demurred and Crossman comments, 'I saw what an awkward cuss Hugh is. There he was, stiffening and rigidifying . . . I think Hugh is a wonderful Director General, but he's certainly no negotiator. On Monday he united the opposition against him.' Crossman also complained that despite their wartime friendship Greene was always 'stiff and rigid'. At a later meeting of the Broadcasting Committee, where a change had been proposed in party politicals, Crossman observed that 'once again Hugh behaved to type. He simply said that this could not be considered and wouldn't budge.' Greene commented on this meeting in a letter to Tatjana: 'I was round at the

276

House of Commons for a meeting with the party leaders about the 1968 series of party political broadcasts. I had a flaming row with Ted Heath (alas, our poor country to have to choose between him and Harold Wilson). I was amused to note that the more heated he got, the cooler I got . . .'

Despite the conflicts and Crossman's general misgivings about the way in which Hugh Greene handled politicians, 1966 ended on a high note, with a considerable level of cooperation with the government, some major new developments, and a feeling of bonhomie between the BBC and the government department responsible for broadcasting. There had been the rows but even constant guerrilla warfare seemed to have done nothing to harm the BBC's programme content. A remarkably abrasive, but brilliantly written and produced, comedy had started on June 6th, called *Till Death Us Do Part*. Satire, first in the shape of *Not So Much A Programme*, *BBC3*, and *The Late Show* continued, if with nothing like the tone of their legendary predecessor, *TW3*, and the coverage of contemporary events showed no obvious diminution. On November 16th the BBC broadcast one of the most controversial and successful plays ever produced, *Cathy Come Home*, which showed the problems of homelessness in brutally stark terms, the rumblings from which are still felt years later.

The BBC had been battered and assaulted time and again. It had gone into the streets, under Greene's tutelage, both to have a look at what was happening and occasionally to make things happen. It had been mugged, spat upon, reviled, laughed at, patted on the back, applauded. To all this, it had felt a large measure of indifference. Its strength was, indeed, the very fact that it could be indifferent. It was a creature of the constitutional monarchy, not of Parliament. It was a body shrouded in history and reputation which possessed a forcefield around it which would always be extraordinarily difficult to breach. It seemed capable of handling direct assaults on its integrity and well-being. It was, however, vulnerable to indirect assault, and one man at least knew that, Harold Wilson.

17

Lord Normanbrook died on June 15th, 1967. On the same day Greene wrote to Tatjana: 'I was very fond of him, and a good Chairman can do so much to help to lighten the burden one inevitably carries. One needs someone to talk things out with and the choice of a new one is always a chancy business.' The past few months had not been easy for Greene as a number of problems had begun to loom large. He had been having difficulties with the union over the introduction of colour TV. At the same time, commercial television had been poaching BBC talent. He was especially hurt by Michael Peacock's departure. As he wrote to Tatjana, Peacock had been 'a man for whom I had done a lot and with whom I had worked very closely in the last few years. For a few minutes I had a feeling of discouragement and bitterness. *Et tu, Brute*. The fortunate thing is that I really do feel physically better when things get tough.'

A few weeks later John Arkell, the BBC's efficient but dour and humourless Director of Administration, approached Hugh Greene at a party. He had, he informed him, heard from a Post Office official that the next Chairman of the BBC would be Lord Hill, the existing Chairman of the ITA. Hugh Greene, controlling his urge to burst into gales of laughter, went over with Arkell to confront the official. With mock solemnity he asked, 'What's this I hear about Hill . . . ?' To Greene, it seemed one of the most ludicrous ideas he had heard in his life. In fact the official said he had merely been pulling Arkells leg. In the 1950s Hill had first become known as the Radio Doctor. He was a former Conservative

Postmaster General and Chancellor of the Duchy of Lancaster. In July 1962 he had been one of the Ministers sacked by Harold Macmillan in a bloody Cabinet reshuffle. In 1963 he was appointed to the chairmanship of the then Independent Television Authority.

On July 25th, 1967, Hill was phoned at his home by Philip Philips, the TV correspondent of *The Sun*. Philips wanted to know if it was true that Hill was to become the Chairman of the BBC. Hill informed the journalist, in his famous gruff but affable manner, that such an idea was 'a load of nonsense'. (Hill perhaps had forgotten that several months before Wilson had sidled up to him at a party and said, 'Charles, when you've finished sorting out the ITV Companies, you'll be ready to tackle a similar job at the BBC.') Intrigued by the reporter's rumour, however, Hill immediately phoned the Postmaster General, Edward Short, to find out how such a story might have started. He says in his memoirs that Short claimed that he knew no more than that there was a rumour and that he himself had heard it from a *Daily Mirror* executive. It now seems highly likely that Short was covering up his real knowledge since he appears to have been the instigator of the extraordinary events which were to break about the ears of Greene and the BBC. Short realised that the well-laid plans of the government, which they had not intended to reveal until some time later, had been leaked. Therefore, he suggested that Hill should come to the Prime Minister's room at the Commons the following day at two thirty pm.

Hill arrived there to find Wilson in a relaxed mood, smoking a large cigar. Short was also present. Wilson proceeded to praise Hill's performance at the ITA, to observe that the chairmanship of the BBC was vacant and then asked if Hill would like the job. The urgency of the proposal, Wilson explained, was that the press had got wind of the idea and he was hoping that Hill would say 'yes' so that they could make the announcement at midnight. Wilson did not add that the press had got wind of the idea because he had told them at an *Economist* party the previous evening. Hill found the idea of heading the BBC totally irresistible. His

279

first action was to inform the Director General of the ITA, Sir Robert Fraser. That evening of July 26th he told the members of the Authority that he would be switching over to run the opposition. They were as mystified and amazed as everyone else was to be.

On the same day, the 26th, Sir Robert Lusty, acting Chairman of the BBC, received two phone calls from Short. In the first he asked if Lusty could call at the Post Office the following day. Shortly after this, Short phoned again and in an urgent voice said that it would be necessary for them to meet that same day, Wednesday, at four thirty pm. When he arrived, Lusty was placed in a room to await his appointment with the Postmaster General. He had no idea at this stage what all the urgency was about. Suddenly Short entered the room looking serious, accompanied by several even more serious looking aides. He told Lusty that the new Chairman of the BBC would be 'Charles Smith'. Lusty looked puzzled since he knew no such man. The aides looked flustered, and one leaned over and whispered in Short's ear, 'Hill, sir, not Smith, Hill.' (Short had that morning been negotiating with Charles Smith, the General Secretary of the Post Office Engineering Union.) He corrected himself and told Lusty that the new head of the BBC would be Lord Hill, that the announcement would be made that evening at ten past eight and that Hill would take up the post on September 1st. In his memoirs Lusty recalls: 'The full horror of the situation numbed my mind. All I could wonder was how to break the news to Hugh Greene and the others. It was the end of the BBC as I knew it and the end of Hugh Greene, too.'

Lusty returned to Broadcasting House with the news, full of foreboding about how Greene would react. When he was told, Greene leapt from his chair with a shout of horror and anger. He said, 'How can I work with a man for whom I have the utmost contempt!' He seized the phone and made an appointment to see the Postmaster General the following morning, intent on telling Short that he would be offering his resignation to the governors. Lusty counselled calm and suggested that they talk through the situation with Oliver

25th February, 1965

1 James Thomas Daily Express	8 Martin Jackson Daily Express	15 Henry Raynor Times
2 Norman Hare Daily Telegraph	9 Peter Knight Daily Telegraph	16 Aldo Nicolotti Evening News
3 Jack Miller News of the World	10 Ken Irwin Daily Mirror	17 John Woodforde Sunday Telegraph
4 Brian Dean Daily Mail	11 Nick Marker Tel. Pub. Org.	18 Stewart Lane Morning Star
5 Colin McIntyre C.P.O. Tel.	12 Clifford Davies Daily Mirror	19 Peter Black Daily Mail
6 Fred Billany Thompson Newspapers	13 Philip Purser Sunday Telegraph	20 Ramsden Greig Evening Standard
7 Douglas Marlborough Daily Mail	14 Peter Dacre Sunday Express	

Farewell dinner for the press, 1969

Whitley, Greene's chief assistant. Whitley had a reputation, both in the BBC and outside, for being the repository of dignity, rectitude and calm common sense. If anyone knew how to respond, it was thought, Oliver would.

Whitley counselled patience and suggested that Greene sleep on the matter before deciding what to do. He also added that if Greene did resign, then the whole of the Board of Management would resign with him, leaving the BBC at the mercy of its new master. Shortly afterwards, Greene received a note from the BBC's lobby correspondent, Peter Hardiman Scott, suggesting that Wilson's motive in appointing Hill had been to force Greene to resign. That sealed it; whatever he did do, he would not resign; he would stay on and fight. He immediately wrote to Tatjana to tell her of Hill's appointment: 'An appalling blow. My first reaction was to resign immediately. My second, to stay and fight it out, but it means the end of all pleasure in my work.'

At eleven o'clock on the morning of the 27th the board of governors met in a state of shell shock. The main feeling was one of puzzlement that Hill found it so easy to transfer from the ITA to the BBC, mixed with a feeling of resentment at what seemed to be an obvious act of political malice. Throughout the BBC a mixture of sadness, anger and sympathy welled up for Hugh Greene, who, it was felt, was the real victim of the appointment. To Tatjana he wrote: 'I thought the morale of the BBC would be completely shattered. Curiously enough exactly the opposite has happened. Everything suggests that I now have behind me 22,000 people, united as never before—from the top down to the drivers and commissionaires, and the remaining governors are in the same state of outrage.'

Hill was piqued by this reaction to his appointment but, as he argued in his memoirs, Greene no doubt had seen how he had strengthened the role of the members of the ITA against the Director General there, and he had no doubt assumed that he would want to do the same at the BBC. Hill had also lunched with Mary Whitehouse, and he knew that that would not recommend him to Greene. 'This was part of the background of suspicion and animosity against which I began at the BBC. Not unnaturally I resented the mood of courteous hostility that greeted me and it was some time before my resentment died.'

The violence of the antagonism to Hill seems overdone, but it was fomented by those who saw that the bell was tolling for Greene. Hugh himself added fuel to the flames. He wrote to Tatjana at the beginning of August:

> So that you should know the ins and outs thoroughly, I should explain that I've ostensibly kept completely quiet and just gone off on holiday as previously arranged. Behind the scenes I've guided the *Observer* and the *Sunday Times*, two papers with which I've got very good and confidential relations. You will have seen by now what they wrote, which I find very helpful. You see, I'm rather a ruffian.

What the *Observer* had said on July 30th under the heading 'The feud that brings Hill to the BBC' was 'The Prime Minister with this appointment has given notice to the BBC that henceforward things cannot be the same again and that the Corporation and the somewhat freewheeling policies it has enjoyed under Sir Hugh will have to change.'

Wilson now says that he made the appointment because he felt that Hill had done a good job at the ITA and had, as he puts it, 'shaped things up and modernised things a bit'. He wanted him to do the same thing at the BBC. He claims that it never occurred to him that there would be any adverse reaction nor that Greene would be upset enough at the idea to think of resigning. It is difficult to grasp this, but it is what he says now!

What then is the evidence that this appointment was a long-laid plan by Wilson to bring down Greene and to change the character of the BBC? Hill denies firmly that he and Wilson discussed any such idea, or that they even discussed Hugh Greene. Crossman, on the other hand, is clear on Wilson's motives in what he describes as 'the most characteristic piece of Wilsonian gimmickry'. He writes in his *Diary* for July 26th: 'So Harold has coolly switched Hill to the BBC to discipline it and bring it to book and, above all, to deal with Hugh Greene.' One should perhaps distinguish between the BBC and Greene, because in the Prime Minister's mind they *were* different. His hatred was for the bad treatment he had received from BBC producers and journalists far below the level of Director General. He must have known, however, that if he were to try to change the BBC, and to mould it to his own preference, he would find Greene putting up a powerful defence for the BBC's political independence. Greene would have to be bypassed or made the victim, even if he himself was not especially guilty in Wilson's eyes.

The slight question mark hanging over this thesis is provided by two relatively new pieces of information. Robert Lusty, who had been the acting Chairman, claims in his memoirs that the post of Chairman had been offered to Herbert Bowden who turned it down on the grounds that he would not be able to 'deal with that fellow Greene'. Lusty had heard this story from members of the Irish Broadcasting Service who had themselves been told by Bowden. Wilson, however, denies that any such offer was made: 'It would have looked very peculiar. I would not under any circumstances have appointed a Labour politician or a Labour minister to the BBC. I thought that most of the criticism would disappear because the man I was appointing was a Tory.' Bowden later told Greene that he had been asked by Wilson to take over the BBC.

The second piece of information belying the 'conspiracy' thesis about Hill's appointment is that Edward Short, now Lord Glenamara, claims that it was he, not Wilson, who thought of asking Hill:

I suggested it to the Prime Minister, and he readily agreed. He thought it was a joke, I think, but he agreed because he didn't like the BBC greatly, though I'm sure he had very good relations with Hugh Greene. Harold was a bit obsessive about people attacking him, ultra sensitive, so I think he was only too glad to accept this suggestion. Everybody believed Hill to be a disciplinarian, who would put the BBC in its place and make the producers do as they were told, and not do their own thing as they had always done at the BBC. That's how Wilson saw it. I didn't see it like that at all. I thought Hill had been an outstandingly successful Chairman of the ITA; that it would be good to have this cross fertilisation. It was not seen by either myself or Harold Wilson as an anti-Greene move; nobody wanted Greene to resign. Harold Wilson had, I think, tremendous affection for him, and so had I.

Robert Lusty, who was both a close friend to the DG and still the acting Chairman, felt that he had to explain to Short formally how he felt. He wrote:

> If I should have left you after our brief meeting yesterday afternoon with any discourtesy, I much regret it. But as one who believes very deeply in public service broad-casting, I must tell you that the information which you kindly divulged in advance of its release filled me with profound dismay and consternation. My basic anxiety is that one man in one lifetime can, with sincerity, accept with conviction two completely different concepts.

He had this statement read out at the meeting of the governors on July 27th and it met with their complete agreement. The rest of that meeting was uneventful. It was the last one before their summer break, and they went off knowing that when they returned, at the beginning of September, Hill would be in the chair. At the end of the meeting Greene asked Lusty if he could have a word in private with him. The curtain was about to come down a little further.

Greene told Lusty that on top of the Hill affair, he had another problem to present to him:

> I am sorry to have to tell you this because you are a friend of both Elaine, my wife, and myself, and I'm very sorry to

have to tell you that our marriage is breaking up and there is going to be a divorce and the news is likely to come out soon. I suppose I can assume that in these liberal days the Board will take a liberal attitude and not regard this with disfavour?

Lusty was saddened at the news since he was genuinely fond of Hugh, a man full of both greatness and mischief. Nevertheless, Lusty did not feel that he could give him such assurance and said, 'I simply don't know, Hugh; it seems to me an extremely difficult situation.'

Lusty was privately filled with great doubt and apprehension. He immediately sounded out individual governors whom he knew to be liberal-minded, and he was not surprised to find that they were uniformly condemnatory of the idea of Greene going through yet another divorce. They were unanimous that this would create difficulties for the board and within the BBC. Lusty never told Greene this and was greatly relieved when legal complications over divorce proceedings delayed the case to such an extent that it passed on to Hill's plate.

Charles Hill arrived for the first board meeting, sought no word of welcome, did not mention Normanbrook's death and merely said, with that voice which had made him famous as the Radio Doctor, 'Let us get on to the Minutes of the last meeting'. Several governors thought, on the basis of the first performance, that it was unlikely that Greene would be able to survive.

Hill was determined to impose his presence within the BBC. He began by breaking with tradition. He wanted to bring in his own secretary, Mrs Fenton, rather than to use one provided by the BBC; he wanted to use his own chauffeur; he wanted to keep the colour TV set which the ITA engineers had only just installed in his home; and he demanded a different room for his office. Traditionally, the Director General's and Chairman's rooms had been adjacent, linked by a common secretarial pool. This allowed them both to know what letters and documents were going through. There was, however, another aspect to the arrangement, which had grown up over the years, and which Hugh Greene in particular had felt had been especially important in his relationship with fforde and Normanbrook. The structure of the rooms, with the secretarial pool acting as the umbilical cord between the Chairman and the Director General, had come to have an almost metaphysical significance, intensifying the relationship between the two, without which the BBC could never be successful.

Hill was adamant that his office reminded him of an oak-lined coffin, airless, and stuffy. He asked for a new one with a room adjacent for his secretary to use. This was eventually found for him on the fifth floor. He comments in his memoirs that it was being suggested in the press,

> that I had deliberately moved to another floor to set up a chairman's establishment in competition with that of the Director General. This was not my last experience of a pastime indulged in by some BBC staff of feeding the press with malicious titbits. The fact is that I would have stayed on the third floor if someone had been willing to move to give me houseroom.

It is difficult to see, despite his denial, that the change of office was anything other than a wish to make himself visibly separate from the Director General. Greene felt that if the old room had been good enough for Normanbrook and fforde, then it should have been good enough for Hill.

Whether Wilson realised or not, there was a touch of genius in his understanding that the key to the BBC lay in the subtle relationship between the Director General and the Chairman. No government this side of revolution could ban a programme, could sack Greene or even issue orders about what programmes they would like to see. The BBC is a creature of the monarchy in that the governors are formally appointed by the monarchy and in turn appoint the Director

General. For any government to interfere with the BBC directly would have been to guarantee a major political and constitutional crisis. Faced with the agonised question from the whole of the British political establishment 'will no one rid me of this turbulent priest?' Wilson had realised that the only way to change the BBC was to suffocate Greene slowly by providing him with a Chairman with whom he could not work. It would later be argued, and accepted, that Hill never sought to undermine the independence of the BBC or to change its forms of finance, indeed, he was a doughty champion of these formal attributes, but it was not the independence which mattered, but what was done with it. Hill's appointment was never intended to leave open wounds or visibly damage the body of the BBC. He was merely required to inject doses of 'responsibility', 'maturity', 'professionalism', 'propriety', and 'traditional values': the patient was being doped into quietude, that was why they needed the doctor.

In his memoirs Hill asked rhetorically, 'Did I yield to lobbies, political, libertarian or other? Did I turn over the BBC professionals to the mercies of the layman? Did I argue for advertising on the BBC? The answers are to be found in the record.' The real answers, however, could not be found from those questions. The truth of the consequences of that appointment in July 1967 could no more be contained within 'the records' than a snapshot from the family album could contain the truth of a life.

Greene's profound influence on the BBC had lain in his being first and foremost an editor concerned with content, rather than an executive administrator beguiled by the sheen on the Corporation's public face. At meetings with the board of governors, or indeed on any occasion where there was someone to listen, he would observe that he was above all a journalist. On one occasion he mildly reproved a questioner who asked, 'As a former journalist . . .' He retorted that he was not, nor ever would be, a 'former' journalist. A small illustration of how true this was occurred at a dinner given by Lord Thomson. George Brown, the main guest, gave an outrageous and offensive speech in which he directly insulted Thomson. Greene immediately found a telephone, contacted the BBC's newsroom and gave them his account of the story. He cared passionately about what was put out by the BBC. The content must always be in keeping with his own sense of values, purpose and humour, and he continued to maintain these ideals despite opposition from those within and without the BBC, who were unlike him in their mood, their humour, and their root disposition.

He could appear sometimes to be high-handed, even arrogant and condescending. It certainly irritated the governors that Greene would make pronouncements on issues such as the licence fee which might more appropriately have come from the Chairman. He had been allowed that prominence by the rather father-like figure of fforde and had simply continued the habit under Normanbrook. Without any question it was this commanding authority which allowed him to have enormous impact on the BBC in the first years of the decade. But the very conspicuousness of his hubris raised profound misgivings among the ruling orders about the turbulent priest. Among the Governors themselves serious doubts were expressed by Duff, Richard Pim, John Fulton and David Milne. That he would shock was inevitable however, since mischief and uncovering cant were at the heart of his character. Glanmor Williams, who admired Greene, nevertheless felt that 'sometimes Hugh was his own worst enemy. He often gave the impression that he was just out to shock the bourgeoisie.' He had been bound to want radically to improve the BBC in directions which were compatible with that character. It was equally certain that he would not be allowed to do so. Therefore, logically, if his authority and influence had flowed from his being the editor-in-chief then the way to diminish that influence, short of a sacking which was politically impossible, was to transfer some of that role to the office of the chairman. This in essence was what happened in the twelve months after Hill's appointment.

There are, therefore, two vital questions which need to be

posed: what was the relationship between the two men; and how did Hill engineer his final victory?

Hill made it clear that he intended to boost the power of the governors. He introduced voting into all board meetings. He set up a series of subcommittees of the governors, the most prominent being that on finance, chaired by Sir Robert Bellinger. Hill became infuriated by what he saw as the reluctance of the members of the Board of Management to allow the governors knowledge of their discussions. Hugh Greene himself had actively lobbied against the governors receiving minutes. Hill much later was to say that 'Greene never told me much, but then he never told the governors very much either'. Greene was trying to fend off the governors from straying into editorial terrain; Hill was saying that if they were to do their job properly, then that was precisely where they had to go. In his memoirs, Hill comments that there was a wide range of subjects raised at their meetings: 'The Wednesday Play came up again and again for scrutiny, for both praise and criticism. Bad language, emphasis on sex, all these matters came up frequently in one form or another. But there the matter seemed to end. We could talk, but that was all. Policy was made by management.'

Behind the jousting over formal procedures lay deeply-felt personal animosity. In particular Greene did not like the way in which Hill worked:

> One could not have confidence that he was not doing things behind one's back, talking to members of the staff, talking to politicians. I remember on one regional tour it was reported back to me that he had said to producers, 'I'm going to show who's master, Hill or Greene.' What I couldn't stand was Hill's way of conducting affairs, that everything was conducted on a count of heads with the majority always of course being counted the winner. I just got fed up.

Incidents, as ever, fuelled the fires. The issue of cigarette advertising in *The Radio Times* had been raised by Lady

Baird, a qualified doctor and a governor. Greene and his chief assistant Oliver Whitley were worried about the loss of revenue if the advertisements were banned. They expressed their anxiety to Hill in private, and he said that they should not worry since it was likely that the governors would support them. He also created the impression that he would be on their side. At the next meeting of the governors, Hill arrived with the BBC's own doctor, who spoke strongly in favour of the ban. The views of the governors were divided and in spite of what he had said before, Hill cast his vote for the ban. Greene seethed, and legend has it that Whitley was so upset by Hill's behaviour that he was physically sick. At lunch that day Greene, perhaps exhibiting a part of his personality which had been summed up by one governor as '*enfant terrible*, sometimes more *enfant* than *terrible*', ostentatiously smoked a cigarette for the first time in years.

A more serious incident occurred shortly before the Christmas of 1967. Mary Whitehouse had complained about a line in a Beatles' song which was to go out in a film they had made for the BBC. The line, in the song 'I Am A Walrus' said 'Crab a locker, fishwife . . . pornographic priestess, boy, you've been a naughty girl, you let your knickers down.' It was the last phrase which was at issue and which Hill had said should come out. Greene enquired whether this was possible, and he was told that it was not, on technical grounds. Hill still insisted that it be deleted and asked Greene what he would do if he, Hill, instructed him to remove the offending phrase. Greene said that he would be unable to accept such an instruction.

Hill now claims that he never discussed the issue with Greene, only with Oliver Whitley, and adds that 'if Hugh Greene says differently, he is a liar'. Greene insists that they did discuss the song, though it was over the phone rather than face to face.

On December 22nd Greene wrote to Tatjana of what he described as, something near to a head-on collision with Hill on what seemed to me to be a very stupid little thing. He regards it as a matter affecting his authority and would, he says, take it to the board of governors in January. If he doesn't think better of it, he will lose. But I don't want empty victories which will just make things more difficult in the future, just when I hoped that a quite good relationship was being established and that he was being educated.

Hill's idea was to reassert what he felt to be the lost authority of the governors, whereas Greene believed that their role entailed the 'right to reprove and restrain'. It was an argument as old as the BBC itself, and involved much of the theology and metaphysics of public service broadcasting.

It was widely felt by his closest colleagues that by this time Greene was 'psychologically and emotionally' over the top. Certainly the job was not quite what it had been. Charles Curran said about Greene:

There is a natural indolence in him. It is not that he will avoid difficult jobs, but he just doesn't like work too much. In the later stages of the 1960s and certainly by the time Hill came, Hugh was freewheeling, and probably assumed that he could ease his way through his last years at the BBC and at the same time control Hill. This was a mistake.

He thought he could freeze Hill out, hold him at bay but Greene couldn't because he was in the wrong frame of mind. There were other more personal factors, Curran implied, undermining Greene's ability to function. The immediate problem of sheer exhaustion was something which Curran, who was to succeed Greene, felt to be especially important. He observed:

Hugh's tough, but not fit. He was bored. My own experience would suggest that the exhaustion increases progressively. It is mainly a question of stress, a gradual wearing down caused not by the work, though that is also hard, but by the constant pressure from outside. In effect you are in a permanent defensive position. As the pressures continue you can quit, you can go and worry, or you can go on and try to ignore it and that latter was what Hugh Greene tried to do.

There was another element to this; Greene did not especially care for the general context of BBC culture. In 1964 he had joined the Board of the Greene King brewery. In a note to Tatjana in April 1967, after a dinner he had given for various sportsmen, he observed: 'It is a curious thing that I enjoy the beer side of my life, the brewery and the sort of people I was with tonight [the sportsmen] so much more in many ways than the more intellectual company in which I have to spend more of my time.'

Glanmor Williams, always an astute and, above all, honest observer, felt that after Hill's arrival, Greene was badly de-flated and was, as he put it, 'never the same again'. On the surface, however, all did not seem as if it was about to col-lapse. From his country house in Suffolk, he wrote to Tatjana on November 18th, 1967, at nine thirty pm:

I've just had a telephone call from London. The Prime Minister wants to make a broadcast to the nation to-morrow night to which of course I say 'yes'. The banks are to be closed on Monday, I suppose it means devaluation of the pound. There's a long announcement just going out from 10 Downing St. so I suppose I shall get it in 10 minutes on the 10 o'clock news. You are joining a very leaky ship. 10:10: well, that's what it is . . .

19/11 12:20 pm: After half an hour in the garden, the telephone started up and hardly stopped since devalua-tion and all that . . . 3:30 pm: Oh, dear, what a day! I've now had 10 minutes without a telephone call—the only interval for about 4 hours apart from half an hour when I just walked to the pub. Ted Heath has been trying to get me to make a row about some decisions I've made—and

I've been trying to get him to enable him to make the row! So far without success. I'm feeling grateful for my ability to remain calm in a storm—or at any rate *appear* to remain calm. 5 pm: It started again immediately and so it's gone on. I wasn't even able to empty my bladder without being interrupted! It's one of those situations in which one enrages either the government or the opposition. Sometimes we've enraged the government. This time it's the opposition's turn. Ted Heath finally came through and was kind enough to call me a liar among other things and talk about 'breaking the tyranny of the BBC'. As if that was the most important thing in the world.

The enjoyment of a row and of rejecting the advances of politicians with cool disdain was still there, even after Hill, as was his pleasure in making life difficult for his enemies. When Mary Whitehouse had appeared and fared rather badly on a discussion programme *Talkback*, he commented, 'My advice had been to give her enough rope to hang herself. I think it went that way.'

He was, however, slowly being undermined not just in particular details or issues, but in the way in which the BBC's role within society was now being presented to the public. The governors announced that they were going to produce a paper which would take account of 'the public mood'. The first draft of this was to be produced by Oliver Whitley, something which allayed at least some of the fears being felt by the Board of Management. The governors, however, found Whitley's draft too diffident, and Hill eventually took over the drafting himself. The original understanding had been that document would be for internal circulation only, but the governors decided to publish it and to give it wide circulation outside the Corporation. The document was called *Broadcasting and the Public Mood*.

In a fascinating and perceptive piece in *Encounter* Christopher Driver pointed to the differences between this document and the ideas and sentiments contained within Greene's 1965 Rome speech:

The Governors: . . . it is no part of our responsibility to appear to deride, or despise, or destroy, merely because they are traditional or conventional, the moral standards to which sections of the public are attached. There are people who are deeply hurt by the intrusion into their homes of what they believe to be the BBC's amoral or anti-moral attitude. We should take care not to offend such people needlessly. If we do not pursue a traditional line, we should not cultivate or appear to cultivate a 'permissive' one.

Greene: . . . the BBC should encourage the examination of views and opinions in an atmosphere of healthy scepticism. It follows that in its search for truth . . . a broadcasting organisation must recognise an obligation towards tolerance and towards the maximum liberty of expression.

The Governors: The problem is particularly acute in sexual matters . . . we must reconcile the dramatist's need to express himself with the nature and susceptibilities of our audience, a large proportion of whom are deeply offended by overt references to or portrayals of sexual behaviour.

Greene: The attempts at censorship come nowadays also from groups . . . which do not claim to be 'guardians' but claim to speak for 'ordinary, decent people' and claim to be 'forced to take a stand against' *unnecessary* dirt, *gratuitous* sex, *excessive* violence—and so on.

The Governors: A fully responsible producer or editor is one who, by reason or instinct, recognises and eschews anything that involves a risk of damage disproportionate to the importance of the objective.

Greene: . . . it is better to err on the side of freedom than restriction. (Driver, *Encounter*, November 1968)

The counterpoints could be continued. But there is enough here to illustrate that the subtleties and emphases of the BBC's moral and cultural responsibilities had changed gear, from a Greene era to a Hill era. The document was published in July, 1968, and in the same month Greene announced his resignation.

18

Shortly before Christmas 1967, Greene told Hill what he had told Lusty back in April, that he and Elaine were about to be divorced. He was worried because the *Daily Express* had got hold of the story and had placed reporters outside his homes. It upset him as much because he felt it to be an intrusion into his private life, as because of any problems it might cause with the governors.

Hill observed: 'He was very worried as to what the impact would be. I told him then that a man's private life is his own affair, that it was of interest to those who employed him only if it impinged on his work for them. I did not regard this as a matter that concerned me or should concern the governors. But he was very worried.' It was, records Hill in his memoirs, 'a matter which was to have important repercussions'. What does seem clear is that, at this stage, Greene had no intention of leaving the BBC. Indeed, it seems likely that he was worried that a scandal would inhibit his ability to work and perhaps badly affect the governors' confidence in him.

On April 26th, 1968, he wrote a letter to Hill about his future. He said that there were persistent rumours about his leaving the BBC, which were affecting the staff morale. He proposed therefore that the BBC issue a public statement:

'In view of recent press speculation the Board of Governors of the BBC wishes it to be known that it continues to be its assumption that Sir Hugh Greene will remain as Director

General at least until his sixtieth birthday in November, 1970. Any possibility of an extension beyond that date will be the subject of later discussion between the Board and Sir Hugh.

The Board believes in principle that the eventual successor to Sir Hugh should be found if possible from within the ranks of the BBC.

I have put in the second paragraph because I know that the speculation about an appointment from outside is bothering people at the top.

This, I know, would be an unusual step, but it seems to me that it would clear the air once and for all.'

Hill regarded this 'unusual step' as a 'remarkable' letter and was appalled by its assumption that the governors would bind themselves both to guaranteeing Hugh Greene two more years, come what may, and to the kind of person who would be his successor. There is, however, perhaps another way of seeing this curious request. Greene realised that there was speculation about his leaving and that if he did go, it would be under the cloud of his divorce. If, on the other hand, he could persuade Hill to accept the terms of the letter, with its agreement in principle of his staying on until sixty, he could choose his own moment to leave with no danger of being seen to have been forced out. A week or so after the letter was drafted, in a discussion about senior appointments and his own future, he left the very strong impression in Hill's mind that he wanted to 'go early'. Greene had not particularly wanted to create this impression, and in a note to Tatjana he mentioned that Hill had asked him if he had thought of doing something else, and that he replied that he had not.

It was in this conversation that Hill sensed a 'nagging doubt' in Greene's mind that if he resigned at the same time as his divorce was going through, it would look as if the two were connected. To get round this problem of 'face' Hill came up with the idea of suggesting to Harold Wilson that Greene be made a governor. Greene remembers:

I'd imagined myself soldiering on till sixty and conceivably longer if they thought there wasn't a successor ready. But I must say that a lot of the pleasure of the job had gone. One day Hill said to me, 'Would you like to become a governor?' . . . I said that I'd like to think about this, but the next time I saw him I said 'yes'. I must say that it was a bribe, so to speak, well-attuned to my character, because it had never happened before. So I took the bait, being quite clear in my own mind that it was bait, but still, why not take it?

Very few people, other than Hill and Greene, felt that his becoming a governor was a good idea. All his closest colleagues told him it was a great mistake, if only because it would embarrass his successor. His decision to accept the offer was also partly vanity, combined with a feeling he had that as a governor he would be able 'to keep an eye' on Hill. In July 1968 he wrote to Sir James Duff, who had counselled him that it was a bad idea: '. . . in normal times there would have been a great deal in what you say . . . but the Barbarians are now across the Danube and I think and believe that my successor may find me more helpful than formidable. I shall certainly do my best not to breathe down his neck.'

The roots of what was happening to Hugh Greene at this time went back to 1946. He had gone to Hamburg largely to escape the pain of his separation and divorce from Helga, neither of which he had wanted. He returned from Germany in 1948 not only with a reputation for having done a very good job at NWDR, but also with Tatjana Sais, the wife of the German theatre director, Günter Neumann, with whom he had begun to have a passionate affair. Together they had set up house in Elizabeth Street in Chelsea, just round the corner from Helga. Hugh had hoped that Tatjana might be able to work on the English stage, but it quickly became clear that this was unlikely because of her lack of perfect English. She eventually decided to return to Germany where she was already well known. Neither of them was sure whether it was the end of the affair, but it left Hugh feeling very lonely.

Hugh Greene had always longed for a stable and loving relationship. There is no shadow of doubt that he had been very much in love with Helga in the way in which he understood being in love. There were two incidents which capture his feeling and his hurt at what happened, like two perfectly painted miniature portraits. In 1935 he had returned home to their ground floor flat in Berlin and had looked in through the window to see Helga standing alone. He sensed, even before he went through the door, that something was wrong. To his utter amazement when he entered, she began to shout that she did not love him, had never loved him, and had only married him to get away from her parents. The episode stayed in his mind even though the marriage lingered on. Early during the year of 1944 Ivone Kirkpatrick, when he was head of the European Services, had called Greene into his office and said that as the remaining part of the war was going to be very taxing, he should take a holiday for a month. Hugh was delighted and went home feeling happy at the thought of his being able to spend a month with Helga and the boys, Graham and James. When he had told her, she had looked at him with coldness and said, 'I'm never going away anywhere with you again'. It was one of the very few occasions in his life when he'd gone away and cried. He had, however, been young enough to get away to Hamburg, to pick up the pieces and to fall in love again. But then disaster had struck, and Tatjana had left. Once more he was hurt and perplexed but all the while determined that somewhere he would find emotional stability and security.

Whether the pain created by Tatjana's departure was equal to, or less than, that caused by Helga's desertion of him is really not the point. He had once more, for a moment, found that passion and happiness which he hungered for and which Tatjana seemed to offer in abundance. When it was over, the possibility of working in Malaya had come up, and so off he'd gone to a new challenge and away from the sadness.

In Malaya he met and fell in love, a little too easily and

quickly, with Elaine Shaplen. Elaine was totally different from Helga and Tatjana, with none of Helga's self-confident assertiveness or Tatjana's sensuality. She was much cleverer than the other two and understood that by giving Hugh a considerable sense of freedom she gained more power over him. He seemed happy enough to his family and friends; they were married, returned home, and had two children, Christopher and Timothy. He had remained in touch with Tatjana, corresponding with her throughout the 1950s. Then came a trip to Germany in the first years of his Director Generalship and a meeting with Tatjana. Suddenly he fell out of love with Elaine and back into love with Tatjana. In reality he had never really been out of love with Tatjana. Somewhere in his mind, he had retained the firm belief that with her he could find a happiness which had always eluded him.

By the autumn of 1966 his marriage to Elaine was finished, even though they lived in the same house and tried to keep the truth from the boys. He was, however, becoming depressed by the whole situation and merely forced himself to stay because of his fear of what a separation might mean to the two children. By the autumn of 1967 he had decided that he would have to leave home. He found a small flat, and in October Tatjana moved in with him. That seemed to break something of the depression, even while he felt that, whatever the outcome, he had done something which was wrong and hurtful to someone who did not deserve to be hurt and to two young children who were totally innocent. He recalled later that 'of all the many bad things I've done in my life, this was the worst'. It was at this moment, in the winter of 1967, when he was waiting for the divorce to take place that he began to be concerned about the publicity. The worry stayed with him and when, in October 1968, he went to a European Broadcasting Union conference in Reykjavik a special operation was put into effect by the BBC's skilled press officer, George Campey. It was known as 'Operation Iceland' and had the specific intention of not only keeping Greene informed of the press coverage, but in particular of keeping the lid on that coverage. The decree was not issued until December 2nd, 1968, on the grounds of his adultery with 'Else Neumann', (Tatjana's real name). It became absolute on March 5th, 1969.

Hugh may never have realised how the situation disturbed people inside the BBC who were cut from a more traditional cloth. One recalled being amazed and appalled when Hugh Greene, with a casual cynicism, said at a dinner party, that he was 'between wives'. The second divorce had triggered off a doubt in some minds which actually went back to Jacob's doubts in 1959; did Hugh have any stable commitments, did he really believe in anything, did he have any values which were solid and permanent? One former senior executive became quite passionate: 'I'm not quite sure what he believes at all. One was never quite sure where Hugh would stick and one felt that there was nothing that he might not betray because of his lack of values and commitments.' This man cared deeply that his Director General had so few certainties in his life: 'He is on the side of freedom but in a somewhat anarchistic way. This is what I meant by absence of values.'

Even among those who admired and liked him, there were serious misgivings about his latest divorce, worry too that the case would be squalid and messy, and would therefore be a stick with which to beat him and the BBC. He took Anne Godwin aside on one occasion to hear her views as a governor. She told him rather bluntly that one divorce was manageable, but that she was not at all sure he would get away with another. A close colleague of Greene's summed the feeling up in a comment to another member of the Board of Management: 'Hugh can't go on doing this. One divorce is OK, but two is going a bit far.' Whatever Hill had said —with, it has to be said, honesty—there was a wide consensus among Greene's colleagues that the divorce, which Elaine had demanded because of his relationship with Tatjana, *was* a political and moral issue both for him and the governors.

Many feared that the reputation of the BBC would be

affected by the divorce. It comes as a surprise to realise that after all the disdain and dismissal of Mary Whitehouse, there were still quite a few BBC executives who worried about what she would make of a sordid divorce case. Hugh Greene himself could not see that the details of his private life were relevant to his professional role, even when he appeared at the BBC functions with Tatjana, rather than Elaine, on his arm.

One of the immediate difficulties for his colleagues, after Tatjana had returned to the scene, was that they all knew and liked Elaine while the new love in his life remained unknown, slightly mysterious, and, it has to be said, slightly improper. One member of the Board of Management re-called how on a number of occasions he had phoned Addison Avenue, only to find Elaine alone with no knowledge of where Hugh was, the assumption being that he was with Tatjana. The whole situation began to create personal and professional difficulties for his friends and colleagues. While affection and loyalty to him remained, there arose a very large questionmark in their minds about the morality of his life.

As Director General he travelled an enormous amount, especially to meetings of the European Broadcasting Union and, with particular pleasure, to the Commonwealth Broadcasting Conferences. His instinctive inclination when abroad on such occasions was wherever possible to avoid the formal junketing and to disappear with his immediate circle of intimates such as Donald Stephenson to local night clubs, bars and the occasional strip club. As one of those travelling with him said, in a rather wry, amused tone, 'I think to some extent this made a rather bad impression on our conference hosts and colleagues'.

Inevitably stories filtered back to London and one very senior and close colleague spoke of how the more staid members of the BBC upper echelons, including the governors, regarded his behaviour as rather 'unbuttoned'. One of those who regularly accompanied him responds to this: 'There are many people who thought the same thing, but if

Hugh was a little unbuttoned it was to relax and it did him good.' The most curious aspect to this is that not only were stories being fed back to the BBC in London—greatly exaggerated versions according to those who were with him—but that according to Charles Curran, who succeeded Hugh as Director General, titbits were being fed to Harold Wilson in No 10 who then passed them on to Hill. There is, not surprisingly, absolutely no evidence for this.

Lord Hill does, however, say in his memoirs, *en passant*, that when he went to see Harold Wilson to discuss the idea of making Greene a governor, 'to my surprise the Prime Minister knew of the impending divorce'. Curran offers insight into how the divorce issue worked itself into the Hill-Greene relationship. It seemed likely that Hugh would be faced with an expensive divorce settlement. In particular he would still have to find the money to put his two young boys, Timothy and Christopher, through school. There is no doubt that the possibility, if not the certainty, of retirement had wandered through his mind. There was however a very important problem which was bound to influence his decision whether or not to go.

There existed a technical qualification concerning the BBC's regulations on pension rights. The BBC rule was that an employee did not get the full pension unless he or she had worked for forty years in the Corporation. Hugh Greene had been with the BBC for twenty-seven years and, therefore, would have received only 27/60th of his salary, which it was assumed would not have been enough to meet the various financial commitments with which he would be faced. He could not afford, quite literally, to leave the BBC even though he may have wished to do so. This meant, as Curran noted—and no doubt he had taken a close look at the issue when he in his turn became Director General—that 'Hill had Hugh by the balls'. A little piece of circumstantial evidence which supports Curran's penury thesis is that after the Board of Management meeting in which Hugh announced that he would be getting a divorce, Hugh asked one of those there whether he could give him some advice on obtaining a flat 'and he added that he couldn't afford much'. On his retirement *The Times* report merely said, 'he will receive a pension of 60 per cent of his salary'. He wrote to Tatjana, on June 13th, 1968, 'It now seems that the announcement about my future will be out about the middle of July. The board today approved my financial treatment. Better even than I had hoped.'

It all seems rather prosaic, even sordid, but Hill's answer to the problem of Hugh Greene was found in special pension arrangements. Of such rather simple, brutal truths is history made.

On July 15th, 1968, Lord Hill announced to the assembled press in Broadcasting House that Hugh Greene would be retiring from the Director Generalship on March 31st, 1969. He also announced that Greene would become a governor of the BBC. Hugh Greene sat smiling next to the Chairman and announced that he was not being 'kicked upstairs but was walking upstairs with pleasure'. He had decided, he said, that he had been in the job long enough and that now was the time to move to give a chance to a younger man. He denied that there had been any row with Hill and added that their working relationship had been excellent. He had done what he wanted to do which, in that well-worn phrase, was to 'open the windows and turn down the central heating'. He added in terms which he had repeatedly uttered in the previous seven years, 'I think my greatest satisfaction has been that in this time the BBC has become more realistic as an organisation and closer to life as it is lived.'

Both Hill and Greene smiled throughout the press conference, but no one believed them. No one imagined that theirs had been a relationship of Flanagan and Allen, and the *Guardian* asked the obvious question, 'Did he jump, or was he pushed?' The truth of the matter was that he had been slowly shuffled out of office by his own ennui, personal anxieties, sheer dislike of Hill, and a subliminal recognition that he had lost.

The announcement came as a relief to him. He wrote to Tatjana:

An interesting thing which Hill told me today is that only one governor asked whether the proposal for my retirement arose in anyway from my private situation. His reply had been that the two things had nothing whatever to do with each other, except in so far as the timing of the announcement was concerned. Not another word on the subject. I must say good for them. Quite a civilised group!

The mood did not last, and he was quickly at odds with Hill and the governors over the appointment of his successor; to him it was obvious that it should be Curran. Once more to Tatjana:

It's been a tiresome day. The board meeting was thoroughly frustrating and irritating. No decision yet. On another minor issue I lost my temper with Hill in a very cold and controlled way. I was so cold and controlled that I have the impression that many of the governors did not realise how angry I was. It's his bland way of dismissing arguments that enrages me as much as his interference with things that shouldn't be his concern. I look forward to continuing the battle as a governor with a longer lease of life than his!

As well as the continuation of his battle with Hill, his mind was turning to other things that he might do in his retirement:

Here I am in my office at 6 pm. The board is still toiling on about the choice of my successor—which should be the easiest thing in the world if enough of them had experience and sense. Another offer today. This time a rather exciting one. The *Sunday Telegraph* wants me to do the occasional special correspondent jobs for them abroad in places that interest me. Can I pick up the old news gathering technique? At least I could try. I am inclined to think that the right approach for me would be not to be in the place where all the news hounds are (as Czechoslovakia at the

305

moment for instance) but to try to think of the places where the news may break later on. I think you will agree that this is much more promising than *Punch*. Later. Thank God, they've chosen the right man.

By July 25th he had been approached by six different publishers to write his memoirs; had been offered the editorship of *Punch*, and the chairmanship of The Bodley Head.

Inevitably, the moment came to leave. The evening of March 31st was the designated moment, but the farewells had begun well before that. His feeling is in his letters:

March 26th, to Tatjana: Tonight's party for drivers, commissionaires, cleaners, etc., went better than I could ever have dreamed. For the first time in this long process of farewell I was really moved and had to fight back tears. Very odd. One was surrounded by love. I had never expected anything like that.

He left, rather as his friend and mentor, Arthur fforde, had left: 'Nostalgia for me isn't really the right word. I hated leaving the BBC and think of it with affection; but with the knowledge also, and without regret, that the end of a chapter is the end of a chapter, and that there are other ways of living and learning.'

Inevitably words of praise came from the press, and more privately and personally from those with whom he had worked. Sir Gerald Beadle wrote:

The newspapers tell me you are retiring from the post of DG tomorrow. I am very sorry indeed. I served under every DG the BBC ever had. There were only three who had the ability and the sensitivity to reflect the mood of the times: Reith, Haley, and Greene . . . The main object of this letter is to tell you how much I have admired your performance as DG. It was quite brilliant and exactly what was required at that moment. I am so involved myself that I feel it would not be out of place to say thank you.

Another wrote:

> My dear DG. On your last day in office I must write you a
> personal note to thank you wholeheartedly for all your
> kindness and leadership over the last eleven years. To me
> you have been the BBC. What you have contributed to us
> all in firmness of purpose and clarity of mind has been of
> incalculable value. That you have given us our marching
> orders and then trusted us to get on with our jobs has
> meant that it has been an adventure in partnership to
> work with you and under you. We all, and I personally,
> shall miss you very much indeed. But I do want you to
> know what respect, gratitude and affection you have
> inspired in those immediately around you, and to send you
> my warmest good wishes for the future. We shall try to be
> true to your trust.

Someone else wrote: 'I have served under many DGs but
never under one so human. That is what it is all about, isn't
it?' John Freeman wrote from the Embassy in Washington:

> . . . as one of your old servants—if only on an *ad hoc*
> contractual basis—for all the earlier years of your Direc-
> tor Generalship, I cannot see the last day of your Director
> Generalship without wishing you farewell and God speed.
> In all affection and respect I want to tell you of my
> certainty that, despite the inevitable frictions of public
> controversy, you will be remembered as the 'other great
> DG'. And in truth I believe you have done as much for
> public service broadcasting as Reith did—and this will be
> recognised . . . What I am trying to say, equally as an
> audience and as an employee, is thank you and good luck.

And finally one must quote from a note not from someone of
exalted status but someone who had worked with him
closely, his chief secretary, Monica Long:

> I know you're not a great one for thank-you letters, and

I'm not much of a one for sorrowful farewells. But I do want to say, very sincerely, how much I've enjoyed working for you, and how much I've respected and admired your work. My time in the office has been very happy and if I achieve anything more, it will be thanks to you for giving me a chance.

The press assessment of his career was overwhelmingly favourable. The most characteristic piece was by Peter Black with the headline 'The Rebel Who Shook Auntie into Success' and a content which showed a careful reading of his Rome speech. Everywhere the comparison was with Reith, of Greene being the only other Director General who had stamped his personality on the Corporation. Nancy Banks Smith in *The Sun* wrote:

> Hugh Greene's genius is that he provided an atmosphere in which other men were encouraged to create. He must have courage, a sense of humour, and a sense of the time for, under him, the BBC had all three. Reith made it respectable. Greene made it exciting. He found a Rolls Royce but made it move so that at times everything else on the TV road seemed to be standing still.

One of the few notes welcoming his departure was sounded by the editorial columns of the *Daily Sketch*:

> Few tears need be shed because Sir Hugh Carleton Greene is ceasing to be Director General of the BBC . . . He presided over a transformation in which staid old Auntie BBC put on mini-skirts and began blurting out dirty words. It has not been an edifying spectacle . . . the sordid wasteland of *The Wednesday Play* seemed calculated to depress and deter [viewers]. Drug addicts and homosexuals were paraded across the screen in seemingly endless processions . . . Anybody with something nasty to say about Britain was assured of good publicity on the BBC.

The Financial Times carried the best review of his career. T. C. Worsley argued that Greene had,

carried the BBC struggling and kicking out of its Auntie image into something much more relevant to the decade. Instead of reflecting the respectable old-fashioned, middle class values of a past that was over and done with, the BBC began to mirror at least equally, the aspirations and attitudes of the generation of the newly enfranchised young who had come up via the grammar schools and red brick universities, and whose voice it was time that we heard. Sir Hugh gave them their chance.

Hugh Greene had achieved this not by any personal *fiat*, but by giving freedom to key executives who themselves had an eye for just the right kind of talent: Baverstock, Wheldon, Peacock, Newman, Goldie, and many more. Jacob had done the same when he made that crucial decision to transform his Controller, Overseas Services from promising material into the heir apparent. Jacob had known that he had to find the man who fitted the moment, who could take the BBC out of the early 1950s into the 1960s. Greene in his turn found the team who could help him do this, and they in their turn found their own teams. All the excitement and controversy flowed from that process of recruitment and encouragement. The roll-call of creative talent is truly remarkable: Frost, Bird, Cook, Moore, Levin, Bennett, Sherrin, Messina, Burton, MacTaggart, Bakewell, Russell, Miller, Loach, Savile, Coleman, Page, Jarrott, Watkins, Pinter, Hopkins, Mercer, Exton, McGrath, Kennedy-Martin, Jones, Cooper, Barton, Owen, Speight: it was a creative soup from which sprang life.

The BBC under Greene covered the whole waterfront, from the arts to hard-nosed journalism, from the writer to the technician, from the poet to the social realist, and found the best, brought them in, paid them reasonably well, and released them on the nation. It was a recipe, however, far too rich even for a Britain in the throes of Beatlemania and Harold Wilson's white hot technological revolution. It was certainly a mixture far too rich for the ladies and gentlemen of the governors for whom the whole experience was like a ride on a roller-coaster. What Hugh Greene had done by encouraging talent, releasing their creativity, was to say that the point of the BBC was not its independence, that most exalted of Reithian legacies, but the quality of the experience of independence. Independence of itself was meaningless; it was what you did with it that counted. That is why he should be considered as important a figure as Reith: the founding father created the structure, Greene showed what you could achieve with it.

This wealth of writing, performing, and producing talent, it must be re-emphasised, actually only influenced a small part of the output, but it was that part which received all the attention, all the accolades and the abuse. They were naughty, outrageous, realistic, sympathetic to the poor and disadvantaged rather than to the rich and powerful; their hearts were with everyone so long as they were not part of the establishment; they hated hypocrisy, enjoyed wit, were slightly seedy, enjoyed sex rather than being fearful of it; they cared about basic liberties that were in practice denied by a society flabby with its own history. They were, in short, rather similar to their boss.

There is something of the agnostic in Greene's make-up; not just lack of religious conviction, but rather an open-mindedness, a great facility, as one of his former German colleagues put it, to listen without having any particular preconceptions. This is the reverse side of that other, often-heard comment about him, that he did not really believe in anything, that he had no fundamental commitments, in other words, that he accepted other people's views because he did not have any of his own.

But he did hold strong beliefs and possessed a clear-cut, distinctive set of values, only they were not linked into any coherent philosophical structure. He believed in freedom, in tolerance, in fairness and in liberal democracy and he quite understood that there were certain attitudes, such as Fascism, which were unacceptable in a free society. So he had recognised that boundaries inevitably existed in a liberal democracy, but he did not feel that the full potential for creativity had yet been reached within those boundaries. He wanted his creative staff, and the numerous clever and extrovert broadcasters under him, to explore those boundaries, to prowl along the borders, to open up the fringe areas. It was inevitable that in so doing he would upset those who instinctively preferred the middle ground, the safer central area. The greatest difference between the middle ground and the fringe areas in English society occurs over sexual values; that is why attitudes towards sex became so controversial at this time.

Greene liked to challenge staider members of the community, particularly if they had power: he enjoyed questioning, probing, exploring, testing. From 1960 to 1965 British society seemed, for a brief moment, to possess sufficient social stability to be able to enjoy the right to doubt, to mock, to pronounce traditional thought and behaviour as absurd. This taunting was accepted and even in some quarters encouraged and welcomed: indeed its acceptance seemed to some an assertion of judicious tolerance on the part of the ruling powers. But Greene's ability to tease and scorn with impunity depended on the political establishment retaining this level of self-confidence and well being. As Macmillan was eventually succeeded by the more difficult Wilson, the confidence oozed away—with some, such as Duff, it had never been there—and the Prague Spring of the early years of the decade gave way to the chill of Hill.

To some the BBC *was* the establishment so its Director General must also be a member by definition, but Greene persistently defined himself as separate from the establishment and tried to distance himself from those who held similar positions in the hierarchy to himself. He refused membership of the Athenaeum, preferring to form his own social circle. He was a founder member of Bushmen, a cricket-playing, eating and drinking club for like-minded souls. It still exists and is often referred to with bated breath as though it were some kind of anti-establishment secret

311

BBC society. His founding of it had been a way of signalling not so much disapproval as disdain for the much more conventional BBC Club. There was, however, another element and that was the way in which this self-sought separateness reflected a fundamental part of his personality, a loneliness which created aloofness. One of those close to him said "He tends to create a loneliness around himself and that is why he likes a coterie of friends. But I should say that generally he tends to envelop himself in a cocoon of isolation and loneliness."

When he was abroad, therefore, the desire to distance himself from many of his senior international colleagues as well as from the great and good in Britain, was natural to him; it was not an engineered ploy. It did, however, have the added effect, and benefit, of creating the legend of the bold, risqué DG which did wonders for his reputation among junior colleagues. What young producer, with an ounce of wit in his soul, could not fail to be stimulated by the knowledge that his boss had the reputation of being a 'bit of a lad'.

This physical distancing was matched by the feeling among some, especially the governors, that he was also psychologically apart. One governor commented: 'Hugh lacked a certain viability with other human beings. I personally never got on close terms with him. Hugh is in some respects a detached cold fish. In other ways very warm. He hadn't quite the human touch somehow. In conversation he was lucid, but he made no small talk, and had very few of the minor human graces.' One of those colleagues who travelled with him a great deal and who became very fond of him said: 'He tends to create a loneliness around himself. He tends to envelop himself in a cocoon of isolationism.'

Greene's detachment reflected in part a deep inward unhappiness; not the misery of self-pity or self-doubt, but of emotional unfulfilment. His ability to distance himself from problems made him a most effective executive and administrator; it also removed him out of the range of his critics'

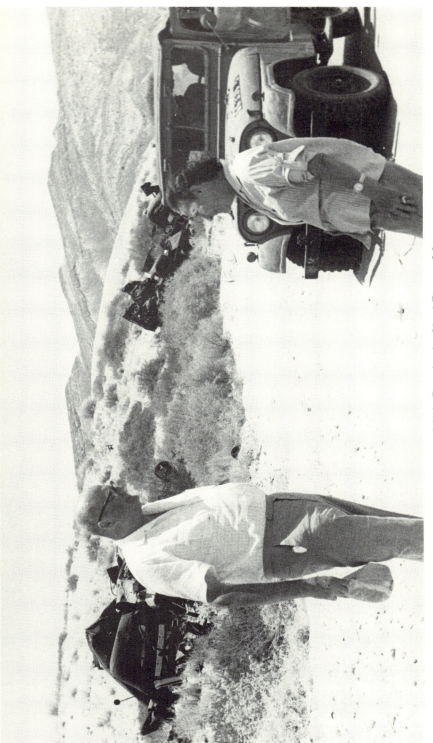

With Tatjana at the Mitle Pass in the Sinai Desert, May 1973

With John Pesmazoglou, former Minister of Finance and John
Lampsas, former Director General of Greek National
Broadcasting (centre)

With George Mavros, former leader of the Greek Centre Union Party

barbs, be they from governors or audience. At the end of the day, he did not care very much if people attacked him or hated his policies, and in an innovative, and therefore controversial, age that was indeed a great strength.

Curran said that fifty per cent of his time was taken up with correspondence with viewers: Greene spent only five per cent. He did not worry what people thought about his programmes. This did not mean that he did not care about programming, just that he did not worry all that much what people thought. Greene recognised that if broadcasting was to mean anything as a cultural force, then it would have to prod the margins of experience. That in turn would invoke cries of pain, not just from moral guardians such as Whitehouse, but from the ordinary man and woman who remained fearful of change and innovation. In this sense the Currans of the world are far more 'responsible' than someone such as Greene. They are also far duller and ultimately more dangerous because in their nervous conservatism are sown the seeds of stagnation.

There was one kind of letter for which he always had time. There are in the BBC's files many such examples as this to a young boy, Jeremy Bournon:

'Dear Jeremy / Thank you very much for your postcard. I am sorry that you miss your favourite programmes on your choir practice night. Perhaps you will find something on another evening which you will grow to like as much. I am sending you a copy of the BBC *Handbook*. There is a nice picture of Joe Hugget and Bobby between pages 48 and 49.

Greene worried even less if the blasts of complaint came from establishment figures, for he did not care for their idea of culture. His tastes did not run to opera, classical drama, or even classical literature, but to cabaret and detective stories. He was not someone who could hide his boredom: his own preferred culture suggested sin rather than sanctity.

He was educated at public school and at Oxford; he came from a long line of sturdy middle-class gentry, interspersed with clergy, educators, stalwart City figures, and the one Caribbean maverick. He held one of the foremost establishment posts. Yet he had always been discontented with the established orders and enjoyed being seen to be out of step with middle-class mores: he possessed the detachment of the outsider with the position of an insider. He liked to use his intelligence, whether it be to solve detective story problems, to defeat the Germans, the Malayan Communists, win Pilkington, or devise successful schemes to sell BBC programmes.

As an outsider on the inside, it was probably inevitable that he would be seen as such by the governors of the BBC, who would then, after the initial moment of relative freedom, gradually tighten control, not because they conspired with Wilson, or even with his appointee Hill, but because, like arthritic sufferers responding to changing weather, they sensed the increasing harshness in the political and social climate. In their bones they felt that Hugh Greene was simply inappropriate to head the BBC when the temperature dropped.

A former governor reflecting on the 1960s asked 'Why didn't Hugh see the need for a new kind of discipline?' The very fact that he could ask the question indicated the differences which ran deep between Greene and the governors. By 'discipline' he meant certain received truths, values, commitments as represented by the board, which should inform and shape the content of programmes. To Greene that would be a recipe for stagnation, because if all that was picked up were the static, existing consensual values, then there would be no potential for truth and growth. Broadcasting was like water; if it flowed forward, it had energy, direction, and strength. But if it stayed as a pool, unmoving, unreplenished, then it would grow mould on the surface and slowly die. For Hugh Greene corporate freedom and public responsibility were as one because the health of one depended upon the health of the other.

Hugh Greene is not an easy man to understand. Even his closest friends would become mystified in an attempt to capture him in their mind's eye. Questions abounded, and continue to abound. Where is he politically? Not a fighter for lost causes, he was a liberal, but not a Liberal. Radical but not socialist, a close friend of Gordon Walker (whose daughter his son Graham married) and of Richard Crossman, but with little use for Gaitskell, Wilson, and especially Benn. The one person he did identify with politically was Roy Jenkins, although he did not feel especially friendly towards him as a person. He was attracted by Butler's sardonic wit and Macmillan's skill, but he had absolutely no time for Home or Hailsham. He much preferred Maudling to Heath, and positively liked Whitelaw.

He was an effective adversary of ITV and yet had amiable relations with Grade and the other moguls of commercial television. He could not stand Robert Fraser and stuffily refused to talk to him direct, insisting that all contact be through Oliver Whitley, his Chief Assistant. One is sometimes tempted to conclude that he preferred rogues to intellectuals, but then one has to allow for his fondness for fforde and his friendship with Normanbrook.

One of his very closest colleagues spoke of his naïveté in personal relationships: 'I thought he sometimes overestimated people's regard for him. He himself believed in straight dealing and with great equanimity he seemed to me to assume that others would be equally undevious. Or perhaps he simply didn't care.'

He hated tyranny and oppression, yet he warmed to Lee Kwan Yew of Singapore who had imposed dictatorial restrictions on the press. He was against obscurantism, pomposity, and too rigid principles. He loved personal challenges, good living, travel, freedom, getting his own way, women. He was apparently totally indifferent to schools broadcasting (despite being the son of a headmaster), religion and religious broadcasting (despite being the brother of Graham), and music. Donald Stephenson and Hugh made a visit to Vienna, where they bumped into Graham Greene at the airport. The conjunction of author and city obviously turned Stephenson's mind to *The Third Man*. That first evening Stephenson decided to take Hugh round the Bier-kellers; in each one he bribed the band to play the haunting Harry Lime theme. Five times the tune was played. At the end, Hugh said, 'By the way, what was that tune they kept playing?'

Why was he such an impressive and attractive leader? He was for a start totally confident and competent in whatever he did. He was accessible and decisive. He had an easy, unpretentious, straightforward manner. He had no ego problems in harnessing other people's talents to a common purpose, as long as he defined that purpose. He enjoyed life, at least he appeared to do so, and that was something many people found attractive. He was certainly different from his predecessors, with none of Reith's formidable élitism, Haley's mixture of shyness and pomposity, or Jacob's military manner.

One of the more curious aspects of his career is that those who watched him work and chewed over his career arrived at a judgment which combined admiration for his abilities with sadness at how he had employed them. Time and time again one comes back to concern at the absence of any visible moral allegiances in his make-up, tinged with doubts about his occasionally 'unbuttoned' behaviour abroad. His agnosticism was actually known to very few people—hence the question in 1959 from fforde of whether he was a Catholic —because he did not flaunt it, but it was perhaps assumed by more people. His preference for iconoclastic figures against more establishment-minded characters—his obvious relish in some of the demolition jobs which *TW3* did on such characters as Henry Brooke would be an example here—was too much for some stomachs. His clear patronage of what became known as the 'permissive society' was bound to evoke wrath. It was also often assumed that he too easily dominated the board of governors. This was simply not the case, but it does attest to his skills in creating that impression. He may have been so successful in this that he even began to believe it himself at times.

His strengths and weaknesses were related. His rather boyish enjoyment at poking fun at the establishment allowed him to accept the work of his young producers on which so much of the reputation of the BBC in the 1960s rests. His very unorthodoxy put him in tune with the times. His indolence allowed him to be relaxed enough to encourage change and innovation which would inevitably cause hue and cry and which might have led a lesser man to worry too much about public reaction. His independence of mind allowed some great television to be made, but inevitably sowed the seeds of his own downfall.

Hugh Greene is now over seventy. He makes the occasional TV documentary, writes the occasional review or reminiscence, is still proud of his journalistic skills which seem to have lost none of their sharpness. He has his books—those he publishes, those he reads. There is a captivating quality to him which still makes him enormously attractive to younger people. One can understand how he was able to generate that confidence in others because he can still create that effect today. If the angels are young, he is definitely on their side. He is charming, kind and unpretentious. One can understand how women might have fallen for him in his prime because one can still witness the same effect today, not because of any good looks on his part, but because of a gentle power. It is, however, his sheer humanity which lies there beneath the apparent aloofness which is his most appealing quality. He is still a private man, so private that his true qualities are often missed by those who think they know him.

He is, however, a sad figure, lonely as presumably only old people can be lonely when all they have are memories. Tatjana is no longer there, and her absence once more raises black spectres. She had offered him what he always sought, a romance. They married in 1970 and even though her continuing career kept her away much of the time, that merely added to the effect, since to him each return was like a honeymoon. He had always been able to fill the emotional

317

gap in his life with an affair or a new wife. But after Tatjana, there really could be nothing more. She had said to him in her last letter before she died that she hoped he would find someone new to spend his old age with. He knew that that would be impossible. He had searched and for a moment found his ideal love, only to have it slip away once more.

He has the pride and self-perception of having lived a life well, of knowing that others now look to him as having embodied fine qualities of leadership and caring. Even the dark spectres cannot extinguish that side of his character which makes his eyes twinkle, which leads him to chuckle, to enjoy the occasional mischief. He still likes pubs, even if he no longer drinks the amounts which made him famous. He still enjoys being seen to be slightly naughty, slightly wicked. That is why this story ends not with a mighty flourish, not by trying to capture in one stroke a canvas of seventy years, but with a snapshot of one scene.

The scene is a conference hall in Iceland. A rather stark, colourless place, its mood matched by the dullness of the meeting which is taking place within it. A sub-committee of the European Broadcasting Union, of which Greene is chairman, is assembled to discuss the mind-splittingly boring details of how to aid developing countries. It is October 1968. Greene sits there a little tired, certainly bored, concerned, even anxious about the divorce case, of whether it will explode about his ears with gory details in one of the Sunday newspapers. He knows that his days at the BBC are numbered. Certainly the excitement is gone. There is nothing more to do because there is nothing more he can do, and all that remains is to withdraw with dignity without being seen to be forced out by Hill. His eyes scan the room and alight on a face which is familiar, a face to stare at, to create idle dreams. Laurianne Guéry, the translator. He produces pen and paper and begins to write. The sounds of debate around him are reduced to a background hum. Finished, he passes the paper across to her to read. This is the quintessential Greene, still more *enfant* than *terrible*, still slightly naughty, still the lonely romantic:

318

Laurianne, whose mane is white
But whose heart is always young,
Tell me, please, the French for tight
And the Japanese for hung—

over. Now the Conference sleeps,
The Chairman has begun to snore.
Tell me, please, the French for weeps
And the Japanese for bore.

Over Iceland falls the mist.
Muffled now the geyser's roar.
Tell me, please, the French for kissed
And the Japanese for—more.

EPILOGUE

There is just one more story to tell. In April 1972, the entertainer Hughie Green flew into Athens to appear at a show at the new Athens Hilton. Passing through customs he was peremptorily arrested and whisked off to an interrogation room. After several hours of aggressive questioning, he suddenly became aware that he was the victim of mistaken identity. No, he tried to tell his captors, I am not Sir Hugh Greene, I am Hughie Green, Canadian entertainer and no I have not been trying to overthrow the Greek government. The Canadian ambassador was summoned from his bed in the early hours of the morning to identify Hughie Green.

Retirement for Hugh Greene had not been quiet. He had become Chairman of the publisher Bodley Head, and of the Greene King brewery. He began to publish his popular series of books, *The Rivals of Sherlock Holmes*, and to see them produced as a successful series for Thames Television, much to the chagrin of the governors of the BBC. His membership of the board of governors had been a short-lived and unenjoyable appointment. In May 1973 he had made a report on the operations of the Israel Broadcasting Authority.

He had also become an active opponent of the colonels who had come to power in Greece in 1967 after a military coup. The story is pure 'Greeneland': opposition to a particularly vile dictatorship; meetings in a seedy flat above the Golden Girl club in Soho; tramping through the streets of London in the dead of night, pockets stuffed with banknotes from a sympathetic but anonymous Greek shipowner; burglaries by Greek agents and the threat of violence.

320

Following his retirement from the BBC Hugh Greene had been commissioned by *The Sunday Telegraph* to prepare major interviews with public figures who were not normally accessible to journalists. He obtained interviews with Willy Brandt, not that he was particularly inaccessible, and Yasser Arafat, the latter involving his being picked up from a hotel in Amman late at night, and driven through the streets in a car with drawn blinds to a secret rendezvous with the PLO leader.

The really important meeting, however, was with the Greek dictator, George Papadopoulos, on July 22nd, 1970. His article, based on the interview, appeared in *The Sunday Telegraph* on August 2nd and was a passionate and clever indictment of the particularly nasty government of army colonels, headed by Papadopoulos, which had seized power in Greece on April 21st, 1967. It appears that Papadopoulos was persuaded to grant the interview by the Greek ambassador in London, General John Sorokos, on the grounds that *The Sunday Telegraph* was a tame right-wing newspaper. Certainly that paper's editorial policy on the junta in Athens had since 1967 been less than aggressive. On this occasion, however, the situation was very different, as Greene's opening paragraphs made his own view of the dictator very clear:

He abandoned the phrases he has previously used, particularly for the benefit of the Americans, about a timetable, however gradual, for the restoration of parliamentary democracy, and he justified the continuation of martial law as a means of keeping the Greek people under the control of his régime.

Mr Papadopoulos is not noted for the clarity with which he uses the Greek language. But no other interpretation can be put on what he said to me. In other words, the dictator was dropping the mask.

I felt myself in the presence of a man who is full of self-confidence after more than three years' absolute power and who no longer considers it necessary to maintain some of his previous pretences. He is, I would judge, a man who is emerging from the chrysalis stage of the consummate conspirator he used to be into an absolute ruler fanatically convinced of the blessing and protection of God as well as of the tanks of his army and the massive security apparatus of his police state.

The article had a considerable impact. It received wide attention in Britain, was translated into Greek by a leading opponent of the colonels, and himself a political prisoner, John Zigdis, and circulated among the Greek underground opposition to the junta. It was also given wide currency in Greece when the pro-junta official press attacked Greene without actually mentioning what it was he had said. George Mangakis, later Minister of Justice in the Papandreou Government, who was at that time in prison as a result of his opposition to the colonels, recalled how the article 'showed the monstrous face of the régime'. John Pesmazoglou, another prominent opponent of the junta, and himself imprisoned and exiled, described the interview as 'the first comprehensive article, clear, and at the same time shrewd, intelligent and full of very significant remarks published in a major international newspaper, which at the same time constituted a condemnation both of the régime and of the man who was responsible'. The article brought him to the attention of Greek exiles based in London, such as the well-known journalists Takis Lambrias and Helen Vlachos.

Someone else who had seen the article was Professor John Spraos of University College, London. He was a Greek who had lived in London for twenty-five years and had been an active opponent of the colonels since 1967.

Two strategies of opposition to the régime had emerged. On the one hand there was a grass-roots resistance with an emphasis on public demonstration, leaflets, and so on, specifically aimed at what were regarded as 'soft' targets such as the Council of Europe, from which Greece was eventually expelled. On the other hand was the 'corridors of power' strategy which aimed to push rather 'harder' targets such as the British and American governments, and NATO, into an actively hostile attitude towards the Greek junta. The Greek opposition, both inside and outside the country, was divided over the appropriateness of this strategy, though obviously both forms of open opposition and subtle subversion were engaged in at one and the same time. Some felt that NATO in general and the Americans in particular deliberately supported the colonels, and that there was nothing that could be done to change their attitude. The logic of this position then was that the only way was to fight the colonels openly and not to try to burrow into the foundation of their support. Andreas Papandreou in particular believed that open opposition rather than subtle subversion was the correct way to deal with the colonels. His view had been strengthened with the death of Robert Kennedy, who had promised him that his administration would withdraw US support for the Greek government. The assassination of Kennedy and the emergence of Richard Nixon seemed to indicate to Papandreou and those who thought like him that trying to lobby the major Western powers into influencing the direction of the Greek junta was pointless.

John Spraos did believe in the 'corridors of power' strategy. Spraos puts it like this:

What did one hope to achieve? Not obviously to change the course of events dramatically from one day to the next. But more to create problems that would bring Greece up into the forefront of international issues in such a way as to maintain the morale of the Greeks inside Greece because ultimately it was they who were going to topple the colonels—morale which was otherwise adversely affected by the appearance of international support for the colonels and by a feeling of hopelessness that there was nothing you could do because the Americans, NATO, or whatever were in favour of the régime.

Spraos' view was that there were sufficient contradictions within NATO over Greece which entailed doubts not just about the morality of the régime but about its basic stability and therefore importance to the organisation. These contradictions would allow opponents to agitate and lobby and thereby create a sense of Greece being a constant irritant in need of a solution. Pressure from the NATO countries would so encourage the internal opposition that the régime would be destabilised and ultimately fall.

Spraos then was advocating taking on the Western establishment, and to do that he realised that he would need another establishment body. A meeting was organised at the Hotel Corona in The Hague on November 6th, 1970, with Max van der Stoel, a prominent member of the Dutch Parliament in the chair. Also at the meeting were parliamentarians from all over Europe, including Sir Geoffrey de Freitas and John Morris from Britain. The minutes of that meeting state:

> Concerning NATO, it was recognised that governmental refusal or reticence to undertake any initiatives in the direction of measures leading to the exclusion of Greece from the alliance, or even strong and effective pressure on the junta, are and are likely to continue to be serious obstacles to any concerted action. However, it was generally felt that pressure from NATO can have a decisive effect on developments inside Greece. It is therefore important to impress on NATO member governments the need for action in this direction and it is the duty of all those concerned with the cause of democracy in Greece and in Europe to work towards the adoption of such measures.

The members of the meeting concluded by agreeing that it would be desirable 'to establish some standing body which could perform these and other similar tasks . . . the conclusion was reached to organise a European-Atlantic Action Committee for Greece, with membership from all countries which were members of the Council of Europe, as well as from Canada, and the United States.'

324

John Spraos set about finding an appropriate chairman who had to be sympathetic to the cause, widely respected, with no party political commitments. Touring the political 'salons' of London he found no one with any particular ideas on who that person might be. He began to suggest, therefore, his own candidate, Hugh Greene, whose article on Papadopoulos had so impressed him. It was an idea which once mentioned was recognised as a good one, and so he visited Greene to ask if he might, as it were, come out of retirement to lead a campaign to help destabilise the government of the colonels. Greene welcomed the idea, attracted by the fine sentiments and morality which so obviously motivated Spraos and his colleagues, but also by the sheer sense of adventure which such a campaign would clearly generate.

Spraos had found the public figure for his campaign, but he needed someone to act as the 'workhorse' and administrator. Peter Thompson had lived in Greece from 1963 until a few months after the coup in 1967. Thompson was a poet, a politically sensitive man who found the junta odious, and so on his return to London he became involved with a number of rather marginal groups of Greek exiles and British opponents of the régime. He then went to live in Cyprus only to return to London once more with an even greater distaste for the colonels' régime than before. Thompson, who had already met Spraos, was just what the Committee needed. He was energetic, extremely able and bilingual, not kept too busy by his occasional teaching, and above all passionately opposed to the junta.

The years in Greece were particularly important for me. I was learning to write. I was given this tremendous opportunity to live very cheaply in a very friendly country, whose landscape and people were lovely and whose literature I liked. And they were very formative years, between 23 and 27. I felt I had a debt to these people, besides which I don't like tanks, I don't like colonels, and I don't like people who seize power. A lot of friends of mine got thrown into prison and nastily treated. Greece had become bound up with my life and it simply became impossible to stand and do nothing, even though what one did was perhaps fairly limited.

By February 1971 the Committee had its heads of the organisation: the well-respected public figure; the strategist; and the administrator. The first meeting with Greene in the chair was held at the Hotel Terminus-Gruber in Strasbourg, on January 26th, 1971, again attended by a large number of European parliamentarians. The Minutes of the meeting include an outline of the Committee's agreed strategy:

There will be an inaugural declaration which will serve as framework for policy and for which the signature of eminent individuals will be sought. All signatories will be *ipso facto* members of the Committee. The announcement of their names will have an impact and thereafter, with their help, a growing momentum will have to be generated. Names which will impress the US will be particularly sought.

The main point of this first meeting was to discuss the draft of the Declaration, prepared by John Spraos who, while not formally a member of the Committee, was its adviser on strategy. This the Committee would eventually ask prominent figures in Western public life to sign. The most important point to emerge from the discussion was the Committee's wish to combine a moral stance with a recognition that a more pragmatic appeal to the interests of the Western nations was ultimately likely to bear more fruit:

The first point to be discussed related to the assertions of the draft declaration that the integrity of one nation cannot be defended at the expense of the liberty of another. The view was expressed that this was an admirable sentiment but not an accurate description of big power practice . . . The prospects of the campaign's success came under discussion when a pessimistic view of this matter was expressed. One reaction was that we must persevere anyway because moral solidarity has great practical value . . . A view which found general support was that the lesson of Greece was that democracy was fragile even in the post-Second World War climate and in a country which was politically part of Western Europe. It was for this reason that it was in the self-interest of all those who value democracy to help in the struggle for its restoration in Greece.

Even while the Declaration was still being finalised, Hugh Greene began the long task of lobbying establishment opinion. In March, 1971, he was host at a dinner in London for a number of prominent MPs such as Denis Healey, Douglas Jay, Monty Woodhouse and Frank Judd. In the same month he visited Washington and New York, contacting such political luminaries as Edward Kennedy, Fulbright, Pell, Hartke, Javits, Muskie, and Birch Bayh. He addressed a large luncheon meeting of congressmen in the Speaker's Dining Room at the Capitol. His visit prompted the *Evening Standard* Washington Correspondent, Jeremy Campbell, to write an account of the visit with the headline, 'The Crusade Against the Colonels Gets the Greene Light'.

He also contacted representatives of the TV networks and of *The New York Times*, *The New York Post*, *The Washington Post*, and *The Christian Science Monitor*. He promised them all advance copies of the Declaration and of the list of signatories. His memo on the trip notes: 'Unless the story breaks elsewhere they will all hold their horses until we have held our press conference and will all, I hope, give the story a good run.' He also lobbied Arthur Schlesinger, Fred Friendly, and Mayor John Lindsay of New York. In April he took his lobbying campaign to Germany, where he obtained support from various prominent members of the SPD and the CDU.

The Declaration, sent out for signature in May 1971, with a view to the list of signatories being published at a press conference on June 1st, reiterated the belief that the governments of Western Europe and North America must unite to get rid what it described as 'a blot on the political map of Europe'. Crucially it argued: 'While it is deeply offensive on moral grounds, in practical terms it is a dangerously weak link in the community of democratic nations with which it continues to be associated.'

By June 1st, 1971 the Committee had 160 signatures to its Declaration, a veritable Who's Who of Western politics. Interestingly enough, and a portent of the difficulties to come for Hugh Greene, the British list contained not a single senior member of either main party.

The press coverage on June 2nd was wide and positive with such headlines as 'Sir Hugh Confronts Colonels'; 'Sir Hugh Squares Up to the Greek Colonels'; 'Bid to Topple Greek Colonels'; 'Former BBC Chief Opposes the Colonels'. One small item in *The Times* of June 3rd indicated that John Spraos' tactical analysis might well prove to be correct. The paper's Athen's correspondent wrote: 'Representatives of the three main Greek political groupings today welcomed the formation of the European-Atlantic Action Committee on Greece as a move "strengthening our struggle for democracy and the respect of human rights in our country".' The official Greek press in their attacks on the formation of the Committee described Greene as 'an aged communist with nothing better to do'.

The next stage of the campaign saw Hugh Greene, using arguments developed together with John Spraos and Peter Thompson, launching out to persuade the NATO powers that Greece was being militarily weakened by the dictatorship. In an appearance before the European Sub-Committee of the Foreign Affairs Committee of the US House of Representatives, he offered a detailed account of the state of affairs inside Greece and of the damage it was doing to the alliance. He quoted figures on the number of army officers who had been forcibly retired because of their suspect loyalties.

The same points were made at a press conference of the Committee, chaired by Hugh Greene, in December 1971, on

328

the day before a meeting of the NATO Foreign Ministers' meeting in Brussels. In the previous months John Spraos had visited Denmark and Norway to persuade parliamentarians in those two countries that their foreign ministers should continue to raise the question of Greece at the Council of Ministers. A note he prepared at the time of his lobbying activities stated:

> The particular issue through which the Greek question can be pressed on to the agenda and the communiqué of the next meeting of the Council of Ministers is not material at this moment. What matters is the admission of the subject on the agenda and in the communiqué. Once admitted, the subject will acquire its own momentum and the pressure on the Greek régime will grow stronger and stronger.

He realised nevertheless that at some point a specific issue would need to be chosen. The likeliest issue, though certainly not the only one, was the question of aid to the junta. The Committee's tactical note, prepared at the end of 1971, states:

> The hard core men of the junta will not be turned into reluctant democrats by international pressure. The object of such pressure must be to deprive the régime of its sources of support inside Greece so that it is forced to surrender power. Essentially this means depriving it of the support of the army. Only a small minority of officers are firmly committed to the régime . . . their tolerance depends *inter alia* on the belief that NATO and the US are solidly behind the régime and on the conviction that under this régime the continuing flow is assured of the tools of their trade—the modern military hardware without which they would feel second-class officers in a second-class army . . . If forced to choose between the junta and the Western alliance, there is little doubt that the Greek officer corps will choose the latter.

There was never much hope, nor indeed expectation, that major political initiatives would follow from the Committee's lobbying. It did, however, succeed in keeping the issue alive and feeding back to Greece that most vital of juices, hope. In this it seems to have been remarkably successful.

Greeks who were prominent in the opposition to the colonels, such as Takis Lambrias, Helen Vlachos, John Pesmazoglou, George Mavros, George Mangakis, all attest to the importance of the moral support which the Committee provided. No one suggested that it was in any way ultimately responsible for the downfall of the régime, merely that it helped with support from afar. For example, in January 1973 Greek students revolted against the junta and so laid the basis for the beginning of the end. Throughout that year opposition grew and on November 17th, 1973 came the final and most acute revolt by the students at the Athens Polytechnic. Papadopoulos over-reacted; the students gained a large measure of public support, and the dictator fell, to be replaced by another member of the junta, Ioannides. John Pesmazoglou assessed the role of the Committee during these particular events: 'During those crucial periods the Committee and Sir Hugh were of the greatest value because they went on explaining the danger of the situation in Greece.'

At the end of May 1972 the Committee held a press conference in Bonn, on the eve of the meeting of the NATO Council of Ministers. Hugh Greene was in the chair, and he had with him to address the press Professor George Mangakis, who had just been released from prison by the Greek régime and had rather spectacularly been spirited out of the country by a German air force plane, and the novelist Günter Grass. Greene once more emphasised the moral illegitimacy of the régime, as well as what he described as the increasing evidence of discontent and disruption in the armed forces. Mangakis argued that the régime was rejected by the vast majority of Greeks. He also said that the continued support for the Greek régime by the great powers represented a

330

double danger: it could lead to the preservation of a totalitarian state in Greece, and at the same time, by putting matters of strategic convenience first, erode the deeper meaning of NATO, an alliance of free people designed to protect their freedom and their democratic institutions. The toleration of the régime, he concluded, was 'a permanent insult to the Greek people'.

A similar effort was made prior to the NATO Council meeting in Copenhagen on June 14th, 1973. As well as Hugh Greene, the press conference also heard from Captain Nicholas Pappas, the commander of a Greek destroyer, *Velos*, which had sought political asylum in Italy in May 1973. Pappas was ideal in the sense that he could talk with particular authority about the weakness and divisions within the Greek armed forces. It was a message which Greene, following Pappas, emphasised to the assembled press men: that Greece was now a military liability to NATO as well as a political embarrassment. Pappas was to become Admiral and Commander-in-Chief of the Greek navy.

It has to be said that in concrete terms, the Committee was achieving little. The problem lay not with the parliamentarians at whom much of the lobbying was directed, but with the appallingly pragmatic governments of NATO and in particular the administration of Nixon. It was widely held at the time that the only problem with the junta in Nixon's eyes was that there were not more régimes like them propping up the Western *status quo*.

Despite Hugh Greene's prominent role in the Committee, the British government was totally unresponsive to overtures about Greece. Indicative of this was a letter sent by the Conservative government's Foreign Secretary, Sir Alec Douglas Home, to James Callaghan, MP, the Labour party's spokesman on foreign affairs. Callaghan had sent a memo to Home drafted by the Action Committee. Home replied:

The memorandum argues that disagreements within the régime, unrest among students and in the Church, and problems in the economy have led Mr Papadopoulos to rely more than ever on the armed forces to keep him in power. It suggests that if it were made clear to the officer corps that the régime and NATO were incompatible, the great majority of them would opt for the alliance. I judge that there is a good deal of wishful thinking in this. It is true that Mr Papadopoulos has his problems. But there is no evidence at all that a substantial proportion of the Greek armed forces are waiting for a suitable occasion to dissociate themselves from or actively to oppose the present régime. The failure of the attempted naval mutiny last month to win widespread support is evidence of this. Moreover, however much we may regret the abolition of the monarchy, its disappearance is likely to be popular in the army (far and away the most important of the services in Greece) where Republican feeling is strong.

I do not therefore think that discussion of Greece at the NATO Ministerial Meeting would have any effect on the policies or position of Mr Papadopoulos. On the contrary, past criticism of this kind has only caused resentment among the Greek armed forces. In any event, we believe, as you know, that it is not appropriate for the internal affairs of member countries to be discussed in NATO. I think the Labour party took a similar line when last in office.

More generally, we take the view (which, again, I think is in line with the policy of the Labour administration) that Greece is very important to the Western Alliance, and that to call in question or to undermine her position in NATO would jeopardise the security of the Alliance without advancing the restoration of democracy in Greece.

Not surprisingly Peter Thompson describes the Conservative government as 'a dead loss, and Alec Douglas Home more of a dead loss than anybody else. Douglas Home was a brick wall in so far as pursuing our aims was concerned.' In February 1974 the Conservative government fell, replaced by a Labour administration with Harold Wilson as Prime Minister and James Callaghan as Foreign Secretary. Greene and his colleagues might have expected more understanding and cooperation from the new government; they were to be largely disappointed. First moves augured well, when on March 14th, the Foreign Office announced that a four-day courtesy visit to Greece by two Royal Navy warships had been cancelled. Later in a parliamentary debate, James Callaghan said: 'There are nations whose internal repression of their citizens we deplore. Whether such nations fall on the right or the left of the political spectrum, the case for speaking is even stronger when silence might be deemed to be consent or indifference.'

The cancellation of the naval visit was welcomed by opponents of the régime in Greece, particularly by Panayotis Kanellopoulos, who had been Prime Minister at the time of the coup, and by the former Centre Union Leader, George Mavros. Kanellopoulos was kept under house arrest and Mavros was exiled to a remote island, but they still regretted the absence of more positive support for opposition to the Colonels.

In May 1974 Hugh Greene and Peter Thompson got a very different response when they went to see a junior minister at the Foreign Office, Roy Hattersley. They were there to ask him to persuade Callaghan to join the Scandinavian and Canadian foreign ministers in speaking out against Greece at a forthcoming NATO meeting. They put to Hattersley the case that the officers' corps in Greece only tolerated the régime and that a clear sign from NATO that they did not welcome the régime would be an important blow against the colonels.

Hattersley had with him a civil servant, Charles Wiggin, who later died while Ambassador in Spain, and as Greene and Thompson finished he turned to his advisor and said: 'I have two questions to put to you. The first concerns the propriety of Her Majesty's Government in considering action which might be aimed at leading to the downfall of a régime of which we disapprove, and the second is, would it work?' Wiggin replied: 'Minister, on the first score, you need have no worries. On the second, I share your doubts.' Hattersley refused to help them.

A few weeks later, in July 1974, they visited Hattersley again, the day after the coup against Makarios in Cyprus, a coup which had been carried out by the Greek-officered National Guard on the island. They argued with him that Britain should issue a formal demand that Greece withdraw her troops and warned of an invasion by Turkish troops. They also suggested that British troops on the spot should be used to restore order. Hattersley's enigmatic reply was: 'We can't because of Northern Ireland.'

When the dictatorship was finally removed and Karamanlis returned to head a government of national unity, Greene, Thompson, Spraos, and those various parliamentarians could take some pleasure and credit in what they had achieved. They had kept the issue alive in the corridors of power and, vitally, had provided moral support for those who ultimately mattered, the Greeks who opposed the junta. Most Western governments could take credit only for having in effect supported a brutal, despicable and ultimately incompetent group of thugs.

John Spraos was in the United States when he heard the news of the return of Karamanlis on his car radio. Greene and Thompson were in London and that very night proceeded to the Lord Byron Taverna in Beak Street where, as they entered, Hugh Greene was heard to demand: 'Let there be a constant stream of bottles.'

The Committee itself, despite its global designs and grand supporters, was a shoestring affair run from Peter Thompson's small flat above the Golden Girl Club in Soho. This flat was broken into, apparently by Greek agents, as was Greene's house in Suffolk. There were vague threats of violence in the air. At the flat Greene, Spraos and Thompson would meet to plan their tactics, draft documents, and decide on next moves. Financially they were dependent on the generosity of some Greek exiles, including the Greek shipowner who must remain anonymous, on Hugh Greene and John Spraos reaching into their own pockets and on Peter Thompson's willingness and ability to live on virtually nothing. Hugh Greene would visit the shipowner late at night to receive payments in cash towards the campaign funds. The same man offers another footnote to history. When Karamanlis was returning to Greece from Paris, he asked that Takis Lambrias, in exile in London, should fly to Paris to return with him on the plane provided by the French government. Lambrias, who was to become Undersecretary for Press and Information, had no money to pay for the fare, and so arrangements were made for him to go to Heathrow and just wait. At the terminal ticket concourse a small boy approached, tapped him on the arm and handed him an envelope. It was the shipowner's son, and inside the envelope was the money to purchase a ticket to Paris.

He and others took with them a considerable wealth of feeling and respect for Hugh Greene. One of Lambrias' first actions was to ask Hugh Greene to prepare a report on the future organisation of Greek broadcasting.

When Lambrias announced this decision in Parliament, the opposition spokesman was George Mangakis. He approved of the invitation to Hugh Greene to prepare the report on broadcasting, and added:

I believe we are all characterised by a high degree of distrust towards foreign consultants and technocrats. But in this specific case there is no reason whatsoever for us to be distrustful because Sir Hugh is no foreigner to us in the broader sense of the word. He is the man who stood at the side of the Greek people during the years of struggle against tyranny, and indeed he offered most valuable services to our cause . . . he is the carrier of the liberal democratic spirit, and this precisely implies that he is no technocrat but a man who indeed can enjoy the full confidence of all the sides and wings of this chamber.

335

Hugh Greene was sitting in the gallery during this, and as Mangakis finished his statement, the whole of the assembly rose and applauded.

When he presented his report to the Karamanlis government on January 22nd, 1975, his principal recommendation was that the National Broadcasting Service, EIRT, should be re-constituted as a corporation functioning under private law. The main advantage of this would be that the staff of EIRT would cease to be civil servants or bound by civil service regulations, something which he believed would be of great psychological importance: 'The civil service mentality and the creative outlook on which good broadcasting depends are like oil and water. Promising men and women will never be attracted to a broadcasting system which strangles initiative with civil service regulations.'

The rest of the report was a detailed description of the possible future organisation of Greek broadcasting. This would include an Advisory Council, representing all the various elements within society; an Administrative Council consisting of a Chairman and six members, appointed by the government, but only after consultations with the opposition parties:

The members of this body should be chosen as individuals because of their standing in the community and not as representatives of any party, ministry or other organisations. They should not include members of Parliament or civil servants . . . They should concern themselves with major matters of programming, financial and administrative policy. Above all, they should regard themselves as the trustees of Parliament and of the nation, in the maintenance of political objectivity, fairness, and impartiality in the news and other programmes of EIRT.

The final important recommendation for EIRT was that the Director General of EIRT should be appointed by the Administrative Council and not by the government and should only be, if necessary, removed by the Administrative Council. In another potentially very difficult issue, he

336

recommended that the military broadcasting service, YENED, was an anomaly and should be amalgamated with EIRT.

It was all very familiar. Hugh Greene was trying to create a broadcasting body which was independent, objective and impartial, in charge of its own affairs, with a supportive rather than subordinate relationship to the state. It was, in short, an attempt to create an Hellenic BBC, and as with his similar efforts in Germany and Rhodesia, it ran into trouble almost immediately.

When the government published its Law 330 on the formation of 'Greek Radio-Television [ERT]', it was only a very pale imitation of Hugh Greene's recommendation. In particular, while ERT was a legal entity of civil law, and its employees no longer civil servants, the government retained extensive, and in all likelihood choking, control over administrative, financial and editorial aspects of its work. Most ominously the Director General was to be appointed by the government.

At the time Hugh Greene put on a brave face in an effort at least to encourage whatever progressive elements remained within ERT. He knew, however, that the new birth of Greek broadcasting had produced a deformed creature. He was encouraged by the appointment of John Lampsas as ERT's first Director General, only to be appalled when Lampsas was removed in an overtly political move.

Hugh Greene's report was never debated by the Greek Cabinet. Lambrias only discussed its contents with Karamanlis, George Rallis, another leading member of the government, and two or three of the Prime Minister's advisers: 'They were rather afraid that the report was not adjustable to Greek reality.' There was in effect a failure of nerve and a lack of confidence in the stability and maturity of the new Greek democracy in which the only sources of power and authority were the political parties. The last thing they were willing to do in that context was to allow a truly independent and creative TV organisation. At the same time Karamanlis and his colleagues undoubtedly believed that TV was the

337

key to the Greek mind and therefore to the future of the new state—a fantasy commonly held by politicians.

They also believed that if a plurality of voices were allowed into positions of power in ERT, then what would follow would not be social harmony and debate, but dissension and disruptiveness. For example, Lambrias says of Greene's idea for a council of fifty people reflecting the many diverse aspects of Greek society and culture:

> I know that if you get fifty Greeks of different cultural, spiritual or political views in a room, you can never obtain in two or three years a decision. For Sir Hugh the representative of the Church in London is a personality. The representative of the Church here is not a personality; he is an obscurantist trying to say a monologue and never in a position to collaborate with the others. We were afraid that it was not easy to implement the ideas in full. No foreigner can fully understand the possibilities and the realities of Greek life. I knew that what Sir Hugh could give to us would be the idea and I wanted to have the ideal model. I knew that I could not put this into practice in full.

Members of the opposition thought at the time that the rejection of the council meant that a great chance was missed.

Hugh Greene's report threw into sharp relief the fact that the new Greek establishment, one which had shown considerable courage during the years of the dictatorship, did not have the courage to allow a separate, independent and objective voice to television. When the government of Andreas Papandreou came to power, exactly the same attitudes prevailed. Once more Hugh Greene's version of broadcasting had failed, but once more out of the failure he himself had emerged with a reputation not just intact, but enhanced amid the wreckage of another attempt to achieve the elusive reality of liberal democracy.

INDEX

340

343